THE CLASSICS
OF **WESTERN**
SPIRITUALITY

THE CLASSICS OF WESTERN SPIRITUALITY
A Library of the Great Spiritual Masters

President and Publisher
Lawrence Boadt, C.S.P.

EDITORIAL BOARD

John Baptist de la Salle
THE SPIRITUALITY OF CHRISTIAN EDUCATION

EDITED AND INTRODUCED BY
CARL KOCH, JEFFREY CALLIGAN, FSC, AND JEFFREY GROS, FSC

PREFACE BY
THOMAS H. GROOME

PAULIST PRESS
NEW YORK • MAHWAH, N.J.

Cover art: John Baptist de La Salle: untitled work painted by Pierre Léger, most likely the second such work. It is currently preserved in the Archives of the Generalate. Dated 1734, it has been adopted as the official portrait of the founder. It reminds us of Blain's description: "His face was always happy, tranquil, and imperturbable....The image of kindness that characterized him also produced a joy among those around him" (*Life* by Blain, Book 4, 308).

Cover and caseside design by A. Michael Velthaus

Book design by Sharyn Banks

Library of Congress Cataloging-in-Publication Data

John Baptist de La Salle : the spirituality of Christian education / edited and introduced by Carl Koch, Jeffrey Calligan, and Jeffrey Gros ; Preface by Thomas H. Groome.
    p. cm.
    Includes bibliographical references and index.
    ISBN 0-8091-4162-0 (alk. paper); ISBN 0-8091-0557-8 (cloth)
    1. La Salle, Jean Baptiste de, Saint 1651–1719. 2. Spiritual Life—Catholic Church. 3. Christian education. I. Koch, Carl, 1945– II. Calligan, Jeffrey. III. Gros, Jeffrey, 1938–
BX4700.L3J635 2004
248.41'82—dc22

2003021530

Published by Paulist Press
997 Macarthur Boulevard
Mahwah, New Jersey 07430

www.paulistpress.com

Printed and bound in the
United States of America

Contents

Editors of This Volume

CARL KOCH is director of the Master of Arts in Servant Leadership Program at Viterbo University and program coordinator for the Franciscan Spirituality Center in La Crosse, Wisconsin. He holds master's degrees in English, human development, and religious education, and a doctorate in English from the University of Michigan. Carl has authored over thirty books, including: *Praying with John Baptist de La Salle, Garden of a Thousand Gates: Pathways to Prayer, A Popular History of the Catholic Church* (Saint Mary's Press), and is the general editor of the *God Knows* series from Sorin Books. He gives retreats and conferences on a wide variety of topics, including Lasallian spirituality for teachers. The US/Toronto Region of the De La Salle Christian Brothers named him Outstanding Lasallian Educator.

JEFFREY L. CALLIGAN, FSC, currently serves as US/Toronto regional director of religious life studies for the Brothers of the Christian Schools. Recognized as an authority on De La Salle, Brother Jeffrey has given seminars and retreats on Lasallian spirituality all over the world. He has been a school administrator, associate vicar for religious, president of Commission Internationale Catechetics in Rome, and has been published in *Lasalliana*, the journal for international Lasallian studies.

JEFFREY GROS, FSC, is associate director of the Secretariat for Ecumenical and Interreligious Affairs for the U.S. Conference of Catholic Bishops. He holds master's degrees in theology and biology education and a Ph.D. in theology from Fordham University. For ten years before coming to the USCCB, Brother Jeffrey was executive director of the Faith and Order Commission of the National Council of Churches of Christ. He won the James Fitzgerald Award from the National Association of Diocesan Ecumenical Officers and was awarded the Doctor of Pedagogue *honoris causa* by Manhattan College. He has authored dozens of journal articles and eight books, including *That All May Be One: Ecumenism* (Loyola University Press) and, most recently, *The Fragmentation*

of the Church and Its Unity in Peacemaking, co-edited with John Rem-
ple (Eerdmans). Brother Jeffrey has participated in ecumenical
dialogues all over the world and lectured on ecumenism at many
national and international gatherings.

To

Luke Salm, FSC—a pioneering theologian who opened doors of leadership in the church to all the people of God, a scholar always and a teacher first.

John Johnston, FSC—a Lasallian leader in the church, advocate for the poor, laity, and for a global spirituality, and superior general of the Brothers of the Christian Schools (1986–2000).

Augustine Loes, FSC—a visionary leader in bringing these texts into English and in interpreting a new vision of Lasallian spirituality.

Acknowledgments

We gratefully acknowledge the indispensable, generously given help of Paul Grass, FSC, executive director of Lasallian Publications, without whom this volume would not have come to fruition. Likewise we thank his predecessors in this role: the late Francis Huether, FSC, and William Quaintance, FSC. In addition, we owe profound thanks to Luke Salm, FSC, who chaired the editorial board and whose Lasallian scholarship has guided all of us.

Next, we must recognize and give thanks for the wonderful work of those who translated and edited the selections collected in this volume: Richard Arnandez, FSC, and Augustine Loes, FSC, for *Meditations of John Baptist de La Salle;* Augustine Loes, FSC, and Ronald Isetti for *Rule and Foundational Documents;* F. de La Fontainerie and Richard Arnandez, FSC, for *The Conduct of the Christian Schools;* Richard Arnandez, FSC, and Gregory Wright for *The Rules of Christian Decorum and Civility;* Colman Molloy, FSC, and Augustine Loes, FSC, for *The Letters of John Baptist de La Salle;* Richard Arnandez, FSC, and Alexis James Doval for *The Duties of a Christian to God;* Richard Arnandez, FSC, and Donald C. Mouton, FSC, for *Explanation of the Method of Interior Prayer;* Richard Arnandez, FSC, and Luke Salm, FSC, for Jean-Baptiste Blain's *The Life of John Baptiste de La Salle, Founder of the Institute of the Brothers of the Christian Schools.*

We would be remiss if we did not express our gratitude to others who have steadfastly served on the editorial board of Lasallian Publications—Daniel Burke, FSC, Miguel Campos, FSC, William Mann, FSC, and Joseph Schmidt, FSC; and to the scholars and translators who over decades have collected, studied, and made available the works by and about John Baptist de La Salle in the *Cahiers lasalliens* (Rome).

The Christian Brothers Conference, Landover, Maryland, holds the copyright to the English translations of De La Salle's works. To the Brothers Visitor of the Christian Brothers Conference of the United States-Toronto Region, our sincere thank you for permission to reprint the texts in this volume and for your steadfast support and encouragement of the Lasallian Publications Board.

Finally, we give thanks to and ask God's blessings on the thousands of Brothers of the Christian Schools and their associates who have kept and continue to keep the ministry of Christian education of the poor alive throughout the world. May Jesus live in all of our hearts forever.

Preface

✛

It is a great blessing to have readily available in this one volume the core writings of John Baptist de La Salle. The church of today needs them as much as that of seventeenth-century France. This volume rightfully takes its place within the Classics of Western Spirituality, for it is a rich and time-tested proposal for how educators can put their faith to work through their vocation—as a spirituality for life. All who educate from a faith perspective—parents as well as teachers and administrators—owe a debt of gratitude to Carl Koch, Jeffrey Calligan, and Jeffrey Gros for giving us this fine selection of De La Salle's original writings.

Since the risen Christ gave "the great commission" to the first Christian community on a hillside in Galilee (Matt 28:16–20), the church has recognized that education is an integral aspect of continuing God's work of salvation in the world. The Catholic community has been more convinced than any other that this includes general as well as religious education, that the church should educate in the humanities, arts and sciences, as well as in Christian faith itself. To echo Irenaeus (130–200), anything that enables the human person to become "fully alive"—the intent of good education, surely—"gives glory to God."

Plato understood the function of educators as to "turn the soul" of students toward the true, the good, and the beautiful. Education that humanizes, that enables people to make and keep life human for themselves and others, must engage the "souls" of learners, and the educator's own soul as well. If this is true of all good education, it must be eminently so for education motivated and shaped by Christian faith. So, the actual practice of Christian education needs a philosophy that becomes a spirituality precisely because it is grounded in faith and put to work.

The church has educated people in the "three R's"—as well as religion—since the earliest monastic schools. Yet, De La Salle was

1

the first to set out a comprehensive spirituality for teachers, crafted precisely to ground and guide the work of education. In sum, he proposed that Christian educators be motivated by their faith and allow it to permeate every aspect of their teaching, entrusting the outcome to God's provident care.

For De La Salle, educators so grounded in Christian faith must have a deep commitment to the personhood of learners in order to respect and nurture their dignity and responsibility as made in God's own image and likeness. Most urgently, Christian teachers must favor the people whose human dignity is most denied by society, making what we call today an "option for the poor." To this reader, at least, faith-based education of the poor will always define the Lasallian charism.

For De La Salle, the key to such humanizing education is that teachers have a life-giving relationship with their students. And, as if coming full circle, the quality of this relationship depends most upon the spirituality of educators themselves. In other words, the touchstone of life-giving education is the teachers' spirituality—that they put their faith to work in what they do. And as teachers allow their faith to ground their educating, not only are they instruments of God's grace for the salvation of students, but they grow in their own holiness of life. Such an educational apostolate is the means of grace for both teachers and students. "It is a good rule of life to make no distinction at all between the work of our vocation in life and the work of our salvation and perfection" (Rule 3 of *Rules I Have Imposed on Myself*, 8.1).

Though thoroughly convinced that its foundation is spiritual, De La Salle had a very practical sense of education as well; it is eminently a praxis, something done with great intentionality. And teachers can learn to do it well by reflecting on their own best efforts, by sharing with and learning from each other's experiences. Yet, the reflections on praxis by Christian educators should arise from and return to more than a philosophy—to their spirituality.

In De La Salle's time spirituality was taken very seriously as the foundation of priestly ministry—part of the reforms put in place by the Council of Trent. But he insisted that as much was needed for the ministry of teachers, though they were lay people (he always insisted that the Brothers be a lay movement). In this he was revolutionary for his day, and maybe still for ours. De La Salle left the legacy of a powerful statement of what such a spirituality might look like, not just "in the air" but "on the ground," down to the details of the curriculum.

As with all classics, De La Salle's spirituality for educators can be read afresh in every age; it transcends its original time and place. Of course, we need to read him in his context and be aware of what we bring to it as well, allowing his horizon to fuse with our own, stretching both. So, for example, his *Rules of Christian Decorum and Civility* could be dismissed as dated etiquette, unless we remember that he was trying to raise up the dignity and self-worth of impoverished urchins, educating them to have respect for themselves and others. Then we need to imagine how to reflect and encourage such a positive anthropology in our own praxis of education, perhaps honoring the need for a bit of civility in our time, too.

All educators will find an invaluable resource here. It will stimulate our imaginations about how to care for our own spirituality and then to put it to work through our vocation. This will surely enhance our potential to be instruments of God's saving work and likewise our own holiness of life.

Beyond educators, the emerging lay ecclesial ministries in our time are searching urgently for a spirituality to sustain them. This makes the writings of De La Salle essential reading. As they have given rise to and sustained one of the richest charisms of Christian education over the past three hundred odd years and a community of Brothers of the Christian Schools that have been extraordinary educators, now they can be a rich treasury for the whole church.

—Thomas H. Groome
Professor of Theology and Religious Education
Boston College

Introduction

✠

John Baptist de La Salle was proclaimed a saint in 1900 by Leo XIII and named the patron of all teachers by Pius XII in 1950. De La Salle's educational and spiritual works are today being read not only by the members of his religious family, called "Brother," but also by lay, priest, and religious associates across the world engaged in educational works centered on young people, especially the poor.

The God of De La Salle is a provident God with a plan for the salvation of all, especially young people who are "far from salvation," far from wholeness. This God is found among the poor and the marginalized. The means this God uses is a community of teachers who create schools where salvation through education and relationships is the raison d'être.

What we offer in this volume of the Classics of Western Spirituality is a taste of De La Salle's writings. We have tried to include foundational texts, which point to the role of the teacher as one called by God for the salvation of young people—especially poor young people—through education.

A classic is often a seminal or a source reality. In classics, people read their lives and their times in all ages of civilization and religion. De La Salle's writings are a reality of this nature, hence classic.

DE LA SALLE'S STORY

In a memoir written later in his life, John Baptist de La Salle still wondered at the mysterious ways of God's providence. It had led this son of privilege to dedicate himself completely to the Christian education of poor children, to found a community of lay teachers dedicated to that mission, and to articulate a spirituality of educational ministry as a way to holiness. Reflecting back, he declared:

> Indeed, if I had ever thought that the care I was taking of the schoolmasters out of pure charity would have made it my duty to live with them, I would have dropped the whole project. For since, naturally speaking, I considered the men whom I was obliged to employ in the schools at the beginning as being inferior to my valet, the mere thought that I would have to live with them would have been insupportable to me. In fact, I experienced a great deal of unpleasantness when I first had them come to my house. This lasted for two years. It was undoubtedly for this reason that God, who guides all things with wisdom and gentleness, whose way it is not to force the inclinations of persons, willed to commit me entirely to the development of the schools. God did this in an imperceptible way and over a long period of time, so that one commitment led to another in a way that I did not foresee in the beginning.[1]

God led, De La Salle followed. And, in following, John Baptist de La Salle spearheaded a revolution in education and gave voice to an apostolic spirituality for laypeople, particularly teachers.

The France of De La Salle

In 1651, when John Baptist de La Salle was born, Louis XIV, the Sun King, reigned in France. For the rich and powerful, this was *Le Grand Siecle* (the great century). For the poor, by far the majority of French people, life continued to be a constant, grinding struggle to feed, clothe, and shelter themselves.

A middle class of merchants, bishops, and government officials was developing in France. It, along with the guilds of artisans and tradespeople, wielded considerable influence within French society. Somewhat analogous to today's unions, the guilds regulated their membership and ensured proper training of new members, but they also exercised monopolies over their crafts and merchandising areas. While some movement into the guilds and middle class was possible, the masses only dreamed of upward mobility.

INTRODUCTION

Two-thirds of French citizens depended on the land. Crop failures frequently led to widespread starvation and subsequent outbreaks of disease. Unable to raise their own food, the poor of the cities found basic foodstuffs impossibly expensive. Contagion quickly spread through the ranks of the poor crammed into slums. French peasants and the poor had no security. When crops thrived or businesses prospered, they had just enough food to stay alive and some shelter. When times were bad, they starved and were homeless. Some monasteries and parishes offered assistance, but even this was undependable.

In addition, France seemed to be continually at war. The tax burden for these wars and the lavish lifestyle of the nobility fell squarely on the shoulders of the peasants and the poor in the cities. Occasionally riots erupted in protest, but these were harshly suppressed. Taxation continued inexorably.

In the world of De La Salle, only the nobility and the middle class had access to adequate schooling. Wealthy children received tutoring at home, went to grammar schools attached to a university, or attended a school for the boys singing in the cathedral choir. Less advantaged children attended "Little Schools" taught by teachers belonging to the Guild of Schoolmasters. A diocesan superintendent oversaw the Little Schools, and the boys paid modest fees. Some convents maintained schools for girls. Other children received classes in writing, reading, and basic bookkeeping in Writing Schools staffed by members of the Guild of Writing Masters. Children in the Little Schools and the Writing Schools attended for perhaps two or three years.

Like their parents, the majority of poor children were illiterate. Even if the local poor house or parish operated a charity school, children either had to work to help their families or lacked the proper clothes to wear—or both. Even if children went to school, their teacher often had only rudimentary learning, no pedagogical training, and took the job as a last resort. Schoolmasters beat children as standard practice and gave lessons to one child at a time, while the other students milled around waiting. If these obstacles to education were not bad enough, the children were expected to learn Latin first, not their native French.

In De La Salle's France, church and state were inextricably related. The Catholic Church claimed over one-quarter of the nation's wealth. Bishops held sway over many functions of public life: education, health care, and other services.

Catholicism was the religion of France, and Louis XIV suppressed reform religions through draconian laws and force of arms. In villages and small towns the parish priest wielded enormous power, second only to the local nobility. On the other hand, the French king controlled the appointment of bishops, and any religious group required "letters patent" from the king in order to become a legal entity.

John Baptist de La Salle could have lived a comfortable life, born as he was into a wealthy family. But he was called to follow a different path, one that would challenge the way poor children were treated, challenge the clericalism of the day, and challenge his culture's concept of ministry and religious life.

The Early Years

John Baptist de La Salle's family had earned its wealth as merchants. His father served as a magistrate in Reims. Though John Baptist's family did not belong to the nobility, the family lived well in a fine home. As the eldest of eleven children—seven of whom survived into adulthood—John Baptist could have been expected to move among the privileged class of French society.

Private tutors instructed John Baptist until he was nine. Then, until he turned eighteen, he studied at the College des Bon-Enfants connected to the University of Reims. His curriculum consisted of classical subjects: grammar and syntax, Latin, Greek, and philosophy.

Nearing his eleventh birthday, John Baptist received the tonsure, the first step toward ordination. At age fifteen a canonry at the cathedral of Reims was offered to John Baptist. This appointment brought a tidy income and considerable honor to John Baptist and his family: "Three popes, 23 cardinals, more than 30 bishops and most distinguished of all perhaps, Saint Bruno," founder of the Carthusians, had been cathedral canons before him.[2] As a canon of the cathedral, John Baptist prayed the Divine Office in choir several times each day, took part in liturgical celebrations, and consulted with the archbishop.

INTRODUCTION

In 1670 John Baptist started seminary training at Saint Sulpice in Paris. Founded two decades earlier by Jean-Jacques Olier, who had been deeply influenced by the French School of spirituality of Cardinal Bérulle, Saint Sulpice and the society of priests who directed it sought to train self-disciplined, committed, competent clergy. The seminarians followed a rigorous regimen of prayer, studies, silence, and pastoral work among poor Parisians.

Over a year after settling into the rhythms of Saint Sulpice, John Baptist's life took an unexpected turn. During the summer of 1671 his mother died. Nine months later his father died. At age twenty-one, John Baptist returned to Reims to assume charge of his sisters and brothers and the family estate.

The Work Begins

During his first year at home, De La Salle spent all his efforts in managing family matters. Then, in 1673, under the guidance of his spiritual director, Father Nicolas Roland, a fellow canon at Reims, De La Salle resumed his studies for the priesthood. He finished his bachelor's degree in theology in 1675 and was awarded a licentiate in 1678 and a doctorate in 1680.

On Holy Saturday 1678 the archbishop of Reims ordained De La Salle a priest. Now twenty-seven, De La Salle seemed ready to move into positions of prominent service in the church. However, his mentor and friend Nicholas Roland died only two weeks after De La Salle's ordination. In his will Roland designated De La Salle as executor of his estate and protector of the Sisters of the Holy Child Jesus, a community founded to educate poor girls. De La Salle dutifully assisted the sisters in gaining legal recognition and acted as their chaplain and supporter.

One day De La Salle arrived at the front door of the sisters' community at the same time as Adrien Nyel. The sister superior introduced the two men, and the direction of De La Salle's life changed forever. Upon the invitation of Mme. Jeanne Dubois Maillefer, related to De La Salle by marriage, Nyel had come to Reims to start a charity school for boys. Nyel outlined his intentions to De La Salle, who then offered to help. Since Nyel had no place to stay, De La Salle invited him into his home.

Nyel set to work. In short order a pastor in Reims consented to establish a school for boys in his parish. Then another patron wanted Nyel to open a school across town and agreed to support it because Nyel used De La Salle's name when asked for his credentials. Nyel found teachers and opened the second school, and De La Salle's name became irrevocably linked with the project of these teachers and schools. Nyel then opened a third school. However, as was his habit, Nyel's zeal out-paced his planning. The teachers soon outgrew their living quarters, and it became apparent to De La Salle that they were ill prepared to teach overflowing classes of poor boys. The young men Nyel recruited had little education, no training, and less direction.

In an attempt to remedy the situation, De La Salle invited the teachers to have their meals in his home. At mealtime he offered instruction in manners, methods, religion, and tried to provide inspiration. It worked. These schoolmasters, who one contemporary of De La Salle's described as "gamblers, drunkards, libertines, ignorant, and brutal," grew more disciplined and capable. However, this success raised new questions for De La Salle: If the schoolmasters continued to need supervision, was he willing to extend such involvement? What would this mean for him and his family?

As usual when De La Salle had weighty matters to discern, he turned to a spiritual director. He asked Father Nicholas Barré for advice. Barré, who had helped establish schools for poor children in Rouen and Paris, suggested that De La Salle bring the schoolmasters into his own home. In that way he could closely supervise them.

Distressed at the prospect of living with men that he ranked "inferior to [his] valet" and despite the angry protestations of his relatives, in 1681 De La Salle brought the teachers to live with him. Under pressure, two of his younger brothers moved into the homes of relatives. Eighteen-year-old Jean-Louis stayed with John Baptist and the schoolmasters.

The sacrifices De La Salle made to ensure that poor boys would receive an education are best explained in these passages from his *Meditations for the Time of Retreat*, written years later. The Brothers, he believed, must first dedicate themselves to teaching the good news: "God is so good that, having created us, he wills that all of us come to the knowledge of the truth [1 Tim 2:4]. This truth is God himself....We cannot be instructed in the mysteries of our holy religion unless we have the good fortune to hear about them, and we cannot have this advantage unless someone preaches the word of God." The Brothers must also prepare the poor boys to work. The Christian schools were to be places "where the children are kept all day, learn to read, to write, and their religion, and are always kept busy, so that when their parents want them to go to work, they are prepared for employment."[3]

To share this vision with the schoolmasters, De La Salle set a schedule for the group. They prayed together, kept regular hours, and De La Salle gave the schoolmasters instruction in educational methods that seemed best suited for poor boys in the charity schools. Living in a central house, they could share their experiences and learn from one another. Gradually this ragtag collection of men became a community. The central house served as the base for teachers of the several schools throughout the city. This would become an established practice as the community spread to other cities.

As the schools succeeded, De La Salle received more requests to open charity schools. When possible, he sent teachers, but the community was fragile. Food was rough fare, and the work and living conditions were hard. While some of the men willingly embraced the lifestyle, many left. De La Salle encouraged the men to rely on divine providence, but they countered that if the enterprise failed, he still had his personal wealth and canonry to depend on. They had nothing.

Realizing that he had reached another defining moment, De La Salle prayed about what he should do and again consulted with Father Barré. As a consequence, in August 1683 De La Salle resigned his canonry. That winter famine struck France. De La Salle responded by giving away his personal savings to the lines of poor people who came to his door. Soon he was as poor as they were. He is recorded as praying, "If you [God] endow the schools, they will be well endowed; if you do not, they will be without endowment. I beseech you to make your holy will known to me."[4]

Expansion

God's will quickly became known. Sponsors continued to ask that De La Salle send teachers to them. The community slowly grew in numbers and in a sense of identity. Around this time the schoolmasters became known as the Brothers of the Christian Schools. And, to signal their identity as a group of laymen dedicated to gratuitous schools, they chose to wear a plain black robe cut somewhat differently than a priest's cassock. In the "Memorandum on the Habit," De La Salle explained: "The members of this Community, being for the most part rough, unrefined, and uneducated men who ordinarily respond to feelings and impressions, need some tangible token of membership in the Community to draw them to it, to retain their allegiance once they join, and to lead them to observe its Rule." With the robe, they wore thick-soled, peasant shoes, a tri-cornered hat outdoors, and a short mantle: "The long mantle would get in the way of their work....People have mentioned that with this mantle there is a danger of knocking over most of the small children on one side or the other while trying to place them in order."[5] The selection of the habit illustrates two key characteristics of De La Salle: his desire to signal the lay nature of the community and his practicality.

In 1686 De La Salle gathered the Brothers and persuaded them to select one of their own to be superior of the community. The Brothers resisted, but at De La Salle's insistence they eventually chose Brother Henri L'Heureux. At this assembly a group of key Brothers also took a private vow of obedience. The archbishop, however, had other ideas. He ordered De La Salle to remain superior, because he believed that a priest should never submit to a lay Brother as his superior. In what became a recurring issue for the community, ordained clergy with little respect for the Brothers' competence and religious dedication would often seek to control and direct the affairs of this group of laymen. By resisting their efforts, De La Salle was often accused of being exceedingly stubborn.

Even so, young men continually joined De La Salle's community. In 1687 he created a separate formation community. This, de facto, became the first novitiate of the Brothers.

The same year that De La Salle was establishing this formation program, priests from rural communities asked him to prepare teachers for their parish schools. So he opened a teacher-training school. Twenty-five men came from the countryside to learn pedagogy under the direction of Brother Henri L'Heureux. They studied practical educational methods, basic composition and mathematics, and other subjects necessary for teaching poor children. This teacher-training school only lasted until the parishes had sufficient teachers. Then it closed. However, it provided a model for similar schools that the Brothers would establish later.

Paris

By 1687 Brothers conducted schools in Reims, Guise, Rethel, and Laon. Now, De La Salle received an invitation from one of his former seminary teachers to staff a school in Paris. The parish of Saint Sulpice was extensive and included some of the worst slums of the capital city. Wishing to see the ministry expand, De La Salle and two Brothers moved into the school on Rue Princesse on February 24, 1688.

Once they began directing the school, the Brothers rapidly created order from the chaos that had reigned before their arrival. They imposed a firm schedule for the boys, grouped them by age, and regularized the teaching of religion and other subjects. However, as was often the case, the pastor who had invited De La Salle and his successor as pastor sought control over the community and the running of the school. Even so, the school thrived and the Brothers subsequently opened other schools in the sprawling parish.

Over the following years the pastor's interference caused continual trouble for De La Salle and the Brothers. He pressured De La

Salle to change the Brothers' habit, tried to interfere in the formation of new Brothers, and even appointed a priest superior of the community. De La Salle quietly resisted these manipulations.

One of the chief reasons that the schools succeeded was De La Salle's practicality. In constant dialogue with the Brothers about the best practice for teachers, he collected their wisdom and methods and disseminated this information to all the communities. Eventually, this collected wisdom was published as *The Conduct of the Christian Schools*, an instruction manual for the Brothers about the specifics of running schools; for example, "What Is Done During Breakfast and Afternoon Snack," "Training to Write Well," and "How to Ask Questions During Catechism." Throughout his instructions for teaching, De La Salle grounded each aspect in the Sacred Scriptures.

Another key to the Brothers' success with the children was their use of French as the language of instruction. During this era children typically learned Latin first. De La Salle saw that this was counterproductive. Since most poor children stayed in school a maximum of two or three years, they needed to learn reading, writing, arithmetic, and religion as quickly as possible. They learned most readily in their native tongue. While critics, including some otherwise supportive priests and bishops, objected to French as the medium of instruction, De La Salle held his ground.

Opposition to his methods of instruction was not the only problem facing De La Salle and the Brothers. In 1690 the community was accused of admitting boys able to pay fees for schooling. The diocesan supervisor claimed that the Brothers were luring pupils away from the Little Schools. Much the same protest came from the Guild of Writing Masters, who wanted to preserve its monopoly on the teaching of penmanship. These guilds filed suits against De La Salle, seized the furniture of the schools, forced the closure of the schools for a while, and continually harassed the Brothers.

Life for the Brothers was hard enough without such strife. Diseases spread easily in the schools. Exhausted and stressed from the hard work and poor diet, the Brothers struggled to stave off illness and discouragement. Many men left the community and, employing the skills learned as Brothers, made a better living on their own. In

1690 De La Salle almost died himself. Just after he was back on his feet after months of illness and recuperation, he suffered the sudden death of Brother Henri L'Heureux.

Hoping that Henri could replace him as superior, De La Salle had been preparing him for ordination to the priesthood. Badly shaken by Brother Henri's death, De La Salle meditated upon its meaning. He concluded that the community should remain all Brothers. An early biographer, Jean-Baptist Blain, described De La Salle's thinking in this way: "Would such priests be humble enough to confine themselves to the limitations of a vocation which has nothing flamboyant about it in the world's eyes?...It must be admitted, therefore, that the priestly state is not compatible with that of a teaching Brother."[6] Once again, a crisis became a defining moment for De La Salle and the new community.

By 1691 the community seemed ready to collapse. The workload was burning the Brothers out. De La Salle realized that they needed time and a place for retreat and renewal. Eventually he found a house in Vaugirard, a suburb of Paris. De La Salle gathered the Brothers there and instructed and reviewed with them the essential elements of their life as a religious community. This practice of bringing experienced Brothers together for some months of renewal became a feature of the early community's life and continues to this day.

When the Brothers left Vaugirard, De La Salle asked them to write to him regularly. Through their letters back and forth, De La Salle acted as spiritual director to all these men. His words were both practical and inspirational and illuminate the character of De La Salle and the community at the time.

By Association

Members of the community had been pronouncing annual vows as a sign of their commitment. Toward the end of the first retreat at Vaugirard, De La Salle and two of the senior Brothers took what became known after De La Salle's death as the heroic vow, which declared in part that they "make the vow of association and union to bring about and maintain the said establishment, without being able to withdraw from this obligation, even if only we three remain in the said Society, and if we were obliged to beg for alms and to live on bread alone."[7] During the summer of 1694 De La Salle and twelve key Brothers pronounced perpetual vows.

Men continued to join the community, and new schools opened in Chartres, Calais, Troyes, Avignon, Rouen, and several other cities. As the Society spread, the Brothers initiated new educational programs. Many poor young men had started working in childhood. Deprived of even basic education, they could neither gain better employment nor learn about their religion. Recognizing this need, De La Salle started a Christian Academy on Sundays and holidays. The young workers could learn reading, writing, arithmetic, drafting, and religion. And, in response to requests to supply trained lay teachers to village parishes, De La Salle opened another teacher-training program for country schoolmasters.

When King James II fled England into exile in France, De La Salle was prevailed upon by the archbishop to provide lodging and education to fifty boys in the king's entourage. Thus, De La Salle opened the community's first boarding school.

In Rouen, De La Salle opened a different sort of boarding school in which the young men took commercial courses so that they could enter the world of business. This was a clear break with the traditional classical curriculum. These students took advanced mathematics courses, drawing, and so on. Indeed, many historians consider this the first "commercial" school of its kind.

Also in Rouen, De La Salle admitted delinquent boys to the boarding school. While they followed the regular classes, they lived separately, and their movements were closely supervised. Eventually, the Brothers accepted young men in trouble with the law into another facility. Instead of being plunged into French prisons and forgotten, these men—while clearly prisoners—received some education and, more important, religious instruction.

Wanting to gain papal approval for the growing community, De La Salle chose two Brothers to establish the Institute in Rome. One of the Brothers abandoned the journey, but Brother Gabriel Drolin arrived in the Eternal City. For the next twenty-six years, Drolin—all alone—faithfully carried out his mission of teaching and tried to gain papal recognition. De La Salle continually assured Drolin that he would soon send another Brother, but he never accomplished this.

During this time of expansion, De La Salle also started composing essential texts for the community. In 1694 he wrote a draft of a rule for the Society. He worked on catechisms; revised *The Conduct of the Christian Schools*; composed *The Rules of Christian Decorum and Civility*, outlining the proper manners of a French gentleman; and provided other needed texts and documents.

Enemies Abound

Even as De La Salle and the Brothers expanded their good work, De La Salle's enemies actively sought his ruin. By all accounts his chief nemesis was the pastor of Saint Sulpice, Father de La Chetardie. While Chetardie wanted the community to teach the children of the parish, he also wanted control of the Brothers. Father La Grange, a priest aware of the conflict, drew this conclusion: "His [De La Salle's] great crime, as far as I can find out, is that he does not act according to the views of the pastor of Saint Sulpice....If De La Salle could agree with him, there would be no trouble with the archbishop."[8]

Chetardie prosecuted a quiet war against De La Salle that lasted for years. The pastor submitted surreptitious reports to the archbishop of Paris that were filled with accusations against De La Salle. Investigations by church officials followed. When the archbishop tried to replace De La Salle with a priest-superior, the Brothers resisted. The cardinal threatened to exile De La Salle. Hearing this, La Grange records that De La Salle said that he would go "wherever His Eminence might care to send him, and that this would afford him much consolation since he could find God everywhere. As for food and clothing, he could hardly be worse off than he already was."[9] In the meantime, the Brothers determined that they would abandon Saint Sulpice rather than De La Salle.

Chetardie quickly backed down, pleading with the Brothers to stay. The archbishop withdrew the decree of banishment. Chetardie muted his opposition but continued to subvert De La Salle by various means.

Other enemies—the writing masters and the masters of the Little Schools—united to destroy the community. The legal status of these two guilds gave them certain rights and powers. Not having gained letters patent from the king, the Brothers had no legal status. Thus, the two guilds charged that the Brothers accepted students who could pay for schooling. Indeed, the Brothers' schools gave a better education, were more disciplined, and were free. Naturally, parents wanted this superior and gratuitous education for their sons. For several years De La Salle was embroiled in legal struggles. The furniture of the schools was seized twice. The Brothers were forced to leave the schools for a time. And the Brothers faced harassment on the streets from members of the guilds.

With Chetardie and the guilds actively fighting against the community and having established the novitiate at Saint Yon in Rouen and dispersed the Brothers to other schools, De La Salle decided to leave Paris entirely. Many other cities sought the Brothers' services, and the Brothers had formed new communities in Darnetal, Marseille, Mende, Ales, Grenoble, Saint Denis, Les Vans, Moulins, and Boulogne-sur-Mer. Chetardie faced upset parishioners who wanted the Brothers back. Finally, Chetardie recognized that he needed the community and not the other way around. He guaranteed that he would not interfere with the community. The Brothers returned to Saint Sulpice. To deal with the guilds, Chetardie assumed responsibility for ensuring that all boys in the schools were unable to pay fees.

While circumstances improved in Paris, other trouble was brewing. A wealthy young man had pledged to fund a teacher-training center. De La Salle moved ahead with the project. When the young man reneged on the agreement, he accused De La Salle of owing him a substantial sum. Being well connected, the man's family prevailed in subsequent legal action. De La Salle was fined and might have been jailed had he not set out to visit the Brothers' communities in southern France.

Despite being circled by enemies wishing to destroy him and the community he had founded, his biographers describe De La

Salle as never losing either his equanimity or his determination. De La Salle worked hard and planned well but ultimately left matters in the hands of Providence. De La Salle declared: "If my work does not come from God, I would consent to its ruin....But if [God] declares himself its defender, let us fear nothing....If contradiction is proof that an enterprise comes from God, let us be happy; our Institute is indeed his creation. The cross which follows it everywhere gives us assurance that this is so."[10]

The Final Chapter

De La Salle's faith sustained him, but the troubles in Paris, his age, periodic illnesses, and the new challenges in the south all compelled him to retreat into solitude. When he reached Marseille, De La Salle found a faction of priests demanding that seminarians teach in the charity schools. Many people who had supported the Brothers' novitiate in Marseille withdrew their help when they realized that these Brothers could be sent anywhere in France. Some of the Brothers harshly criticized De La Salle for his leadership.

De La Salle retreated to a monastery and shrine nearby to pray, meditate, and to discern God's will in his regard. Some have called this his dark night of the soul. While he never recorded what happened during this period, he subsequently continued his visits to the communities in southern France.

Arriving at Mende, the Brothers refused him admission to the house. Realizing that he would correct their lax observance of the Rule and the poor conduct of the school, they used his embattled status in Paris and conflict with the Brothers in Marseille as excuses to bar his entry. The Capuchin friars offered him shelter, and then a wealthy woman in the city asked him to assist her in establishing a community of women.

Eventually, at the behest of the Brothers, Brother Timothy found De La Salle and convinced him that the community needed his leadership. With some hesitation De La Salle traveled to Grenoble, where he lived with the Brothers for nearly a year. During this time he revised some of the texts, substituted in classes, and suffered through the cures for his chronic rheumatism. He also spent time in retreat at Parmenie under the guidance of Sister Louise, a hermit known for her powers of discernment.

In the north of France the community was in chaos. Once again the Sulpician pastors tried to control the workings of the Institute. In desperation the senior Brothers sent this letter, dated April 1, 1714, to De La Salle:

> We, the principal Brothers of the Christian Schools, having in view the greater glory of God as well as the good of the Church and of our Society, consider that it is of the greatest importance that you return to the care and direction of God's holy work....We very humbly beseech you, and we command you in the name and of the part of the body of the Society to which you have vowed obedience, to take up at once the general government of the Society.[11]

After some delays De La Salle made his way back to Paris. Arriving at the Brothers' community, he asked, "Well, here I am. What do you want of me?"

While De La Salle left Brother Barthélemy to run the day-to-day affairs of the Institute, De La Salle's presence and guidance helped the community right itself. After some months De La Salle moved to St. Yon's in Rouen to help guide the novices and work among the delinquent boys. He continued writing various texts.

Wishing to hand over the direction of the Institute, De La Salle supported the call for a general assembly of the Brothers so that they could formally elect a superior. In 1717 delegates chose Brother Barthélemy to lead the community, which now numbered over one hundred members.

In his last two years De La Salle fended off any attempts to involve him in direction of the community, deferring all questions to Brother Barthélemy. Many people came to him for spiritual direction and the sacrament of reconciliation.

After a long illness, De La Salle died on Good Friday, 1719. In answer to a question from Brother Barthélemy, his last words were typical of the way in which he lived his whole life: "I adore in all things the guidance of God in my regard."[12]

INTRODUCTION

CENTRAL THEMES OF LASALLIAN SPIRITUALITY

John Baptist de La Salle is situated squarely in the center of the French School of spirituality.[13] The theological themes of Lasallian spirituality are common to other figures of the period: Christocentrism, theocentrism, reliance on providence and the action of the Holy Spirit.[14] Throughout his writings De La Salle kept coming back to the following three core values:

The Spirit of Faith: De La Salle made the spirit of faith the spirit of the community. In one of his many letters to Brothers, he explains: "The spirit of faith is a sharing in the Spirit of God who dwells in us, which leads us to regulate our conduct in all things by the sentiments and truths that faith teaches us. You should, therefore, be wholly occupied in acquiring it."[15] For classroom teachers this meant trying to make all decisions about the welfare of their students in the manner that Jesus did with his disciples. To help nurture faith, De La Salle developed simple practices of prayer and meditation on the gospels and regular reminders of God's sacred presence for the teachers that would help them be "ambassadors" of Christ to their pupils.

Zeal in Their Ministry as Teachers: True faith should overflow with abundant zeal. After all, Christ lives in each child in the classroom. Teachers are God's "ambassadors" to their students. Therefore, De La Salle emphasized that disciples of Jesus, especially teachers, should be recognized by their zealous love of God and their students: "If you want the instruction you give to be effective in drawing those you are obliged to teach to the practice of good, you too must practice these same truths. You must be so full of zeal that your students can share in the communication of the same grace for doing good that is in you. Thus your zeal will draw down on you the Spirit of God to inspire them with the same Spirit."[16] In De La Salle's spirituality, faith and zeal went together inextricably, as can be seen dramatically in the "Rules I Have Imposed on Myself" (see Chapter 8). Faith without action was dead. Work not rooted in faith would be fruitless.

Trust in God's Providence and Holy Will: Part of living in the spirit of faith is relying on the providence of God. Even when his enemies encircled him, allies abandoned him, and famine emptied the pantry, with complete confidence De La Salle urged the Brothers to rely on God's providence. Tied to this reliance was his practice of praying to know the will of God in all things. He discerned this will with spiritual directors, friends, study of the scriptures, and constant prayer. Even at the end of his life De La Salle's prayer was to know God's will: "To my mind, what I must ask of God in prayer is that he tell me what he wants me to do and that he inspire me with the disposition he wants me to have."[17]

ENDURING CONTRIBUTIONS OF DE LA SALLE'S SPIRITUALITY

The particular genius of De La Salle's work and its lasting contribution come not from his theological innovation, but from his concrete adaptation of this spirituality to a barely literate community of teachers and their illiterate charges.[18]

As patron of all teachers, Roman Catholicism recognizes him as a universal spiritual model. Not only his personal example but his teachings have an enduring value for the spiritual life, especially for teachers and those in the direct service of the economically poor. His work is "a proven source of continual human and Christian enrichment, theoretically and practically."[19] The patronage of John Baptist de La Salle applies to all who see the gospel as a force motivating the Christian community to become what it is called to be: the body of Christ.

Meditating on the texts, but also the rituals, practices, disciplines, institutions, and methods of both the interior life and of ministry, helps us fully understand a spiritual legacy.[20] All of these give us access to the relationship with God and with Christ's church, which is the core of that spirituality. This is why this volume includes occasional memoirs on issues such as habit and language, rule selections, instructions for running a school, and politeness, in addition to meditations and spiritual advice.

The charism of a religious leader or community offers a gift to the whole Christian community. In the Christian context, charism is rooted in the biblical understanding of grace. Rather than solely the gift of an individual, charism is the response of an individual or community to God's grace in Jesus Christ for the service of the church in the midst of a complex confluence of events that can be spoken of as a crisis.

For John Baptist de La Salle, the response was to a providence he could not foresee, to promptings he often resisted, to a group of men he originally considered "inferior to [his] valet," and to poor young people neglected by both church and society. In his book on characteristics of Lasallian schools, George Van Grieken declared: "To do justice to De La Salle's charism in the contemporary world, one must do justice both to the nature of that charism and to the nature of the contemporary world, placing them in critical dialogue with each other."[21]

The doctrine of abandonment to divine providence is a case in point. A central motif in the French School, for De La Salle it meant taking the risk of faith to enter practically and creatively into the world of the poor, even when it necessitated burning the bridges of clerical culture, social class, security, and even family. God's reign and its service through the ministry of education supplied the confidence teachers need to risk their own future. To discern God's providence is to interpret the events of life not as obstacles and pitfalls, but as challenges and opportunities given by grace. Facing these challenges brings dignity to the calling of the educator.

For De La Salle, reliance on providence did not mean passivity. Rather, he had the wisdom to work out detailed educational structures and financial and spiritual supports for his teachers. Indeed, a century later the community survived the French Revolution by transcending the control of local bishops or the confinement of the nation-state.

De La Salle's spirituality continues to have a lasting impact because of three essential features:

1. *His educational focus.* He mined the gospels, the expertise of his period, and his own inspiration and experience for practical models of educational reform;

2. *His option for the poor.* He developed spiritual disciplines for the internal life and community that enabled teachers to love and serve the poor;

3. *His rationale for a lay movement.* De La Salle aided men and women to stand with equal dignity before God and in the church's mission with any other member of the Christian community, no matter how exalted in hierarchy or education.

His Educational Focus

De La Salle adapted the insights and vision of the gospel, as embodied in the French School, to the needs of educators with the simplest spiritual and educational formation. The spirituality is missionary; that is, Christian activism and the details of care, respect, and discipline for the young charges of the teachers are as integral as the extensive regime of prayer, meditation, and sacramental life. For instance, De La Salle designed spiritual practices for the schools that reminded everyone of the presence of God. Each hour and half-hour a student rang a bell announcing the prayer "Let us remember that we are in the holy presence of God." Every interaction or encounter began with the greeting "Live, Jesus, in our hearts!" and was answered with "Forever."

During the period of De La Salle many initiatives for the foundation of schools and assembling teachers to support them were undertaken.[22] However, a firm prayer life, a community support system, and zeal welded faith and active ministry together, thus enabling the Christian Schools as De La Salle developed them and an educational spirituality to support them to endure. Jean-Guy Rodrique notes, "Rather than turn the teacher's focus away from their daily work, the interior life that he developed led them to be aware that school was the very place in which to meet God, in the concrete events of their personal experience."[23]

De La Salle's practical educational approach is most noted for his introduction of group cooperative learning methods to replace the tutorial approach of his time and for his introduction of the vernacular for teaching and, where possible, for prayer, rather than the traditional Latin.[24] The innovative classroom methods, his spiritual formation of teachers, and his integration of chapters on the Mass, prayer, and catechesis as integral and complementary elements of the school have made a lasting contribution to the understanding of the school as a faith community, nurturing the human and religious formation of its students, faculty, and administrators.

His spirituality for educators is always person-centered: "De La Salle is more concerned in the teaching of catechism with teacher-student interaction than with a body of doctrine."[25] Catechesis and the whole spiritual environment of the school are concerned about conversion, touching hearts. He did not avoid doctrine. However, catechetical instruction was not about abstract learning but was a means of salvation, a faith nurtured by community, example, and the practice of the Christian life.[26]

His Option for the Poor

De La Salle's spirituality not only integrates the mission of the teacher into a spirituality for educators, but it also provides a gospel base for a return to the church's mission to the poor. In seventeenth-century France this option was a particular challenge, because the crossing of class lines was as difficult as crossing racial boundaries was a half century ago in US culture. While a number of religious communities of women were developing an educational mission, bringing men into educational work at this popular level was an important innovation.

For some, the education of the masses in pre-revolutionary Europe was seen as a threat to society. After the Council of Trent many developments in support of education of the poor were initiated. Parish education was often conducted in such a way as to make the poor children adornments for the Latin liturgy, paying scant attention to their development and progress in human and religious knowledge. In Louis XIV's France clergy were still the "second estate," with many of the bishops sequestered at the court in Versailles. For De La Salle to find himself identified with the poor eventually meant resigning his ecclesiastical preferment in Reims, moving from his middle-class family home, and eventually dying suspended from his church functions.

Nevertheless, he developed a spirituality that linked the love for and service to and with the poor to the central mysteries of Christ. Like the spirituality initiatives in health care and social welfare initiated by Vincent de Paul (1625–60) and Louise de Marillac (1591–1660), De La Salle avoided sentimental attachment to the marginalized. Instead, he created institutions, internal disciplines, and lifestyles that were able to stand up to the Baroque cultural Catholicism of the day and to recognize God's call among the ignorant and neediest segments of his society.[27] This is a spirituality formed not only by biblical ideals but also by concrete experiences.

The recognition of Christ in the person of the poor, as demonstrated in so many of these texts, required rigorous internal spiritual discipline, reinforced by prayer, reflection, and discernment. Commitment to the educational service of the poor required continual conversion and a communal structure for support.[28]

That his community of Brothers grew to only about one thousand in the century before the French Revolution illustrates that De La Salle's movement toward popular education of the poor was well ahead of its time.[29] In one of history's ironies, the suppression of the Brothers of the Christian Schools with the French Revolution unleashed a desire for educational equality and society's investment in the development of its people. In the wake of the revolution, such desire prompted Napoleon to invite the Brothers to reconstitute French primary education. By the mid-nineteenth century, when popular education was only beginning in England, De La Salle's Brothers and similar congregations in France were integrated into a comprehensive system of state-controlled primary schools.[30]

Lasallian spirituality focused the Brothers narrowly on educational work. While this focus did not always encourage adaptability to the times, their fundamental, counter-cultural commitment to educational service of the poor filled a vacuum in the enlightenment ideology that made both De La Salle's educational ideas and the spirituality that supported them flourish in the nineteenth century.[31] Not only were enlightenment philosophers ill-adapted to popular education, but some were, in fact, hostile to the service of the poor through education.[32]

His Rationale for a Lay Movement

The fact that De La Salle's spiritually is uniquely crafted for the layperson only gradually dawned on him. He spent eighteen months at the seminary of Saint Sulpice, a center for the reforms of the Council of Trent. It nurtured the development of a high doctrine of the priesthood and a serious approach to the clerical state. A case can be made for the fact that a central gift of the French School was reform of the priesthood and a strong, clerical-centered ecclesiology.[33]

De La Salle opted to build a spirituality designed for lay professional educators whose ministry was rooted in their calling to be disciples of Jesus and servants of human need[34]: "The spirituality that results is thus apostolic and not monastic, a lay rather than a clerical way of seeking the perfection demanded by the Gospel, a spirituality accessible to beginners as well as beneficial to the spiritually mature."[35]

His development of lay ministry came from his own theological reflection and not from an institutional designation, as would emerge later with the specialized Catholic Action movement of the early twentieth century.[36] The church only received the Brotherhood that he founded and the wider lay influence it presaged over a long period of time. Certainly the utilization of ministry language to speak of his teachers was uncommon during this period in the life of the church and became quite controversial in the Catholic Church in the years before the Second Vatican Council.[37] Indeed, at the time of De La Salle's canonization, his meditations where these passages occur were considered spirituality and not theology, and therefore were not scrutinized for their orthodoxy.

THE TEXTS

Meditations for the Time of Retreat: Sometime after 1707 and before his death in 1719, De La Salle wrote a set of sixteen meditations for the Brothers to use at their annual eight-day retreat. These meditations provide the most complete, cogent, and inspiring formulation of De La Salle's spirituality for educators. Beginning in the mind of a provident God who creates the Christian School for the salvation of children far from salvation, the meditations take those praying through the lived vocation of a Christian teacher even to the final reward in heaven. All sixteen meditations have been included and form the centerpiece of this volume.

Meditations for Sundays and Feasts were not published during De La Salle's lifetime, and when they were published, they were not meant for distribution beyond his Brothers. However, they demonstrate the integration of his spiritual vision for educators, especially of the poor. The meditations do not depart from the themes of the French School: theocentrism, providence, Christocentrism, and the action of the Holy Spirit. However, the skillful integration of these themes into practical directives for lay educators, always linking the relationship to God with the relationship of educators to their students, makes them a unique contribution to a mission-oriented spirituality.

The 1718 Rule and *Memoranda:* The passages from the 1718 Rule describe the spirit of faith and the spirit of zeal, which together form the spirit of the Institute. "Memorandum on the Beginnings" is the title given to a reflective document that the biographers Bernard and Blain tell us was written by De La Salle himself. The manuscript that the biographers were using is a reflection on the period 1679–80 and 1693–94. For De La Salle, God is intimately involved in the fabric of living, busy about the work of salvation, completing creation. In the "Memorandum on the Habit," De La Salle's biographers tell us, he composed a document around 1690 intended to justify the choice of the habit worn by the Brothers. De La Salle submitted his ideas to "the directors and superiors of the seminary of Saint Sulpice," who agreed with him wholeheartedly. It affirms the lay character of the group and the "gratuitous" character of the schools they conduct. "The Memorandum on Not Using Latin to Teach Reading" defends the practice of teaching in French. The children in the Brothers' schools might only be there for two years. Learning Latin first would preclude them learning religion and the most basic skills they would need.

The Conduct of the Christian Schools: This volume evolved over many years as De La Salle and the Brothers examined their experience of what worked well in conducting schools for poor boys. They took what was "best practice" from other educators of the day and revised it. To this they added their own experience and insights gained through their daily encounter with the poor children of their schools. The earliest extant manuscript of the *Conduct* is dated 1706, but it went through many revisions during De La Salle's lifetime. Indeed, the *Conduct* was still being revised and followed into the last century. The volume shows Lasallian spirituality in action.

The Rules of Christian Decorum and Civility: De La Salle wrote this as a text for boys in the Christian Schools. First published in 1703, it underwent many editions in De La Salle's lifetime and remained in continuous publication until 1875. De La Salle wanted to teach manners to boys, but more important, ways of acting that would create the harmonious relationships that are the fruit of living in a Christian way. Politeness and civility, being a "gentleman," integrated the gospels into everyday life. Unlike the other works about manners that focused on civil virtue, De La Salle gave decorum and civility an underpinning of Pauline theology.

The Duties of a Christian to God: The first members of the society of the Christian Schools were simple laymen. Their task of religious instruction demanded that they be versed in the Tridentine theology of the church. To accomplish this, De La Salle wrote a series of "catechisms" that, by Rule, the Brothers studied daily. The excerpts included in this volume show not only something of the content of religious thought of his day, but also the approach De La Salle took in communicating it.

Explanation of the Method of Interior Prayer: The principal spiritual exercise of the Brothers was interior prayer. In this exercise God was to teach De La Salle's Brothers how to see as the provident God sees and to act as the God desirous of the salvation of all acts. This *Explanation* was a beginner's introduction to the art of interior prayer.

Letters and Personal Documents: The document "Rules I Have Imposed on Myself" marks out the spiritual journey of John Baptist de La Salle in a forceful and personal way. De La Salle composed the "Heroic Vow" that was taken by two Brothers and him in 1691. They pledged to hold fast to the mission of the community even if they were alone and had to live solely on bread. De La Salle's letters offer another unique insight into the spirit of the man and the life of the Institute. By Rule, all Brothers were instructed to write to De La Salle monthly in order to report on their lives. Undoubtedly, De La Salle must have composed thousands of letters during his lifetime, but only 134 have been verified as his. The last texts are De La Salle's final words to the community.

Language and Style

The English words "to translate" and "to be a traitor" come from the same root word. This speaks to the difficulty of trying to take what is said in one language, with its own vocabulary, idiom, and mindset, and put it into another language, with its own vocabulary, idiom, and mindset. This is important in reading the English translations of De La Salle's writings that follow. They represent not only a language translation but a time translation as well.

For the most part De La Salle was writing for a group of men who were little schooled in literary style and sophistication. De La Salle, the son of a lawyer and court magistrate, was most comfortable in writing direct but long sentences. Those who have put his work into the present English format have attempted to be faithful to his meaning and genius while being sensitive to the current English-speaking audience.

At the same time, the translators have tried to create a type of consistency in the English words chosen to translate the French words and ideas. Thus, when we read *instruction* in English, it is important for readers to understand that De La Salle always uses the French equivalent of this English word to mean "the teaching of religion." When we read the English word *prayer*, this is almost always a translation of the French word *oraison*, which means "interior prayer," as distinguished from vocal prayer or *prière*. It was this *oraison* that was at the heart of the Brother's continual conversion to be an instrument of God in the work of the salvation of the young people entrusted to him by God.

De La Salle's own vocabulary grows and develops as he comes prayerfully to understand this "work of God" called the Christian Schools. Young people move from being called children or *enfants* to being named "disciples" of the teacher, even as the teacher is the disciple of Jesus Christ. Rarely does De La Salle use the word *élève* (pupil).[38]

Finally, the translators attempted to be as faithful to the original as possible. Readers are reminded that De La Salle was writing hundreds of years before present sensitivities to gender in language and male language for God were considerations.

A CONTINUING SPIRITUAL CHALLENGE

The school as faith community, Lasallian methods of teaching classrooms of children, and the spiritual formation of teachers have become standard practices in Christian schools. Popular education has become almost universal. The major ecumenical churches of the West have incorporated the option for the poor in their teachings. The Catholic Church has joined Protestants and Anglicans in promoting ecclesial lay ministry and a vernacular spirituality for both worship and formation. The Catholic Church has incorporated active lay communities of women and men into its governance. Community organization, global interdependence, and social transformation are affirmed as gospel values.

If we look closely at the spiritual itinerary of De La Salle, the living legacy of the movement he left, and his writings, there are many elements for opening the heart to the Holy Spirit's call to mission. Here we will note only three: the legacy for a socially sensitive spirituality, lay ministry resources, and a particular contribution to an ecclesial spirituality. The timeliness of this legacy is apparent in discerning the times in which we live:

> The hopes, the searching, the aspirations, the anguish of the youth at the close of [the last] century live with us; they worry and stimulate us. At the same time, we are preoccupied by the

disillusioned relativism of some young people, by their fatalism caused by a feeling of helplessness, and by their allergy to long-term commitments.[39]

Major changes have occurred in the history of Christian spirituality that give new cogency to the Lasallian legacy. The legacy is significant because of its contribution to the needs of the poor and marginalized in our day, and to the life of the spirit among the educators who will respond to this call of the reign of God.

A Socially Sensitive Spirituality. In his day De La Salle provided a spirituality to support educators' mission to serve the poor. His integration of faith and zeal in a spiritual community gave substance to this evangelical ideal. His systematic approach to building faith community in the school and his spiritual support system for a missionary lifestyle continue to provide nourishment for those who would take the risks to identify with the poor and their educational needs. De La Salle's *Meditations for the Time of Retreat* demonstrate how the details of ministry, the signs of the times, and strategies for change are appropriate content for discerning God's will in ministry. His *Method of Interior Prayer*, when interpreted in the context of contemporary biblical, sacramental, and social scholarship, provides a useful, analytical resource for discerning God's presence in the lives of the individual, the community, and the world. Applying the mysteries of Christ's life to the plight of the poor, international conflict, or the struggles in church and society enables the gospel to come alive and to give practical guidance to current events, just as it did for the educational world in which the *Method* was originally used.

A Resource for Lay Ministry. Like Francis of Assisi and Waldo before him, and McCauley and Wesley after him, the most tangible embodiment of De La Salle's legacy is the community that incarnates his spirituality:

> The spiritual vision of De La Salle could never have survived to enrich future generations of Brothers, students and colleagues, if the community had not achieved institutional form. Its formally approved and clearly defined juridical character is a necessary and important guarantee that the legacy of De La Salle will have stability and permanence, that the spirituality and the

charism of the Founder can be kept alive, developed, and trans-
mitted from one generation to the next. Thus it is the Institute
[of the Brothers of the Christian Schools] itself that constitutes
the total legacy of John Baptist de La Salle.[40]

However, the lay movement he initiated was only gradually institu-
tionalized: by papal approval in 1725, civil approval the same year,
and incorporation into canon law in 1917. Nevertheless, it provided
collateral support for the many active religious communities of lay-
women and laymen that emerged during the nineteenth century in
the wake of the French and Industrial revolutions. The lay character
of his contribution and legacy was acknowledged with the Catholic
Church's recognition of De La Salle as patron of *all*, not just religious, teachers.

While he was not involved in questions of lay governance, liturgical participation, or parish and diocesan support for ecclesial lay
ministries, his spirituality is a rich resource for these lay developments
of our own day. He did provide formation for lay teachers. He did
struggle to provide both spiritual and institutional support for his lay
community, often against strenuous clerical and secular pressures.

De La Salle grounded the important theological framework for
the dignity of lay ministry, especially in his *Meditations for the Time of
Retreat* and other meditations, like the one for the feast of Saint
Marcellinus in this volume, in a careful reading of Paul's epistles.
Little direction could be found in the ecclesiology of ministry of his
day.[41] With the shifting demography of the Catholic Church and the
increase of ecclesial lay ministers in education and other sectors of
the church's mission, this spirituality remains an important resource:

> In 1998, there were 6,694 Brothers. Of these, a total of 2,777
> Brothers worked with 64,687 partners and 784,061 students
> among 904 educational institutions throughout the world. In
> the United States alone, there were 969 Brothers. Of these, a
> total of 187 Brothers worked with 3,123 partners and 69,311
> students among 94 educational institutions.[42]

These figures, when compared with the burgeoning needs
of poor communities around the world and the advance of lay

educational ministry, demonstrate the importance of this spirituality for a much wider range of ministers in the church.

An Ecclesial Spirituality for a Reform Era. De La Salle was loyal to a church more universal than the Gallican nationalism of his France. His training at Saint Sulpice supported the reforms of the Council of Trent at a time when the majority of French bishops did not embrace them. In fact, the reform decrees of that council were not promulgated in France until Napoleon's concordat of 1801. De La Salle's contribution lay in his catechetical work and his Christo-centric spirituality grounded in biblical fidelity and loyalty to an international vision of Catholic unity. The dominant view of the church in his day focused on the image of the institutional church as a perfect society. De La Salle's catechetical emphasis in the *Duties of a Christian to God* is more balanced among communal, spiritual, and institutional aspects of the church: "The bonds of unity in the Spirit, in charity and in the end or 'mission' are communal elements, while the unity expressed in sharing the same sacraments and obeying common authorities is more institutional."[43]

De La Salle's spirituality can nourish reformers that today live in the hopes for realizing the dreams of the Second Vatican Council and its biblical, liturgical, ecumenical, catechetical, and social reforms. As characterized by one author, "De La Salle leaves an old, immobile Church to accede to a new one, or at least having freely consented to the creative force acting in and beyond him, he allows himself to be reborn to a new way of living the Church."[44] De La Salle believed in a missionary church, a church for the world, a serving church, a church of the people of God, and a church liberated for universal service while inculturated in a host of contexts.

His ecclesial spirituality has been spoken of as an "existential ecclesiology."[45] This view of the church grows out of the tradition but is likewise drawn from the vision of mission, needs of the poor, and the resources of the whole people of God, rather than solely from particular social institutions of ministry and communion in place in the culture of the time: "The Brothers' ministry is apostolic and evangelical, not primarily because of their being commissioned by the Church, but because the very nature of that ministry resembles what Jesus himself did first and what the apostles did after Jesus."[46]

INTRODUCTION

The spiritual legacy of John Baptist de La Salle offers all educators a grounding for their ministry, a ministry at least as important today as it was three hundred years ago when De La Salle was gathering the ragtag group of schoolmasters into his home. What he said then, still applies, "You are the ambassadors and the ministers of Jesus Christ in the work that you do."

Chapter 1

Meditations for the Time of Retreat

━━━━━━━━━━━━ ✠ ━━━━━━━━━━━━

EDITORS' INTRODUCTION: *This set of meditations stands at the center of the Lasallian corpus. In it we find the central themes of the Lasallian charism: the teacher as ambassador of Christ, the provident God, and the union between work for teacher's salvation and the ministry of teaching. The grounding of the retreats in Pauline theology demonstrates De La Salle's profound knowledge of Sacred Scripture and in particular of Saint Paul. For the first Brothers, these retreats showed clearly how they were to live their vocation as teachers and ambassadors of Jesus Christ to the poor children they served. It is significant that De La Salle's most frequently used words in the meditations are "dieu" (God) and "enfant" (child). In effect, the meditations urge the Brothers to view their ministry to the children as one with their love of God: the two are inseparable. Meditating on God and the children led De La Salle and the first Brothers to understand what they were doing and how they were cooperators in this great work of God—salvation. The meditations were written as pairs. The first of each pair was intended for morning interior prayer and the second meditation of each pair was intended for the evening interior prayer. Each year the Brothers came together for the eight-day retreat. Each year they would make these same sixteen meditations in order to renew their faith in a loving God and their zeal in being Christ to the children who are Christ's presence to them.*[1]

First Meditation

God in his providence established the Christian Schools.

193.1 First Point

God is so good that having created us, he wills that all of us come to the knowledge of the truth (1 Tim 2:4). This truth is God himself and what he desired to reveal to us through Jesus Christ, the holy apostles, and his church. As a result, God wills all people to be instructed so that their minds can be enlightened by the light of faith.

We cannot be instructed in the mysteries of our holy religion unless we have the good fortune to hear about them, and we cannot enjoy this advantage unless someone preaches the word of God. "How can people believe in someone," the apostle says, "about whom they have not heard anyone speak, and how can they hear him spoken about if no one proclaims him to them?" (Rom 10:14–17).

God does this by using human ministers to diffuse the fragrance of his teaching throughout the whole world (2 Cor 2:14). Just as he commanded light to shine out of darkness, he enkindles a light in the hearts of those destined to announce his word to children so that they can enlighten these children by unveiling the glory of God to them (2 Cor 4:6).

Because God in his mercy has given you such a ministry, do not falsify his word but gain glory before him by unveiling his truth (2 Cor 4:1–2) to those you are charged to instruct. Let this be your whole effort in the instruction you give them, looking upon yourselves as the ministers of God and the dispensers of his mysteries (1 Cor 4:1).

193.2 Second Point

Although one of the main duties of fathers and mothers is to bring up their children in a Christian manner and teach them their religion, most parents are not sufficiently enlightened in these matters. Some are preoccupied by their daily concerns and the care of their family; others, with their constant anxiety to earn the necessities of life for themselves and their children, cannot take the time to teach their children their duties as Christians.

It is characteristic of God's providence and vigilance over human conduct to substitute for fathers and mothers other persons who have sufficient knowledge and zeal to bring children to the knowledge of God and of his mysteries. In accord with the grace of Jesus Christ that God has given them, they are like good architects who give all possible care and attention to lay the foundation (1 Cor 3:10) of religion and of Christian piety in the hearts of these children, a great number of whom would otherwise be abandoned.

You, then, whom God has called to this ministry, work according to this grace he has given you to instruct by teaching and to exhort by encouraging those entrusted to your care, guiding them with attention and vigilance (Rom 12:6–8) and thus fulfilling toward them the principal duty of fathers and mothers toward their children.

193.3 Third Point

God wills not only that all come to the knowledge of truth but also that all be saved (1 Tim 2:4). He cannot truly desire this end without providing the means for it and, therefore, without giving children teachers who will assist them in the fulfillment of his plan. This, says Saint Paul, is the field God cultivates, the building he is raising, and you are his chosen ones to help in this work by announcing to these children his son's gospel (1 Cor 3:9) and the truths contained in it.

Therefore, you must honor your ministry and keep trying to save some of these children (Rom 11:13–14). Because God has made you his ministers to reconcile them to him, according to the expression of the same apostle, and has entrusted you for this purpose with the word of reconciliation for them, exhort them as if God were urging them through you, for you have been destined to cultivate these young plants (Ps 128:3; 144:12) by announcing the truths of the gospel to them (2 Cor 5:18–20) and to procure for them the means of salvation appropriate to their development.

Do not teach them these truths with scholarly words, lest the cross of Christ, the source of our sanctification, become void of meaning (1 Cor 1:17) and all you say to them produce no benefit in their minds and hearts. Because these children are simple and for the most part poorly brought up, those who help them save themselves must do so in such a simple manner that every word will be clear and easy for them to understand.

Be faithful to this practice so that you can contribute as far as God requires of you to the salvation of those he has entrusted to you.

SECOND MEDITATION

The means that those responsible for the education of children must use to procure their sanctification.

194.1 *First Point*

Consider that the practice only too common among workers and poor people is to allow their children to live on their own, roaming all over like vagabonds as long as they cannot find them some work. These parents have no concern about sending their children to school either because their poverty does not allow them to pay the teachers or else, obliged to look for work outside the home, they have to abandon their children.

The results of this condition are regrettable, because these poor children, accustomed to leading an idle life for many years, have great difficulty adjusting when it comes time for them to go to work. In addition, through their association with bad companions, they learn to commit many sins that later on are very difficult to stop because of persistent bad habits contracted over such a long time.

God has had the goodness to remedy so great a misfortune by the establishment of the Christian Schools, where the teaching is offered free of charge and entirely for the glory of God, where the children are kept all day to learn reading, writing, and their religion, and where they are always busy, so that when their parents want them to go to work, they are ready for employment.

Thank God, who has had the goodness to employ you to procure such an important advantage for children. Be faithful and exact to do this without any payment so that you can say with Saint Paul, "The source of my consolation is to announce the gospel free of

charge, without having it cost anything to those who hear me"
(1 Cor 9:18).

194.2 Second Point

It is not enough that children remain in school for most of the
day and be kept busy. Those given to children to instruct them must
be especially dedicated to bring them up in the Christian spirit,
which gives children the wisdom of God, something that none of
the princes of this world has known (1 Cor 2:7–8). It is completely
opposed to the spirit and the wisdom of the world, which you must
inspire children with a great horror of because it serves as a cloak for
sin. Children cannot ever be too far separated from such a great evil,
which alone can make them displeasing to God.

Let this be your primary concern, then, and the initial effect of
your vigilance in your work: always to be attentive to your students
to forestall any action that is bad or even the least bit improper.

Help them avoid anything that has the slightest appearance of
sin. It is also of great importance that your vigilance over your students serves to make them self-controlled and reserved in church
and at the exercises of piety performed in school. Because of the
great number of graces piety brings to those who have it, piety is
useful in every way (1 Tim 4:8) and provides great facility for avoiding sin and practicing other acts of virtue.

Do you behave in this way with your students? Adopt these
practices in the future if you have not been sufficiently faithful in
the past.

194.3 Third Point

To bring the children you instruct to absorb the Christian
spirit, you must teach them the practical truths of faith in Jesus
Christ and the maxims of the holy gospel with at least as much care
as you teach the purely speculative truths.

Although it is true that to be saved we must absolutely know a
number of these speculative truths, what use would it be to know

41

them if we did not take the trouble to practice the good to which we are bound?

"Faith without good works is dead," Saint James advises (Jas 2:17). Saint Paul says, "If I knew all the mysteries and had full knowledge and all the faith such that I could move mountains from one place to another, but I do not have charity," that is, sanctifying grace, "I am nothing" (1 Cor 13:2).

Is your main care, then, to instruct your disciples in the maxims of the holy gospel and the practice of the Christian virtues? Have you anything more at heart than helping them find their happiness in these practices? Do you look upon the good you are trying to achieve in them as the foundation of all the good they will practice for the rest of their life? The habits of virtue a person cultivates during youth, encountering less resistance in corrupt nature, form the deepest roots in the hearts of those in whom they are developed.

If you want the instruction you give to be effective in drawing those you are obliged to teach to the practice of good, you too must practice these same truths. You must be so full of zeal that your students can share in the communication of the same grace for doing good that is in you. Thus your zeal will draw down on you the Spirit of God to inspire them with the same Spirit.

THIRD MEDITATION

Those who teach the young are cooperators with Jesus Christ in the salvation of souls.

195.1 First Point

Although Jesus Christ died for everyone, the benefit of his death is not effective in everyone, for all do not make the effort to apply it to themselves. For our part, the response of our will is necessary to make it effective. Although the death of Jesus Christ was more than sufficient to wipe out and to be a complete reparation for the sins of all—for God has reconciled us to himself by Jesus Christ (2 Cor 5:18)—nevertheless, the grace Jesus merited for us effects our salvation only insofar as our will is brought to correspond with it. Each of us must achieve and complete the work of our own redemption.

This makes Saint Paul say very well, speaking of himself, "I accomplish what is lacking in the passion of Christ" (Col 1:24). Is there something lacking, then, in the passion of Christ? There is nothing, certainly, on the part of Jesus Christ, but on the part of this holy apostle, as well as of everyone else, what was lacking was acceptance by his will, that is, the union of his sufferings with those of Jesus Christ as one of his members suffering in him and for him.

Because you are obliged to help your disciples save themselves, you must engage them to unite all their actions to those of our Lord Jesus Christ so that their actions, made holy by his merits and his consecration, can be pleasing to God and their means of salvation. This is how you must teach them to benefit from the death of our Lord Jesus Christ and to make effective in themselves the advantages and the merits of his death.

195.2 Second Point

Because you are the ambassadors and the ministers of Jesus Christ in the work that you do, you must act as representing Jesus Christ. He wants your disciples to see him in you and to receive your instructions as if he were giving them (2 Cor 5:20). They must be convinced that Jesus Christ is speaking his truth through your mouth, that you are teaching only in his name, and that he has given you authority over them.

They must also be convinced that they are the letter Jesus Christ has dictated to you and that you are writing each day in their hearts, not with ink but with the Spirit of the living God (2 Cor 3:3), who acts in you and by you through the power of Jesus Christ. God helps you triumph over all the obstacles that oppose the salvation of these children by enlightening them in the person of Jesus Christ (2 Cor 4:6) to make them avoid all that could displease him.

To fulfill this duty with as much perfection and exactness as God requires of you, frequently give yourselves to the Spirit of our

Lord so that you work only under his influence and your own spirit has no part in it. This Holy Spirit, then, will descend on the children generously to give them full possession of the Christian spirit.

195.3 *Third Point*

All your care for the children entrusted to you would be useless if Jesus Christ did not give the necessary quality, power, and efficacy to make it useful. "Just as the branch of the vine cannot bear fruit of itself," our Lord says, "unless it remains attached to the stem, neither can you bear fruit if you do not remain in me. This will be the glory of my Father, that you bear much fruit and become my disciples" (John 15:4–8).

What Jesus Christ says to his holy apostles he also says to you to make you understand that all the good you are able to do in your work for those entrusted to you will be true and effective only insofar as Jesus Christ gives it his blessing and you remain united with him. It is the same for you as for the branch of the vine, which can bear fruit only if it remains attached to the stem and draws its sap and strength from the vine, the source of all the goodness of the fruit.

Jesus Christ wants you to understand from this comparison that the more your work for the good of your disciples is inspired by him and draws its power from him, the more it will produce good results in them; therefore, you must ask him earnestly that all your instructions be given life by his Spirit and draw all their power from him. Just as he is the one who enlightens everyone coming into the world (John 1:9), he also is the one who enlightens the minds of your students and leads them to love and to practice the good you teach them.

FOURTH MEDITATION

What you must do to be true cooperators with Jesus Christ for the salvation of children.

196.1 First Point

Be convinced of what Saint Paul says, that you plant and water the seed, but God through Jesus Christ makes it grow (1 Cor 3:6) and brings your work to fulfillment. So when it happens that you encounter some difficulty in guiding your disciples, when there are some who do not profit from your instructions and in whom you observe a certain spirit of immorality, turn to God with confidence, and most insistently ask Jesus Christ, because he has chosen you to do his work, to make his Spirit come alive in you (1 Cor 3:9).

Consider Jesus Christ as the good shepherd of the gospel, who seeks the lost sheep, places it upon his shoulders, and carries it back (Luke 15:4–5) to restore it to the fold. Because you take his place, look upon yourselves as obligated to do the same thing, and ask him for the grace needed to obtain the conversion of their hearts.

To succeed in your ministry, therefore, you must devote yourself very much to prayer. You must constantly represent the needs of your disciples to Jesus Christ, explaining to him the difficulties you have experienced in guiding them. Jesus Christ, seeing that you regard him as the one who can do everything in your work and yourself as an instrument that ought to be operated only by him, will not fail to grant you what you ask of him.

196.2 Second Point

Jesus Christ, speaking to his apostles, told them that he had given them an example so that they could do as he had done (John 13:15). He also wanted his disciples to accompany him at all the conversions he effected so that seeing how he acted, they could be guided and formed by his conduct in all they would have to do to win souls to God.

You, whom Jesus Christ has chosen among so many others to be his cooperators (1 Cor 3:9) in the salvation of souls, must do the same. In reading the gospel you must study the manner and the means he uses to lead his disciples to practice the truths of the gospel.

Sometimes he proposes as happiness everything the world holds in horror, such as poverty, injuries, insults, slander, and every kind of persecution for the sake of justice, even telling his disciples that they ought to be glad and rejoice (Matt 5:3, 10–12) when such things happen to them.

At other times he inspires horror for the sins into which people ordinarily fall, or he proposes virtues to practice, such as gentleness, humility (Matt 11:29), and the like.

He also makes them understand that unless their justice surpasses that of the scribes and the Pharisees (who bother only about externals), they will never enter the kingdom of heaven (Matt 5:20).

Lastly, he wants the rich and those who have their pleasures in this world to be regarded as unfortunate (Luke 5:24).

You must teach the Christian young people entrusted to you according to these and all the other practices of Jesus Christ.

196.3 Third Point

In carrying out your service to children, you will not fulfill your ministry adequately if you resemble Jesus Christ only in his guidance and in his conversion of souls. You must also enter into his purposes and his goals. He came on earth, as he says, only that people might have life and have it to the full (John 10:10). This is why he says in another place that his words are spirit and life (John 6:64); that is, his words procure true life, which is the life of the soul, for those who hear them and after hearing them gladly, act on them with love.

This must be your goal when you instruct your disciples: that they live a Christian life and that your words become spirit and life for them, first, because they will be produced by the Spirit of God living in you, and second, because they will procure for your disciples the Christian spirit.

In possessing this spirit, which is the Spirit of Jesus Christ, they will live the true life that is so valuable to humanity because it leads surely to eternal life.

Guard against any human attitude toward your disciples; do not pride yourselves over what you do. These two things are capable of spoiling all the good in the performance of your duties. What have you in this regard that has not been given to you? If it has been given to you, why are you boasting as if you had it on your own? (1 Cor 4:7)

Therefore, keep the goals of your work as completely pure as those of Jesus Christ; by this means you will draw down his blessing and grace upon yourselves and all your labors.

FIFTH MEDITATION

Those chosen by Providence for the education of children must fulfill the function of guardian angels for them.

197.1 First Point

We can say that children at birth are like a mass of flesh. Mind does not emerge from matter in them except with time and becomes refined only little by little. As an unavoidable consequence, those who are ordinarily instructed in school cannot yet by themselves easily understand Christian truths and maxims. They need good guides and visible angels to help them learn these things.

Angels have this advantage over humans: They are not bound to a body and to all the functions of the senses without which the human mind ordinarily rarely operates. Angels, therefore, have intelligence far superior to human intelligence and can contribute much to human understanding, no matter how completely unsullied the level of human intelligence might be.

The angels who guide humans share with them their own understanding and the knowledge they have of the true good. By sharing in this enlightenment of the guardian angels, humans can have a more penetrating knowledge of God, of his perfections, of all that pertains to God, and of the means of going to him.

If this is true of all humans, it is incomparably more true of children, whose minds are more unrefined because they are less free of their senses and of matter. They need someone to develop for them the Christian truths—which are hidden from the human mind—in a

47

more concrete fashion and in harmony with the limitations of the mind. Without this help they often remain all their lives insensitive and opposed to thoughts of God and incapable of knowing and appreciating them (1 Cor 2:14).

For this purpose the goodness of God has provided children with teachers to instruct them in all these matters. Admire the goodness of God for providing for all the needs of his creatures and for taking the means to procure for humanity the knowledge of the true good, that is, everything concerning the salvation of the soul. Offer yourselves to God for this purpose to assist the children entrusted to you as far as he will require of you.

197.2 Second Point

To be saved it does not suffice to be instructed in the Christian truths that are purely speculative. As we have said, faith without works is dead (Jas 2:17); that is, it is like a body without a soul; consequently, it is not sufficient to help us achieve our salvation.

Therefore, it is not enough to procure for children the Christian spirit and teach them the mysteries and speculative truths of our religion. You must also teach them the practical maxims found throughout the holy gospel, but because their minds are not yet sufficiently able for them to understand and practice these maxims, you must serve them as visible angels in two ways.

First, you must help them understand the maxims as they are set forth in the holy gospel; second, you must guide their steps along the way that leads them to put these maxims into practice.

To do so, they need visible angels who by their instructions and good example will inspire them to appreciate and to practice these maxims. By these two means, these holy maxims will make a strong impression on their minds and hearts.

Such is the function you ought to perform for your disciples. It is your duty to act toward them as the guardian angels act toward you: to win them to practice the maxims of the holy gospel and to give them means that are easy and accommodated to their age. Gradually accustomed to this practice in their childhood, they will be able, when older, to confirm them as a kind of habit and practice them without great difficulty.

197.3 Third Point

People encounter so many obstacles to salvation in this life that it is impossible to avoid them if left to themselves and their own guidance. This is why God has given you guardian angels to watch over you, to prevent you, as the prophet says, from falling by tripping against a stone (Ps 91:12), that is, some obstacle to your salvation, and to inspire and help you avoid a path where you might encounter an obstacle.

How much easier it is for children to fall over some precipice because they are weak in mind as well as in body and have little understanding of what is for their own good. Therefore, they need light from watchful guides to lead them on the path of salvation, guides sufficiently understanding of matters concerning piety and the ordinary faults of young people to help them be aware of and to avoid pitfalls.

God has provided this help by giving children teachers whom he has charged with this care and to whom he has given enough concern and vigilance (Rom 12:8), not only to prevent anything whatsoever harmful to their salvation from capturing their hearts, but also to guide them through all the dangers they meet in the world. The result is that under the guidance of these attentive leaders and with God's protection, the devil dare not approach them.

Ask God today for the grace of watching so well over the children confided to you that you will take every possible precaution to shield them from serious faults.

Ask God to be such good guides for them by the light you will procure for yourselves by recourse to God and by the fidelity with which you do your work that you will clearly see every obstacle to the good of their souls and keep away from the path of their salvation everything that could harm them.

This is the principal care you must have for the children entrusted to you and the main reason God has entrusted you with so holy a ministry, one that he will summon you for a very exact account on the day of judgment.

SIXTH MEDITATION

How you fulfill the function of guardian angels in the education of youth.

198.1 First Point

Through the guardian angels, who are highly enlightened and know the good as it is, God makes known this good and the secrets of his holy will to those he has predestined to be his adopted children in Jesus Christ, by whom he calls them to be his heirs (Eph 1:5, 9, 11). By the light these angels share with those who are called, they teach them the good they ought to practice and what they must do to become heirs.

The ladder Jacob saw in a dream while on his way to Mesopotamia symbolizes this reality. Angels were going up and coming down the ladder (Gen 28:12). They were going up to God to make him aware of the needs of those for whom he made them responsible and to receive his orders for them. They were coming down to teach those they were guiding the will of God concerning their salvation.

You must do the same thing for the children entrusted to your care. It is your duty to go up to God every day by prayer, to learn from him all that you must teach your children, and then to come down to them by accommodating yourself to their level to instruct them about what God has communicated to you for them, both in your prayer and in the Holy Scriptures, which contain the truths of religion and the maxims of the holy gospel.

For this purpose you must not only know all these truths in general but also, and more important, have such a grasp of all of them that you are able to explain them sufficiently to make your disciples understand them clearly and in detail.

Have you studied well all these truths up to the present, and have you been thoroughly committed to impress them firmly on the minds of these children? Have you regarded this responsibility as the most important in your work?

From this moment on, take the steps to make it your main concern to instruct perfectly in the truths of the faith and the practical maxims of the holy gospel those who are entrusted to you.

198.2 Second Point

The holy guardian angels are not satisfied with illuminating the minds of those under their guidance with the light needed to know God's will for them and to be saved. They also inspire their charges and procure for them the means to do the good that is appropriate for them.

God uses the angels not only to deliver those entrusted to them from the powers of darkness and make them grow in the knowledge of God, but also to help them lead a life worthy of God so that they will be pleasing to him in every way and produce good works of every sort. The angels are zealous for the good of those in their care because of the commission they have received from God, the Father of light and of all good. They contribute as far as they are able to make those in their care worthy to share the lot of the saints (Col 1:10–13).

You share in the ministry of the guardian angels by making known to children the truths of the gospel, which God has chosen you to announce (1 Thess 2:4).

You must teach them how to put these truths into practice, and you must have very great zeal to achieve this effect in them.

Imitating the great apostle, you must encourage them to live in a manner worthy of God, for God has called them to his kingdom and his glory (1 Thess 2:12).

Your zeal must go so far in this work that to achieve it you are ready to give your very life, so dear to you (1 Thess 2:8) are the children entrusted to you.

It is your duty, then, to admonish the unruly and to do so in such a way that they give up their former way of life. You must inspire those lacking courage, support the weak, and be patient toward all (1 Thess 5:14). Your purpose is to be in a position to stop and to curb their corrupt inclinations and to establish them so firmly in the practice of good that they give the demon no entry to them (Eph 4:22, 27).

Have you maintained this guidance toward your disciples up to now? Have you been helping them practice the good that is appropriate to their years? Have you shown concern that they practice piety, especially during prayer and in church, and that they receive the sacraments frequently?

You must watch over them a great deal to procure for them the practice of good and the horror of sin, two extremely useful ways to help them achieve their salvation.

198.3 Third Point

If you want to accomplish your ministry as the guardian angels of the children whom you must instruct, to build up with them the body of Christ, and to make them holy and perfect (Eph 4:12), you must work to inspire them with the same sentiments and to put them in the same disposition in which Saint Paul tried to place the Ephesians with the letter he wrote them.

First, see to it that they do not sadden the Holy Spirit of God, with whom they have been marked in baptism and in confirmation as by a seal for the day of redemption (Eph 4:30).

Second, you would be blameworthy if you did not engage them to renounce their former way of life; therefore, you must lead them with the same zeal to renounce lying and to speak the truth to their neighbor at all times (Eph 4:22, 25).

Third, you must help them to be gentle and to have a tenderness for one another, to be as mutually forgiving as God has forgiven them in Jesus Christ (Eph 4:32), and to love one another as Jesus Christ has loved them (Eph 5:2).

Is this the way you have instructed your disciples up to now? Have you inspired them with these maxims? Have you had enough vigilance over them, and has your zeal been ardent enough to bring them to practice these maxims?

Concentrate all your efforts in this regard to be faithful for the future.

SEVENTH MEDITATION

The care to instruct youth is one of the most necessary works in the church.

199.1 First Point

God, having chosen and destined Saint Paul to preach the gospel to the nations, as the apostle says, gave him such knowledge of the mysteries of Jesus Christ (Gal 1:15–16) that he was enabled, like a good architect, to lay the foundation for the building of the faith and of the religion that God raised up in the cities where he announced the gospel according to the grace God had given him (1 Cor 3:9–10). Being the first of all to preach in these places, he says quite justly that those to whom he announced the gospel are his work and that he has begotten them in Jesus Christ (1 Cor 9:1).

Without comparing yourself to this great saint (and keeping in mind the due proportion between your work and his), you can say that you are doing the same thing and that you are fulfilling the same ministry in your profession.

You must, then, look upon your work as one of the most important and most necessary services in the church, one entrusted to you by pastors and by fathers and mothers.

This means that you are called to lay the foundation for the building of the church (Eph 2:22) when you instruct children in the mystery of the most Holy Trinity and in the mysteries accomplished by Jesus Christ when he was on earth.

According to Saint Paul, without faith it is impossible to please God and consequently to be saved and to enter the homeland of heaven, for faith is the foundation of the hope that we have (Heb 11:1–6). Thus the knowledge that everyone must have of the faith and the instruction that must be given concerning the faith to those who are ignorant of it are among the most important aspects of our religion.

How much, then, must you consider yourselves honored by the church to have been assigned by her to such a holy and exalted work and to be chosen by her to procure for children both the knowledge of our religion and the Christian spirit.

Pray that God will make you fit to fulfill such a ministry in a manner worthy of him.

199.2 Second Point

The importance of this ministry is seen in the fact that the holy bishops of the early church looked upon it as their main duty and even considered it an honor to instruct the catechumens and new Christians and to teach catechism to them. Saint Cyril, patriarch of Jerusalem, and Saint Augustine have left us catechisms that they wrote and taught and that they also caused to be taught by the priests who helped them in their pastoral duties. Saint Jerome, whose knowledge was so profound, testifies in his letter to Leta that he considers it a greater honor to teach catechism to a young child than to tutor a great emperor. Gerson, the great chancellor of the University of Paris, had such high esteem for this ministry that he practiced it himself.

These great saints acted this way because teaching is the first ministry Jesus Christ gave his holy apostles, a fact Saint Luke reports when he says that as soon as Jesus had chosen them, he sent them forth to proclaim the kingdom of God (Luke 9:1–2). This work is also what Jesus Christ clearly requested of his apostles just before he departed from them, telling them, "Go, teach all nations, baptizing them in the name of the Father and of the Son and of the Holy Spirit" (Matt 28:19).

This was also the first thing Saint Peter did in the Temple of Jerusalem after the descent of the Holy Spirit, with the immediate result that three thousand people began to embrace the faith in Jesus Christ (Acts 2:14–40).

This was also the special work of Saint Paul, as is evident in his discourses in the Areopagus and those he gave before Felix and Festus, as reported in the Acts of the Apostles. Saint Paul testifies to the Corinthians that it would even be painful to him if he had to come to them without being useful by instructing and catechizing them (Acts 17; 24; 25; 26; 2 Cor 12:14–15).

But Jesus Christ did not limit himself to entrusting his apostles with the work of teaching catechism. He did this work himself and taught the principal truths of our religion, as reported in a great number of places in his gospel, where he tells his apostles, "I must announce the gospel of the kingdom of God because this is why I have been sent" (Luke 4:43).

You can say the same thing: This is why Jesus Christ has sent you and why the church, whose ministers you are, employs you. Bring all the care needed, then, to fulfill this function with as much zeal and success as the saints have had in accomplishing it.

199.3 Third Point

There is no need to be astonished that the first bishops of the early church and the holy apostles had such esteem for the function of instructing the catechumens and the new Christians, and that Saint Paul especially gloried in being sent to preach the gospel not with learned words, for fear that the cross of Jesus Christ would be destroyed, for God turns the wisdom of the world into folly. Saint Paul, enlightened by God's wisdom and inspiration, says that because the world did not recognize God through its wisdom, it pleased God through the folly of the preaching of the gospel to save those who accept the faith (1 Cor 1:17–21).

The reasons Saint Paul gives for this are that God's secret plan was unveiled to him and that he had received the grace of unveiling to the nations the incomprehensible riches of Jesus Christ (Eph 3:3, 8) so that those who previously were deprived of Jesus Christ and were strangers to the covenant of God, without hope in his promises, now belong to Jesus Christ and are strangers no longer. They have become fellow citizens with the saints, servants of God's household, and the structure built on the foundation of the apostles and raised up by Jesus Christ. They have become the sanctuary where God dwells through his Holy Spirit (Eph 2:12, 19, 20, 22).

Such is the result accomplished in the church by the instructions given after the holy apostles by the great bishops and pastors of the church, who devoted themselves to instructing those who wanted to become Christians. This is why this work seemed so important to them and why they devoted themselves to it with such care.

This also ought to engage you to have an altogether special esteem for the Christian instruction and education of children as a means of helping them become true children of God and citizens of heaven. This is the foundation and support of their piety and of all the other good that takes place in the church. Thank God for the grace he has given you in your work of sharing in the ministry of the holy apostles and of the principal bishops and pastors of the church. Honor your ministry (Rom 11:13) by making yourselves, as Saint Paul says, worthy ministers of the New Testament (2 Cor 3:6).

EIGHTH MEDITATION

What must be done to make your ministry useful to the church.

200.1 First Point

Because you must work in your employment to build the church on the foundation laid by the holy apostles, consider that in the instruction you give the children God has entrusted to your care, who are entering the structure of this building (Eph 2:20–22), you must do your work just as the apostles carried out their ministry.

As related in the Acts of the Apostles, they never stopped teaching and proclaiming Jesus Christ daily in the Temple and in homes (Acts 5:42), with the result that every day the Lord increased the number of faithful and the union of those being saved (Acts 2:47).

Because the zeal of the holy apostles to announce the teaching of Jesus Christ caused the number of disciples to increase, they chose seven deacons to distribute alms to the faithful and to take care of their other needs (Acts 6:1–4), so greatly did these holy apostles fear to find any obstacles able to distract them from preaching the word of God.

The holy apostles acted this way because Jesus Christ had given them the example, for it is said of him that he was teaching every day in the Temple, where all the people listened to him with attention (Luke 19:47–48), and at night he would withdraw and go to pray on the Mount of Olives (Luke 21:37).

You, then, who have succeeded the apostles in their work of catechizing and instructing poor people, if you want to make your ministry as useful to the church as it can be, you must teach them catechism daily and help them learn the basic truths of our religion, following the example of the apostles, which is that of Jesus Christ, who devoted himself every day to this task.

Like them, also, you must withdraw afterward to devote yourselves to reading and prayer, to instruct yourselves thoroughly in the truths and the holy maxims you wish to teach, and to draw down on yourselves by prayer the grace of God that you need to do this work according to the Spirit and the intention of the church, which entrusts it to you.

200.2 Second Point

It would have been of little use for the holy apostles to have instructed the first Christians in the essential truths of our religion if they did not lead them to live the Christian way of life and conform to what they had experienced with Jesus Christ. The apostles were not satisfied with teaching speculative truths; they had a marvelous care to bring the first Christians to practice their religion.

God blessed their care in such a way that it is said that those who first received the faith persevered in the teaching of the apostles, in the communion of the breaking of bread, and in prayer, and they continued to go to the Temple daily, united in the same spirit (Acts 2:41–45). In other words, after they were baptized, they were living in harmony with the doctrine of the apostles.

Following his conversion, Saint Paul did the same, for it is said of him that after instructing the people of Ephesus for three months in the Jewish synagogue, he taught every day in the school of a man named Tyrannus and continued this practice for two years (Acts 19:8–10), with the result that the disciples of that city were baptized in the name of the Lord and received the Holy Spirit through the laying on of hands (Acts 19:5–6).

The chief care, then, of the apostles, after instructing the first faithful, was to have them receive the sacraments, assemble for prayer together, and live according to the Christian spirit.

Above everything else, this is what you are obliged to do in your work. In imitation of the apostles, you must devote an altogether special care that those whom you instruct receive the sacraments and in particular that they are prepared to receive confirmation with the proper disposition to be filled with the Holy Spirit and with the graces this sacrament produces. You must see to it that after learning how to do it well, they go to confession often. You must dispose them to receive their first communion with a holy disposition and to receive communion frequently thereafter, thus being able to preserve the grace they received the first time they performed this action.

Oh, if you knew the great good you do for them by procuring the preservation and the increase of grace by their frequent use of the sacraments, you would never cease instructing them about this!

200.3 Third Point

Saint James asks, "If someone says he has the faith and does not have the works, of what use to him is his faith; can it save him?" (Jas 2:14). What would it benefit you, then, to teach your disciples the truths of the faith if you did not teach them to practice good works?

Because faith that is not accompanied by works is dead (Jas 2:26), it will not be enough for you to instruct your disciples about the mysteries and the truths of our holy religion if you do not help them learn the chief Christian virtues and do not take altogether special care to help them put these virtues into practice, as well as all the good they are capable of at their age. For no matter how much faith they may have or how lively it may be, if they do not commit themselves to practice good works, their faith will be of no use to them.

If you want to put them on the road to heaven, you must especially teach this maxim to those you instruct so that you can then say to them that you have acted in a way beyond reproach and that "this has given us consolation" (2 Cor 7:11–13).

Inspire them also with piety and self-control (1 Tim 6:11) in church and in the exercises of piety you have them perform in school. Instill in them the innocence and humility (Matt 11:29) that our Lord recommends so strongly in the gospel. Do not forget to help them acquire gentleness, patience (Col 3:12), love, respect for their parents (Eph 6:2), and, finally, all the conduct proper to a Christian child and that our religion demands of them.

NINTH MEDITATION

The obligation of those who instruct youth to have much zeal to fulfill well so holy a work.

201.1 First Point

Reflect on what Saint Paul says, that it is God who has established apostles, prophets, and doctors in the church (1 Cor 12:28), and you will be convinced that he has also established you in your work. The same saint gives you another expression of this when he says that there are diverse ministries but different operations and that the Holy Spirit manifests himself in each of these gifts for the common good, that is to say, for the good of the church. One person receives from the Spirit the gift to speak with wisdom; another, the gift of faith by the same Spirit (1 Cor 12:5–9).

You must not doubt that this grace he has given you—to be entrusted with the instruction of children, to announce the gospel to them, and to bring them up in the spirit of religion—is a great gift of God. But in calling you to this holy ministry, God demands that you fulfill it with ardent zeal for their salvation because it is God's work, and God curses the one who does his work carelessly (Jer 48:10).

Let it be clear, then, in all your conduct toward the children entrusted to you that you look upon yourselves as ministers of God, carrying out your ministry with love and sincere, true zeal, accepting with much patience the difficulties you have to suffer, and willing to be despised and to be persecuted, even to give your life for Jesus in the fulfillment of your ministry (2 Cor 6:3–9).

The zeal that ought to inspire you is meant to give you this motivation: the view that God has called you, has destined you for this work, and has sent you to labor in his vineyard (Matt 20:3). Do so, then, with all the affection of your heart, working entirely for him.

201.2 Second Point

The fact that you are the ministers not only of God but also of Jesus Christ and the church ought to commit you even further to have great zeal in your state. This is the saying of Saint Paul, who wishes that everyone should consider those who announce the gospel to be ministers of Jesus Christ (1 Cor 4:1); they write the letter he has dictated, not with ink but with the Spirit of the living God, not on tablets of stone but on tablets of flesh, that is, on the children's hearts (2 Cor 3:3).

For this reason and in this spirit, the love and the glory of God must be your single objective in instructing these children. The love of God should impel you because Jesus Christ died for all so that those who live might live no longer for themselves but for him who died for them. This is what your zeal must inspire in your disciples, as if God were appealing through you, for you are ambassadors of Jesus Christ (2 Cor 5:14–15, 20).

You must also show the church what love you have for her (2 Cor 8:24) and give her proof of your zeal because you are working for the church (which is the body of Jesus Christ). You have become her ministers according to the order God gave you to dispense his word (Col 1:24–25).

Because the church has great zeal for the sanctification of her children, your duty is to share in her zeal so that you can say to God what the holy King David said, "The zeal of your house has consumed me" (Ps 69:10). This house is none other than the church, because the faithful form this building constructed on the foundation of the apostles and raised up by Jesus Christ, the main cornerstone (Eph 2:20–22).

Act so that with your zeal you give tangible proof that you love those God has entrusted to you as much as Jesus Christ loves his church. Help them enter truly into the structure of this building and be in condition to appear one day before Jesus Christ, full of glory and without stain, wrinkle, or blemish (Eph 5:25–27). This will make known to future ages the abundant riches of grace given to them by God (Eph 2:7), procuring for them the help of instruction, and the grace given to you to instruct and educate them so that they can one day become heirs of the kingdom of God and of our Lord Jesus Christ (Rom 8:17).

201.3 Third Point

Because the purpose of your ministry is to procure the salvation of souls, your primary concern must be to achieve this goal as far as you are able. In this you must imitate God to some extent, for he so loved the souls he created (Eph 5:1–2) that when he saw them involved in sin and unable to be freed from sin by themselves, his zeal and affection for their salvation led him to send his own Son to rescue them from their miserable condition. This made Jesus Christ say that God so loved the world that he gave his only Son so that whoever believes in him would not die but have eternal life (John 3:16).

Looking at what God and Jesus Christ have done to restore souls to the grace they had lost, what must you not do for them in your ministry if you are zealous for their salvation! How much you must be disposed toward them, as Saint Paul was toward those to whom he preached the gospel, to whom he wrote that he was not seeking anything they had but only their souls (2 Cor 12:14).

The zeal you are obliged to have in your work must be so active and alive that you can tell the parents of the children entrusted to your care what is said in the scriptures: "Give us their souls; keep everything else for yourselves" (Gen 14:21); that is, what we have undertaken is to work for the salvation of their souls. It is also the only reason you have committed yourselves to take responsibility to guide and instruct them.

Tell the parents also what Jesus Christ said about the sheep whose shepherd he is and who must be saved by him: "I came that they may have life and have it to the full" (John 10:10). This must have been the kind of ardent zeal you had for the salvation of those you must instruct when you were led to sacrifice yourself and to spend your whole life to give these children a Christian education and to procure for them the life of grace in this world and eternal life in the next.

TENTH MEDITATION

How a Brother of the Christian Schools ought to show zeal in his work.

202.1 First Point

Consider that the purpose for the coming of the Son of God into this world, to destroy sin, must also be the main purpose for establishing the Christian Schools and, therefore, the primary object of your zeal. This zeal must lead you to allow nothing in the children under your guidance that could displease God. If you observe in them something that offends God, you must immediately do all you can to remedy the problem.

Therefore, following the example of the prophet Elias, you must show your zeal for the glory of God and the salvation of your disciples: "I have been roused with a very great zeal for the Lord God of armies," he says, "because the children of Israel have broken the covenant they had made with God" (1 Kgs 19:14).

If you are zealous for the children for whom you are responsible and are committed to keeping them from sin, as is your duty, you must assume this spirit of the prophet Elias when they fall into some fault. Driven by the same holy ardor that roused this prophet, you must say to your disciples, "I am so zealous for the glory of my God that I cannot see you renounce the covenant you made with him in baptism and the dignity of children of God that you received in this sacrament."

Often urge your disciples to avoid sin with as much haste as they would flee the presence of a snake. Direct your primary attention especially to inspire them with horror for impurity, for lack of reverence in church and at prayer, for stealing, lying, disobedience, and lack of respect for their parents, and for other faults with respect to their companions. Help them understand that those who fall into these kinds of sins will not possess the kingdom of heaven (Gal 5:21).

202.2 Second Point

You must not be satisfied with keeping the children in your care from doing evil; you must also lead them to do well all the good of which they are capable. Take care of this, and see to it that they always speak the truth and that when they want to affirm something, they limit themselves to saying that it is or is not so (Matt 5:37). Help them understand that they will be believed more readily when they use few words than when they swear great oaths, for people will consider that their Christian spirit makes them use fewer words.

Help them put into practice what our Lord says when he commands us to love our enemies and to do good to those who do evil to us, persecute us, and speak unjustly against us (Matt 5:44). Help them completely avoid rendering evil for evil, invoking injury for injury, and taking revenge.

In accord with the teaching of Jesus Christ, you must encourage them not to be satisfied simply with doing good actions and also urge them to avoid doing them only to be esteemed and honored by others, for those who act this way have already received their reward (Matt 6:1, 5).

Most important, you must teach them to pray to God as our Lord taught his followers and to pray with much piety and in secret (Matt 6:6), that is, with much recollection, rejecting all thoughts that could distract the mind during the time of prayer so that they will be occupied solely with God and easily obtain what they ask of him.

Because the majority of your disciples are born poor, you must encourage them to despise riches and to love poverty because our Lord was born poor and loved poor people, with whom he also was glad to be present. He even said that the poor are blessed because the kingdom of heaven belongs to them (Matt 5:3).

You must continually inspire these kinds of maxims and practices in your disciples if you have any zeal for their salvation, and in this way you will show yourselves zealous for the glory of God. Because these maxims, being contrary to human inclination, can come only from God, it is a sign of zeal for the honor and glory of God to inspire children to put them into practice.

202.3 *Third Point*

Your zeal for the children you instruct would neither go far nor have much of a successful result if limited only to words. For this zeal to be effective, you must support your instruction with your example, one of the main signs of your zeal.

Speaking to the Philippians after teaching them various maxims, Saint Paul adds, "Act according to the same maxims, and so be imitators of me, and look to those who live according to the example that I have given you (Phil 3:16–17); do the things I have taught you, what I have said to you, what I have written to you, and of which I have given you the example" (Phil 4:9). Thus the ardent zeal of this great saint for the salvation of souls was to have them observe what he practiced.

This is also the way our Lord acted, of whom it is said that he began to do and then to teach (Acts 1:1). Speaking to his apostles about himself after he had washed their feet, he says, "I have given you an example so that you can do as I have done to you" (John 13:15).

It is easy to conclude from these examples that your zeal for the children who are under your guidance would be quite imperfect if you exercised it only by instructing them; zeal will only become perfect if you practice what you are teaching them. Example leaves a far stronger impression on the mind and heart than words, especially for children, because they do not yet have a mind sufficiently able to reflect and ordinarily model themselves on the example of their teachers. They are led more readily to do what they see done for them than what they hear told to them, above all when teachers' words are not in harmony with teachers' actions.

ELEVENTH MEDITATION

The obligation of the Brothers of the Christian Schools to reprove and correct the faults committed by those whom they are charged to instruct.

203.1 First Point

One characteristic and one effect of the zeal people have for the well-being and salvation of souls is to reprove and correct those in their care when they fall into some fault. This is how Jesus Christ often made his zeal for the Jews manifest in the Temple, when he went there and drove out the buyers and sellers (Luke 19:45–46) of items needed for the sacrifices. At that time he made a whip of cords that he used to chase them out (John 2:15).

Jesus acted similarly toward the Pharisees because he could not tolerate their hypocrisy and false piety (Matt 6:2–5), much less their pride, which led them to esteem and praise their own actions (Luke 18:9–14) while belittling and blaming the behavior of others (Matt 9:11; 12:2). He condemned all their conduct because they satisfied themselves with teaching others but took no pains to practice what they taught (Matt 23:3). In all these encounters Jesus Christ rebuked and blamed them publicly. Note what Jesus Christ did not only to the Pharisees but also to others on several occasions.

Saint Paul, with similar freedom, reproved the Corinthians for tolerating an incestuous person in their midst, telling them that they should have handed him over to the devil to be tormented in his body so that his soul might be saved (1 Cor 5:5).

You too must reprove and correct your disciples when they commit some fault, the more so because it is typical of children often to make mistakes by doing many things without thinking. Reproofs and corrections give them time to reflect on what they have to do and cause them to watch over themselves so as not to keep making the same mistakes.

Be exact, then, not to allow considerable faults in them without providing this remedy for them.

203.2 Second Point

Humans are naturally so inclined to sin that they seem to find no other pleasure than committing it. This tendency appears especially in children, because the mind has not developed yet and they are not capable of much serious reflection. They seem to have no other inclination than to please their passions and their senses and to satisfy their nature.

For this reason the Holy Spirit says that folly would seem to be tied to the neck of children and that correction is the only way to cure them (Prov 22:15). The way to free the souls of children from hell, then, is to make use of this remedy to procure wisdom for them; otherwise, if they are abandoned to their own will, they will run the risk of ruining themselves and causing their parents much sorrow. The reason is that their faults turn into habits that will be extremely difficult to correct. The good and the bad habits contracted in childhood and maintained over a period of time ordinarily become part of nature.

Therefore, those who guide young children must reprove them, as Saint Paul says, with all the force of authority to make them return from their wandering and rescue them from the snares of the demon, who holds them captive to his will (2 Tim 2:25–26). In effect, we can reasonably say that a child who has acquired a habit of sin has in some sense lost his freedom and has made himself a miserable captive, according to what Jesus Christ says, "The one who commits sin is the slave of sin" (John 8:34).

You, who are teachers of those you guide, must take all possible care to bring those under your guidance into the liberty of the children of God, which Jesus Christ obtained for us (Gal 4:31) by dying for us. To do this, you need two qualities in your relationship with them: the first is gentleness and patience; the second, prudence in your reproofs and corrections.

203.3 *Third Point*

What ought to inspire you all the more to reprove and to correct the faults of your disciples is the knowledge that if you fail, you will be reprehensible before God, who will punish you for your weakness and neglect in this matter.

Being substitutes for their fathers and mothers and for their pastors, you are obliged to keep watch over these children as the ones who are accountable for their souls (Heb 13:17). So if you do not watch over their conduct, you must realize that because these children are not able to guide themselves, you will render an account to God for the faults they commit as if you had committed them.

The high priest Eli is a clear and frightening example of this truth. Because he allowed bad behavior in his children, God told him through Samuel that he was condemning his house for all eternity because of his sin (1 Sam 3:13–14) and because he did not correct them, even though he knew that his sons were behaving in an unworthy manner. As a result, God swore that this fault could not be expiated by sacrifices or offerings to the Lord, so serious did God consider the sin to be.

You who hold the place of fathers and pastors of souls, be afraid that God will act the same way toward you if you neglect to reprove and correct your disciples when necessary, for you would have neglected the service with which God honored you when he put you in charge of guiding these children.

God has entrusted you especially with the care of their souls, which is what he had most at heart when he made you the guides and the guardians of these young children.

Be fearful that your negligence might not be pardoned, any more than that of the high priest Eli, if you have not been sufficiently faithful to God in your work of striving to preserve in the grace of God these souls entrusted to your guidance.

TWELFTH MEDITATION

The way we must reprove and correct the faults of those we are guiding.

204.1 *First Point*

Reproofs and corrections would be of little value if those who made them did not take the right steps to administer them well. The first thing to pay attention to is to administer reproofs and corrections only under the guidance of the Spirit of God. Therefore, before undertaking them, it is proper to become interiorly recollected, to enter into God's Spirit, and to be disposed to make the reproof or to undertake the correction with the greatest possible wisdom and in a manner best suited to render it useful to the one for whom it is intended.

Because humans, including the children, are endowed with reason, they must be corrected like reasonable people, not like animals.

We must reprove and correct with justice by helping children recognize the wrong they have done and whatever correction the fault they have committed deserves. We must try to have them accept it.

Also, because they are Christians, we must be disposed to make the reproof or correction in such a way that God is pleased with it and that the children accept it as a remedy for their fault and a means of becoming wiser. This is the result that the Holy Spirit says correction must produce (Prov 12:1) in children.

It is also proper to consider before God what sort of correction the fault deserves, whether the guilty person is truly determined to receive it with submission, or whether you must try to dispose the person to be submissive.

There is no need to fear that corrections will have a bad result if carried out prudently. On the contrary, teachers who reprove and correct those who commit faults draw upon themselves the praise of the people, the blessing of God, and the gratitude of those who have been corrected. For you will have done them more good in this way than if you had flattered them with beautiful words (Prov 28:23), which only serve to deceive them and maintain them in their faults and disorderly conduct.

Have you paid attention to yourself up to the present so that you correct your disciples only with God in view? Have you corrected them with exaggerated zeal, perhaps with impatience and anger? Was this to help them change their conduct, or was it to punish them for some annoyance they caused you? Has charity guided you in this behavior, or have you acted instead to vent your bad humor on them?

Pay close attention to this in the future, so that you will conduct yourself in this important matter only with the desire to please God.

204.2 Second Point

Although Saint Paul warned his disciple Titus to admonish vigorously those who live without obedience, lest they corrupt their faith (Titus 1:10–13), and he also told Timothy to do the same to cause fear in others (1 Tim 5:20), he wrote to him at the same time that he ought to be patient and moderate in correcting those who offer resistance, for God perhaps will give them the spirit of repentance (2 Tim 2:24–25). In fact, this is one of the best ways to win and to touch the hearts of those who have fallen into faults and to dispose them to be converted.

This is how the prophet Nathan proceeded when God sent him to King David to get David to enter into himself and become aware of the two sins, adultery and murder, that he had committed. The prophet began by telling him a parable about a rich man who had a great number of sheep and stole the only sheep owned by a poor man. This simple story Nathan told of terrible injustice aroused David's anger against the guilty man and made David say that the culprit was deserving of death and that he would not grant him any pardon. At this Nathan replied, "You are that very man!" (2 Sam 12:1–12) and immediately applied his story to the two crimes David had committed, representing to him in God's name the graces God had given him and how he had abused them.

You must use this type of method with those you instruct when they fall into some fault and you have to correct them. If it happens that you have been stirred by some passion, avoid making any correction while you experience this emotion, for the correction would be extremely harmful to your disciples as well as to you. In such situations enter into yourself and allow the time of anger to pass without showing it exteriorly. When you feel that you are completely free of passion, you will be able to abandon yourself to God's Spirit and make the correction you planned with all the moderation of which you are capable.

Have you acted this way in the past? Pray to God never to allow you to be carried away by an outburst of anger when you have to punish any of your disciples.

204.3 Third Point

The result that Nathan's wise reproof produced in David should make you realize how much good the corrections you give your disciples will profit them when given with gentleness and charity. David became angry at the man described by Nathan in his parable, but when he realized that he was the one for whom the parable was told, he had no other response than the words "I have sinned" (2 Sam 12:13–22). He at once took upon himself a severe penance. When the child born of his adultery died, David adored God and made it clear that he accepted his holy will. Thus the wise and restrained manner of the prophet toward the sinful David softened the king's heart. He acknowledged his two sins, asked God's pardon for them, and was truly sorry.

As a result of wise correction, the recipients are disposed to correct their faults, whereas correction administered through passion and without God in view serves only to turn the disciple against his teacher and to stimulate his feelings of revenge and ill will, which sometimes last a long time because the effects are generally related and similar to the cause that produces them.

If, then, you want your corrections to have the results they ought to have, administer them in a way that can please God and those who receive them. Take care, above all, that charity and zeal for the salvation of the souls of your students lead you to correct them. Show them so much kindness when you give corrections that they will not be angry at you, although you may cause them some pain, but they will be grateful for the good you have done for them, greatly regret their faults, and firmly resolve not to commit them again. From this very moment, put yourself in the disposition to use the means needed to carry out this resolution.

THIRTEENTH MEDITATION

As a teacher, you must give God an account of the way you have done your work.

205.1 First Point

Because you cooperate with God in his work, as Saint Paul says, the souls of the children you teach are the field he cultivates through you (1 Cor 3:9). Because God has given you the ministry you exercise, when all of you appear before the judgment seat of Jesus Christ, each of you will give your own account to God of what you have done as a minister of God and a dispenser of his mysteries (1 Cor 4:1) to children.

Jesus Christ, having been appointed by God to be your judge, will say to you what the owner said to his manager, "Give me an account of your administration" (Luke 16:2). He will then look into the depths of your heart to examine whether you have been faithful managers of the wealth he has entrusted to you and the talents he has given you to work in his service. The good or the bad use you made of these gifts will then become clear, for the Lord, who is judging you, will unveil what is most hidden and most secret in the depths of your heart (1 Cor 4:5).

If you want to prevent this account that you must give from becoming heavier with the passage of time, make it every day to yourself. Examine before God how you are conducting yourself in your work and whether you are failing in any of your duties.

Come to see yourself clearly. Find fault with yourself accurately and unsparingly so that you will be able to face the judgment of Jesus Christ without fear when he comes to judge you. For when he does come, he will find nothing to condemn in you because you will have anticipated his judgment regarding not only your own person but also the talents and graces you received from God to fulfill well the service he gave you.

For he has made you the guardians and guides of children, who belong to him and over whom he has acquired the right of father not only by creation but also by holy baptism, whereby they are all consecrated to him.

205.2 Second Point

Consider that because the account you will have to give to God concerns the salvation of the souls of the children God has entrusted to your care, it will not be inconsequential, for on the day of judgment you will answer for them as much as for yourself.

You must be convinced that God will begin by making you give an account of their souls before you have to give an account of your own. When you took responsibility for them, you committed yourself at the same time to procure their salvation with as much diligence as your own, because you engaged yourself to work entirely for the salvation of their souls.

Saint Paul brings this to your attention when he says that those who have been put in charge of others must render an account of them to God. He says that they will render an account not of their own souls but of the souls of those for whom they are responsible.

They must watch over those souls because they are obliged to render an account to God for them (Heb 13:17).

The basic reason for this is that in carrying out well the service of guides and leaders of the souls entrusted to them, they fulfill at the same time their own duties before God. God will fill them with so much grace that they will become holy while they are contributing as far as they are able to the salvation of others.

Have you up to the present looked upon the salvation of your students as your personal responsibility during the entire time they are under your guidance? You have spiritual exercises arranged for your own sanctification, but if you have an ardent zeal for the salvation of those you are called to instruct, you will not fail to perform these exercises and to relate them to this intention. In doing so, you will draw down on your students the graces needed to contribute to their salvation. You can rest assured that if you act this way for their salvation, God will be responsible for yours. Develop this disposition for the future.

205.3 Third Point

In making you responsible for the instruction of children and for their formation in piety, Jesus Christ entrusted you with the task of building up his body, which is the church (Eph 4:12). You are likewise responsible, as far as you are able, to make her holy and to purify her by the word of life so that she can appear before him full of glory, with no stain, wrinkle, or defect, but completely pure and beautiful (Eph 5:25–27). This is why he wants you to give him an exact account when he calls for it, for he holds this responsibility very much at heart, having loved his church so much that he gave himself up for her.

Because children are the most innocent part of the church and usually the best disposed to receive the impressions of grace, Jesus Christ desires that you fulfill so well your task of making them holy that all of them will come to the age of the perfect human and to the fullness of Jesus Christ. They will no longer be like children, tossed here and there, turned around by every wind of doctrine, deceit, and trickery, whether by the companions with whom they associate or by the people who lead them into falsehood by their evil proposals.

Rather, in all things they will grow up in Jesus Christ, their head, through whom the entire body of the church maintains its structure and its union. Thus they can always be so united with and in the church that, by the hidden power Jesus Christ furnishes to all his members (Eph 4:12–16), they will share in the promises of God in Jesus Christ (Eph 3:6).

Put yourself, then, in the position to be able to tell him, when he questions you, that you have acquitted yourself well of all these duties. Be assured that the best way to do this and to be pleasing to Jesus Christ when he judges you will be to present to him all those children you have instructed as part of the building of the church and brought by your care into its structure to become the sanctuary where God dwells by the Holy Spirit (Eph 2:22).

Thus you will show Jesus Christ that you have truly fulfilled your ministry and that you have worked effectively to build up and to sustain the church as Jesus Christ engaged you to do.

FOURTEENTH MEDITATION

Matters related to his work on which a Brother of the Christian Schools must give an account to God.

206.1 First Point

Because God has called you to your ministry to procure his glory, to give children the spirit of wisdom and the light to know him, and to enlighten the eyes of their hearts (Eph 1:17–18), you will give an account of how well you have instructed those who have been under your guidance. This obligation is inescapable for you, and you will be punished for their ignorance in these matters (if it is your fault) as if you were also ignorant of them.

You will give an account to God whether you have been exact in teaching catechism on all the days and during all the time prescribed for you; whether you taught your disciples the subjects in the catechism that they should know according to their age and ability; whether you neglected some students because they were the slowest, perhaps also the poorest, and whether you showed favoritism toward others because they were rich, pleasant, or naturally possessing more lovable qualities than the others.

You will give an account whether you have instructed them well how to assist at holy Mass and to confess their sins well; whether you have not preferred to teach secular subjects, such as reading, writing, and arithmetic, though you must not neglect these, since they are strictly required of you; nevertheless, those lessons that contribute to the support of religion are of much greater importance; whether you wasted some of the time available for your assignments on useless activities or even on useful ones that were not your duty; finally, whether you took care to instruct yourselves (during the time assigned to you for this) about what you are obliged to teach those for whom you are responsible.

Are your accounts in good order, and are you ready to give them? If this is not the case, put them in order without delay and examine yourself seriously on what your conduct has been in this regard. If there has been any negligence in your conduct, make a firm resolution to correct yourself. Before God, be determined to do better in the future so that death will not surprise you in such an unfortunate condition.

206.2 *Second Point*

When you appear before God, it will not suffice for you to have instructed the children entrusted to you. You will be found guilty if you have not also watched over their conduct, for it is your duty to supervise them exactly, obligated as you are to give an account to God for their souls (Heb 13:17). Have you carefully considered what it means to account to God for the salvation of a soul that is damned because you did not take care to lead it to what is right and to assist it to live accordingly?

Are you convinced that to prevent your disciples from doing anything even the least displeasing to God, you are obliged to take care of them as much during the entire time they are in church as when they are in school? Is it not also your responsibility to be attentive during the prayers you have them say so that they do so as speaking to God with great piety, decorum, and respect?

Do you perhaps believe that you are responsible for your disciples only during the time of school but that your vigilance need not extend to their behavior outside of school or to helping them during the entire time they are under your guidance, as far as you are able, to live everywhere in a Christian manner and not associate with bad companions?

The saying, "Give an account of their souls," means to give an account of everything that concerns their salvation, and "to watch exactly" means to supervise everything with diligence, omitting and neglecting nothing.

If you have not applied yourself to all these matters, consider yourself guilty before God, and have a great fear to appear before God at the moment of your death, after living in such negligence of all that concerns his service.

206.3 Third Point

What you say and do need not be as great a concern in the account you will have to render to God as the intention and the manner of these actions (for the faults of speaking and acting are usually more tangible and come more readily to mind). Speaking about intention, Saint Paul says that whether we speak or whether we act (Col 3:17), we must do all things in the name of our Lord Jesus Christ, not to please man but to please God (1 Thess 2:4). This is the purpose you must follow and the sole motive God wants you to have in your work.

Is it not true that you have often hardly thought of this at all, that usually you have had no intention whatsoever, or if you have had one, it was purely natural and human? This single fault, then, would have corrupted everything you did, however good it might have been in itself, and would have blocked God's blessing on your action.

Concerning your ministry, you will give God no less an account on whether you have worked with wisdom and seriousness and without undue familiarity with those you teach. Saint Paul strongly recommended this seriousness to his disciple Titus as a minister of the gospel and believed it to be more necessary for him than any other good quality. After zeal for instruction and purity of morals (Titus 2:7), this serious self-control is one of the most useful virtues for those responsible for instructing youth.

Nevertheless, do not overlook the account you will have to give of your patience and of your control over your passions (2 Tim 2:24–25). This again is a most important point to which you must be very attentive, especially when the children in your care do something out of order and you are required to reprove or to correct them. There is nothing you must be more on your guard against than somehow allowing your passions to run away with you.

This must be one of the main points of the examination you ought to make regarding the account that God will ask of you concerning your work; consider it very seriously.

FIFTEENTH MEDITATION

The reward that those who have instructed children and have fulfilled this duty well can expect even in this life.

207.1 First Point

God is so good that he does not leave unrewarded the good work done for him and the service rendered to him, especially for the salvation of souls. If it is true that God rewards so generously, even in this world, those who have left all for him that they receive a hundredfold in this life (Matt 19:27–29), with how much more reason will he reward, even in this present time, those who have devoted themselves with zeal to spread his kingdom!

As a reward for so great a good work and for service he regards so highly, God gives two kinds of recompense in this world to those who commit themselves untiringly to work for the salvation of souls. First, he gives them an abundance of grace; second, he gives them a more extended ministry and a greater ability to obtain the conversion of souls.

The first reward is described in the parable of the man who distributes his goods to his servants and gives one of them five talents to invest for profit. When he learns later from this servant that he has made another five, to reward him according to plan, he orders that the one talent given to the servant who made no profit be taken away and given to the one who now has ten. "For those who have will be given more," the Savior says, "and they will be given riches in abundance" (Matt 25:28–29).

The second kind of reward, an expanded ministry, is well described by Saint Luke in the parable of the lord who receives an account of the money he has given his servants. He rewards the first servant, who told him that his money had increased tenfold, by giving him the government of ten villages (Luke 19:16–17).

Oh, how fortunate you should consider yourselves to be working in the field of the Lord, who says that the reaper will inevitably receive his reward! (John 4:36).

For the future, then, devote yourself with zeal and affection to your work, because it will be one of the most helpful means to assure your salvation.

207.2 Second Point

Another reward in this life for those who work for the salvation of souls is the consolation they have of seeing God well served by those whom they have instructed and of knowing that their work has not been useless but has helped save those they were called upon to instruct.

Thus Saint Paul writes to the Corinthians, to whom he had preached the gospel, that he has begotten them in Jesus Christ (1 Cor 4:15) and that they are his work in our Lord (1 Cor 9:1). Similarly, he finds joy in learning of their goodwill, which makes him boast about them because many others have been inspired by their zeal (2 Cor 9:2). He adds that he hopes their increased faith will attain so much glory that it will extend farther and farther to win souls through the proclamation of the gospel. Yet, it is in our Lord that he boasts. "It is only in Jesus Christ," he says, "that I lay hold to some glory for what I have done for God" (2 Cor 10:15–17).

Thus, the spreading of God's glory by the preaching of the gospel made up all the consolation of this great apostle, and it must be yours as well: to make God and his Son Jesus Christ known to the flock confided to you. Oh, what glory it is for you to resemble this vessel of election! (Acts 9:15). With joy, then, say as he does that the greatest cause of your joy in this life is to proclaim the gospel free of charge and at no cost to those who hear it (1 Cor 9:18). It is indeed a great glory for you to instruct your disciples about the truths of the gospel solely for the love of God. This thought made the doctor of nations always find consolation, and according to the testimony he has given, filled him with overflowing joy in the midst of his afflictions (2 Cor 7:4). You too must consider as your great reward the consolation you feel at the bottom of your heart that the children whom you instruct are well behaved, know their religion well, and live a life of piety. Thank God with all your heart for all these kinds of rewards that he gives you in advance in this life.

207.3 *Third Point*

You can expect yet another reward that God will give you in advance in this life if you devote yourselves generously to your duty and if, through zeal and the grace of your state, you have known well how to give your disciples a foundation in the Christian spirit. This reward is the very special satisfaction you will have when they grow up and you see them living in justice and piety (Titus 2:12), keeping free from evil associates, and performing good deeds.

The instructions you gave them did not consist in words only but were accompanied, for those who profited from them, by a great abundance of grace that will maintain them in the practice of good. Their perseverance in piety will be a great cause of consolation for you when you call to mind the results of their faith and of your instruction, knowing that this makes them dear to God and places them in the number of his elect (1 Thess 1:2–5).

What a joy it will be to see that they received the word of God in your catechism lessons not as a human word but as the word of God powerfully at work in them (1 Thess 2:13), as will be clearly apparent in the virtuous life they continue to live. Therefore, along with the consolation you have of seeing them persevere in piety, you will be able to say that they are your hope, your joy, and your crown of glory before our Lord Jesus Christ (1 Thess 2:19).

Regard this as a considerable reward that God gives you even in this world: to see that by means of the establishment of the schools whose direction God has confided to you, religion and piety increase among the faithful, especially among workers and poor people.

Thank God every day (1 Thess 1:2) through our Lord Jesus Christ that he is pleased to establish this benefit and to give this support to the church. Ask God fervently that he will also be pleased to make your Institute grow and produce good results day by day so that, as Saint Paul says, the hearts of the faithful may be strengthened in holiness and in justice (1 Thess 3:13).

Sixteenth Meditation

The reward a Brother of the Christian Schools ought to expect in heaven if he is faithful in his work.

208.1 First Point

Saint Paul, complaining because some Corinthians were saying they belonged to Paul, and others, to Apollo, tells them that each of them will receive his reward in proportion to his labor (1 Cor 3:4–8). This should make you realize that your happiness in heaven will be greater than that enjoyed by those who have worked only for their own salvation. It will be far greater in proportion to the number of children you have instructed and won over to God.

The work of each one, that is, of those who have labored on the building of the church, says the apostle, will be made known on the day of the Lord because fire will be the test of each person's labor (1 Cor 3:13) (especially of those who have instructed children and formed them to piety). Those who formed them in the Christian spirit and procured for them a solid piety will be recognized. Such teachers will easily be distinguished from others who did not train their disciples in any good practice and were negligent in guiding them. The one whose work will survive, says the apostle, that is, the one whose disciples acquired a strong piety through the teacher's effort and concern, will be rewarded in proportion to his work (1 Cor 3:14).

Consider, then, that your reward in heaven will be all the greater according to the greater good you accomplished in the souls of the children entrusted to your care. In this spirit Saint Paul told the Corinthians, "You will be our glory in the time to come, on the day of our Lord Jesus Christ" (2 Cor 1:14).

If you have instructed your disciples well, and if they have profited from your instructions, you can say the same about them, namely, that on the day of judgment they will be your glory. The lessons you gave them and the profit they made from them will be unveiled before the whole world. Not only on that day but throughout all eternity, you will receive the glory of having instructed them well, for the glory you procured for them will reflect on you.

Therefore, fulfill the duties of your employment so well that you can enjoy this blessing.

208.2 Second Point

What consolation it will be for those who procured the salvation of souls to see in heaven the great number they helped to obtain the advantage of enjoying such unbounded happiness! This will happen to those who have instructed many about the truths of religion, as the angel said to the prophet Daniel: "Those who instruct many in Christian justice will shine like stars throughout eternity" (Dan 12:3). They will indeed shine in the midst of those they instructed, who will eternally bear witness to the immense gratitude they have for so many instructions received from their teachers, whom they will regard as the cause, after God, of their salvation.

Oh, what joy a Brother of the Christian Schools will have when he sees a great number of his students in possession of the eternal happiness for which they are indebted to him by the grace of Jesus Christ! What sharing of joy there will be between teacher and disciples! What special union there will be with one another in the presence of God! They will have great satisfaction in sharing together the blessings for which the call of God had given them hope: the wealth of the glorious heritage of God in the dwelling of the saints (Eph 1:18).

Put yourself in such a position in the future by fidelity to your duty so that at the moment of your death, you will possess such great happiness and also be able to see your disciples, after they end their days, possess this happiness along with you.

208.3 Third Point

The holy King David says that he will be filled with gladness when God grants him the grace to see him and to enjoy the glory of heaven (Ps 17:15), for the sight of God fills all the powers of a person's soul in such a way that all consciousness of self is lost, so to speak. The person is entirely present within the divinity and totally penetrated with God. Those will possess this happiness in heaven who procured the salvation of souls, who did so in a way useful to the good of the church, who by their care restored the robe of innocence to a great number of their disciples who might have lost it through sin, and who helped preserve the innocence of many others who never lost it.

This will happen to those who carried out the role of guardian angels for the children Providence entrusted to them, who had an ardent zeal in their work, who practiced this zeal continually, and who saved a great number of these children.

Oh, what a thrill of joy you will have when you hear the voices of those you have led into heaven as if by the hand, who will say to you on the day of judgment, as well as in heaven, what the girl delivered from the devil by Saint Paul said to the apostle and his companions, "These men are servants of the great God who have proclaimed to us the way of salvation" (Acts 16:17). Then they will testify to the good you have done among them. Some will present to Jesus Christ on the day of judgment the robe of innocence you helped them keep in all its purity. Others who committed sin and with your help washed away their sins in the blood of the Lamb (Rev 7:14) will point out to him the trouble you took to lead them back onto the path of salvation.

All of them will join their voices to obtain for you a favorable judgment from Jesus Christ, praying him not to delay putting you in possession of the happiness you procured for them by your work and your concern. Oh, what glory there will be for those who have instructed youth when their zeal and devotion to procure the salvation of children will be made public before all people! All heaven will resound with the thanksgiving these blessed children will render to those who taught them the way to heaven!

Act in such a way, by your good and wise guidance of those entrusted to you, that you will procure all these blessings and all this glory for yourselves.

Chapter 2

Meditations for
Sundays and Feasts

━━━━━━━━━━━━━━━━ ✠ ━━━━━━━━━━━━━━━━

EDITORS' INTRODUCTION: *Each meditation has three points, which were read aloud in the community, followed by a period of silent interior prayer. The biblical material is integrated into De La Salle's text as he used it rather than isolated and taken from a standard translation. The Sunday meditations began with an exegesis and application of the gospel according to the lectionary of the day. The feasts often draw on the lives of the saint or the event celebrated as well as the biblical texts. De La Salle used a variety of contemporary sources but adapted them carefully to the spiritual needs of the teachers for whom they were written. His doctrine of lay ministry is surprisingly strong and of particular relevance to the spirituality of the educator and those ministering to the poor. In several meditations he clearly identifies the calling of the educator with that of the bishop, as outlined in the New Testament.*[1]

THIRD SUNDAY OF ADVENT
GOSPEL: Saint John 1:19–28

Those who teach others are merely the voice that prepares hearts; it belongs to God alone to prepare them by his grace to receive him.

3.1 First Point

The Jews sent priests and Levites from Jerusalem to ask Saint John who he was: the Christ, or Elijah, or a prophet (John 1:19–21). Saint John told them he was none of these but declared, "I am the voice of one crying in the desert: make straight the way of the Lord" (John 1:23). Saint John wished to leave to Jesus Christ all the honor of converting souls, the task at which he himself labored so constantly. He said, therefore, that he was only a voice crying out in the desert (John 1:23). He thus showed that the substance of the doctrine he taught was not his own and that it was indeed the word of God that he preached; as for him, he was only the voice that proclaimed it. In the same way that a voice is a sound that strikes the ear and makes it possible for a word to be heard, so it was that Saint John prepared the Jews to receive Jesus Christ.

The same is true of those who instruct others. They are only the voice of the One who disposes hearts to accept Jesus Christ and his holy teaching. The one who disposes them, according to Saint Paul, can only be God (1 Cor 3:5–6), who imparts to humans the gift of speaking of him. According to the same apostle, when you speak all the tongues, both angelic and human, if you lack charity (1 Cor 13:1), or rather, if it is not God who makes you speak and who uses your voice to reveal himself and his sacred mysteries, you are nothing but sounding brass and tinkling cymbals (1 Cor 13:1). All you say will produce no good effect and will be incapable of achieving any good results.

Let us then humble ourselves, considering that we are nothing but a voice and that of ourselves we cannot say anything that will do the least good for souls or make any impression on them. For we are a mere voice, only a sound that becomes nothing once it has echoed through the air.

3.2 Second Point

Those who teach are only God's voice. The word that makes God known to those whom they instruct must come from him; God speaks in teachers when they explain him and what is related to him. This is why Saint Peter says, "If any speak, let it always be clear that God is speaking by their mouth; if any fulfill a ministry, let them do so as acting only by the power God communicates to them, so that in all things God may be glorified through Jesus Christ" (1 Pet 4:11).

Saint Peter also says on the subject of the truth he was preaching, "I will never give over warning you of these things, even though you already know the truth about them and it is established in you" (2 Pet 1:12). He adds, "We have the word of the prophets, which is firmly established and to which you do well to attach yourselves, for it is like a lamp shining in a dark place until the day dawns and the morning star rises in our hearts; for it was not through the human will that in times past prophecy was uttered; it was rather by the movement of the Holy Spirit that these men of God spoke" (2 Pet 1:19–21).

It is also by the movement of the Spirit of God that all those who today proclaim his kingdom continue to speak. But if God makes use of persons to announce the truths of Christianity to others and to prepare their hearts to be docile to these truths, it is God alone, as the wise man says, who must guide their steps (Prov 16:9) and impart to their hearts the docility they need to welcome these holy truths he is making known to them.

Do not be content, therefore, to read and to learn from others what you must teach your pupils. Pray God to impress all these truths so firmly on you that you will not have any occasion to be or to consider yourselves to be anything, as Saint Paul says, but the ministers of God and the dispensers of his mysteries (1 Cor 4:1).

3.3 Third Point

Saint Zechariah, the father of Saint John the Baptist, says in the canticle he sang at the birth of his son that the reason why Saint John is to walk before Jesus Christ and prepare the way for him is to bring his people the knowledge of salvation (Luke 1:76–77). But this knowledge is not enough; it is necessary for God, through our Lord Jesus Christ, to show us the path we must follow and to inspire us to walk in the footsteps of his Son.

Although in this life we sigh under the weight of our body and long to be free of this burden (2 Cor 5:2), God created us for this very purpose and gave us his Holy Spirit as a pledge (2 Cor 5:5). It is, then, up to God to direct our path straight toward heaven so that we may surely arrive there. For this reason it was as the Son of God that Jesus Christ became the author of our eternal salvation (Heb 5:9).

Because salvation, as the prophet says, comes from God (Ps 37:39), perfection likewise comes from him. As Saint James assures us, every excellent grace and every perfect gift comes from on high and descends from the Father of lights (Jas 1:17).

Beg God, therefore, to lead you on the way to heaven by the path he has traced out for you. Ask him to help you embrace the perfection of your state because he is the one who brought you into it and who consequently desired and still desires that you find in it the way and the means of sanctifying yourselves.

SIXTH SUNDAY AFTER THE FEAST OF THE KINGS
GOSPEL: Saint Matthew 13:31–35

The great benefit produced by what is done through obedience, however insignificant it seems in itself.

12.1 First Point

In today's gospel Jesus Christ declares that the kingdom of heaven is like a grain of mustard seed, the smallest of all seeds, which, however, when it has grown, becomes a tree such that the birds of the sky come to rest in its branches (Matt 13:31–32).

The same can be said of something done out of obedience, even though it may be quite insignificant in appearance; nevertheless, it is quite considerable because it is done out of obedience.

Eating, for instance, or gathering up the crumbs remaining on the table, or sweeping a room, washing dishes, attaching a pin: all such tasks seem to be trifles in themselves, but when performed through obedience, they become highly significant actions because their object is God, for we obey God in performing them.

As a result this virtue, more than any other, can be associated with the theological virtues, for faith is its principle and guide; it is always accompanied by hope and confidence in God, and it is a result of charity and the pure love of God.

Even the birds of the sky, that is, the virtues belonging to the saints in heaven, rest (Matt 13:32) on those who obey, for they experience joy, consolation, and interior peace that cannot be adequately expressed or found in such perfection in anyone on earth except in those who obey solely in view of God.

Experience for yourself how good the Lord is (Ps 43:9) and how true all this is, for throughout your whole life, you must place all your affection in obeying.

12.2 Second Point

We can attribute to obedience what Solomon says of Wisdom, that all good things come to us along with it (Wis 7:11). Indeed, whoever obeys in a spirit of religion possesses all the virtues: He is humble because he must be humble to submit to another; he is gentle because no matter how irksome the thing commanded may be, he does not complain; he is silent because the truly obedient man has lost the use of his tongue and knows only how to do what is ordered without making any reply; he is patient because he endures everything (1 Cor 13:4–7) and bears all the burdens imposed on him; he is charitable beyond measure because obedience makes him undertake all things for the good of his neighbor.

This is why Saint Bonaventure says that obedience must enter into everything done in a community; without it all the most perfect actions cease to be good. Fasting, which is so meritorious before God, is rejected when inspired by self-will; in this case a person assumes the proprietorship of an action over which God alone possesses sovereign dominion and for which that person has the right only to do what God requires of him.

We should consider ourselves happy to be in a state that requires obedience of us; we should look upon this virtue in itself as the mother and the support of all the other virtues. But if you wish this to be true in your case, you must practice it with all possible perfection, for God gives this grace only to those who have renounced self-will and who look upon his will as the rule and principle of all they do.

12.3 *Third Point*

The main benefit obedience produces in a religious person is that it procures for us the perfection proper to our state, fortifies us in it, and assures perseverance. In fact, says Saint Dorotheus, nothing helps us fulfill our religious duties better than renouncing our self-will. This is the most appropriate means we can use to acquire all sorts of virtues. By often sacrificing our self-will, we acquire great control over our passions and inclinations and possess our souls undisturbed in every sort of circumstance. This is the highest perfection.

This is what makes Cassian say that a person achieves purity of heart and fervor in religion in proportion to the progress achieved in obedience. Saint Ignatius, in the third part of his *Constitutions* (Chapter 1, paragraphs 21, 22, and 23), affirms that it is not just expedient but most necessary in his community for all to practice obedience perfectly if they wish to advance in virtue and in the perfection of their state.

Nor is there anything that renders a religious more firm and unshakable, thanks to the respect and the love that it inspires for all the observances of the religious life. These are the safe and sure paths to acquire fully the spirit of your state and to persevere in it. For why do some fail to persevere? Is it not because they lose their love for the rules and practices of the community, eventually grow disgusted with them, and carry them out only grudgingly?

From this you may conclude how important it is that above all else you love the practice of obedience and give it your best effort. According to Sulpicius Severus, it is the first and most important of all the virtues that enhance a community. Rest assured that you will not love your state and will not have its spirit except insofar as you are faithful to obedience.

Second Sunday After Easter
Gospel: John 10:11–16

How teachers should act toward their pupils.

33.1 First Point

In today's gospel Jesus Christ compares those who have charge of souls to a good shepherd who has great care for the sheep (John 10:11). One quality he must possess, according to our Savior, is to know each one of them (John 10:14) individually. This should also be one of the main concerns of those who instruct others: to be able to understand their pupils and to discern the right way to guide them.

They must show more mildness toward some, more firmness toward others. There are those who call for much patience, those who need to be stimulated and spurred on, some who need to be reproved and punished to correct them of their faults, others who must be constantly watched over to prevent them from being lost or going astray.

This guidance requires understanding and discernment of spirits, qualities you should frequently and earnestly ask of God because they are most necessary for you in the guidance of those placed in your care.

33.2 Second Point

It is also necessary, says Jesus Christ, that the sheep know their shepherd (John 10:14) to be able to follow him. Two qualities are needed by those who lead others and should be particularly evident in them.

The first is a high level of virtue, to be models for others, who would not fail to go astray following their guides if the guides did not walk in the right way.

The second is the great tenderness they must show for those entrusted to their care. They must be very alert to whatever can harm or wound their sheep. This is what leads the sheep to love their shepherds and to delight in their company, for there they find their rest and comfort.

Do you wish your disciples to do what is right? Do it yourselves. You will persuade them much more readily through your example of wise and prudent behavior than through all the words you could speak to them. Do you want them to keep silence? Keep it yourselves. You will make them prudent and self-controlled only insofar as you act that way.

33.3 Third Point

The members of the flock of Jesus Christ are also obliged to hear their shepherd's voice (John 10:16). It is, then, your duty to teach the children entrusted to you; this is your duty every day. They must understand what you say, so you must give them instructions adapted to their capacity; otherwise, what you say would be of little use. For this purpose you must prepare and train yourselves so that your questions and answers in the catechism lessons are understood well and you explain the text clearly and use words that will be easily understood.

In your exhortations explain their faults to your pupils simply, and show them how to correct them. Make known to them the virtues they should practice, and help them see how easy this is. You should inspire them with very great horror for sin and avoidance of bad companions. In a word, speak to them of everything that can lead them to piety. This is how your disciples should hear the voice of their teacher.

ROGATION MONDAY

We are bound to pray for those whom we are appointed to teach.

37.1 First Point

In today's gospel Jesus Christ presents a parable that lets you know the duty you have to be concerned about the needs of those whom you instruct. It is as if one of you, he says, goes at midnight to find one of your friends and tells him, "Lend me three loaves of bread because a friend of mine on a journey has just arrived at my house, and I have nothing to give him" (Luke 11:5–6).

In his explanation of this parable Saint Augustine says that this traveling friend is someone who has walked the way of sin, seeking to satisfy his passions in the world and finding there nothing but vice and vanity, misery and disappointment, who turns to you in distress, looking for help, and is persuaded that you have received the grace to support the weak, to teach the ignorant, and to correct the wayward (1 Thess 5:14). Your friend comes to you like the weary and exhausted traveler, and he begs you to help him in his destitution.

Such is the plight of those whom Providence calls upon you to teach and whom you must train in piety. God has led them to you; God makes you responsible for their salvation (Heb 13—17) and gives you the responsibility to provide for all their spiritual needs. To do this should be your constant effort.

37.2 Second Point

The children who come to you either have not had any instruction or have been taught the wrong things; if they have received some good lessons, bad companions or their own bad habits have prevented them from benefiting. God sends them to you so that you can give them the spirit of Christianity and educate them according to the maxims of the gospel.

You are obliged, says Saint Augustine, to learn these things yourselves; you have reason to be ashamed if you have to teach these children what you do not know or exhort them to practice what you do not do. Ask God, then, for what you lack and to give you what you need in full measure, namely, the Christian spirit and deep religious convictions.

Those who come to you do so in the middle of the night (Luke 11:5), which, says Saint Augustine, symbolizes their great ignorance. Their need is pressing, and you have nothing to satisfy their need. Your simple faith in the mysteries may be enough for you but not sufficient for you to be able to give them what they need. Will you then abandon them and leave them without any instruction? Have recourse to God, knock on the door, pray, and beg him insistently, even importunately (Luke 11:9).

The three loaves you should ask for, continues the same father, represent knowledge of the three divine Persons. If you obtain this from God, you will have what will satisfy those who come to you in their need for instruction.

37.3 Third Point

You should look upon the children you are appointed to teach as poor, abandoned orphans. In fact, although the majority of them do have a father here on earth, they are still as if they had none and are abandoned to themselves for the salvation of their souls. This is the reason God places them as if under your guardianship.

He looks on them with compassion and takes care of them as being their protector, their support, and their father (Ps 68:6), and it is to you that he entrusts this care. This God of goodness places them in your hands and undertakes to give them everything you ask of him for them: piety, self-control, reserve, purity, and the avoidance of companions who could be dangerous to them.

Because God knows that of yourselves you have neither enough virtue nor enough ability to give all these things to the children he has entrusted to you, he wants you to ask him for these blessings for them frequently, fervently, and insistently. In this way, thanks to your care, nothing they need for their salvation will be lacking to them.

EVE OF PENTECOST

Dispositions for receiving the Holy Spirit.

42.1 First Point

In today's gospel Jesus Christ points out to us three requirements to receive the Holy Spirit, which he expresses in these words: "If you love me, keep my commandments, and I will ask my Father, and he will give you another Consoler to be with you always" (John 14:15–16).

The first requirement is to love God and to give yourselves entirely to him. For this you must detach yourselves from all creatures and love God alone. Whoever is attached to the world and its goods is not capable of receiving the Spirit of God, who communicates himself only to those he finds empty of all that is not God. This is why, as Jesus Christ observes, the world cannot receive this divine Spirit (John 14:17) because it loves only the concupiscence of the flesh, the concupiscence of the eyes, and the pride of life (1 John 2:16).

Detach yourselves from all things, then, and attach yourselves to God alone if you wish to be in a state to receive the Spirit of God.

42.2 Second Point

The second requirement to receive the Holy Spirit is to keep God's commandments faithfully and to strive to do his holy will in all things. Jesus Christ says that this divine Spirit will always be in and with those who receive him (John 14:16–17) and that he cannot be pleased except with those who try always to do what God desires of them and to be in harmony with his holy will. We should, then, not expect to receive the Holy Spirit if we do not try to accomplish the holy will of God in all things.

You have left the world, no doubt, to give yourselves entirely to God and to possess abundantly his divine Spirit. Do not expect to achieve this, however, unless you punctually fulfill what you know is God's will for you. Be very careful to observe your Rule exactly.

42.3 Third Point

Nothing disposes us better to receive the Holy Spirit than prayer. This is why Jesus Christ assures us that our heavenly Father will give his Spirit, full of love and goodness for us, to all those who ask him (Luke 11:13). Yet, because he knows that the fullness of this divine Spirit is difficult to obtain and because he desires to give the Spirit to his apostles, he promises them that he will pray to the Father for them (John 14:16) so that they will receive his Spirit in profusion.

If you wish to dispose yourselves as well as God asks of you and to be filled with the Spirit of God on Pentecost day, apply yourselves attentively and fervently to prayer to be filled with God's grace. For this is the day on which he generously pours out his graces; on this day he gave himself to the holy apostles and to all those who then made up the church. Do not fail to pray to him during all these holy days, and often repeat with the church these holy words: "Send forth your Spirit to give us a new life, and you will renew the face of the earth" (Ps 104:30).

FOURTEENTH SUNDAY AFTER PENTECOST
GOSPEL: Saint Matthew 6:24–33

Abandonment to Providence.

67.1 First Point

It is to you especially that Jesus Christ addresses these words of today's gospel: "Strive first for the kingdom of God" (Matt 6:33). In fact, you should not have come to this community except to seek here the reign of God: first, for yourself, and second, for those whose instruction God has entrusted to you. Here you should seek only to establish this reign of God within your soul, both in this life and in the next.

You should not be concerned about anything for this present life except to make God reign in your heart by his grace and by the fullness of his love. You should be living for him; the life of God ought to be the life of your soul.

You nourish the life of your soul with God's life by occupying yourself with his holy presence as much as you are able. What characterizes the life of the saints is their continual attention to God; this should also be true of souls consecrated to God, who seek only to do his holy will, to love him, and to cause him to be loved by others.

This should be your entire preoccupation on earth; to accomplish this should be the goal of all your work. Hence, help those you teach to look upon sin as a shameful sickness that infects their souls and makes them unworthy to draw near to God and appear before

him. Inspire them with love for virtue; impress upon them sentiments of piety, and see to it that God does not cease to reign in
them. Then they will have nothing to do with sin, or at least they
will avoid serious sins, which cause death to the soul.

Often recall to mind the purpose of your vocation, and let this
inspire you to do your part to establish and to maintain the kingdom
of God in the hearts of your students. Do you reflect that one of
your best ways to procure such an advantage is, first of all, to make
God reign in your students in such a way that they no longer act or
have any inclination except by God?

67.2 Second Point

To focus your attention only on how to make God reign in you
and in the souls of those whom you instruct, it is important not to
be taken up with the needs of your body. These two kinds of concerns do not go well together at all; preoccupation with external
things destroys in a soul the care for those things that refer to God
and his service.

This is why Jesus Christ, when he was entrusting the salvation
of the world and the establishment of his kingdom on earth to his
apostles, recommends in the same gospel that they not be anxious
by saying, "What shall we eat? What shall we drink? What are we to
wear?" Such concerns are proper only to pagans (Matt 6:31–32).
Insofar as they are so disturbed by such things, they show that they
have no faith.

To give them a convincing proof of this, he says, "Look at the
birds in the sky. They do not sow or reap; they gather nothing into
barns. Consider also the lilies of the field. They neither work nor
spin; nevertheless, not even Solomon in all his glory was ever
clothed like them" (Matt 6:26, 28–29).

Have you, then, so little faith as to fear that if you accomplish
your duty and devote yourselves entirely to bring about God's reign
in your heart and in the hearts of others, God would allow you to
lack something necessary for you to live and be clothed?

67.3 *Third Point*

Jesus Christ assures you that God will take charge of providing your food and your support. "Your heavenly Father," he says, "knows that you need all these things (Matt 6:32). He is the one who feeds the birds of the sky; are you not far more valuable than they? Are you not far dearer to him than birds?" (Matt 6:26). "If God," he adds, "takes care to clothe the grass of the field, which is underfoot today and will be cut down tomorrow, with how much more care will he not clothe you, O people of little faith!" (Matt 6:30).

"Be convinced," concludes Jesus Christ, "that if you truly seek the kingdom of God and his justice, all these things will be given to you besides (Matt 6:33) because God takes responsibility for the care to provide for you." As Saint Paul says, "You do not muzzle the ox that treads out the grain" (1 Cor 9:8).

If, then, you devote yourselves to work in the harvest of souls (Matt 9:37–38), how can you fear that the One who employs you in this task as his coworkers (1 Cor 3:9) will refuse you the food you need to do his work? The more you abandon yourselves to God for what concerns your temporal needs, the more care he will take to provide for you.

If, on the contrary, you want to provide for yourselves in these matters, God will leave you the concern to do so, and it could often happen that you will be in need; God will want to punish you for your lack of faith and for your distrust.

Do, then, what David says: "Turn your thought to God, and place all your trust in him, and he will feed you" (Ps 55:23).

6 JANUARY
THE ADORATION OF THE KINGS

96.3 *Third Point*

The Magi left the city of Jerusalem and proceeded to the poor village of Bethlehem to find there the king they were seeking. They were led there by the star, which moved ahead of them until it reached the place where the child was and stopped there (Matt 2:9). Then the Magi entered the stable and found a little child wrapped in poor swaddling clothes in the company of his mother, Mary (Matt 2:11).

At this sight how could the Magi not fear to have been deceived? "Are these the marks of a king?" asks Saint Bernard. Where is his palace, his throne, his court? The stable, the saint says, is his palace; the crib serves as his throne, and his court is the company of the most blessed Virgin and Saint Joseph. This stable does not appear to them deserving of disdain; these poor swaddling clothes are not shocking in their eyes; they feel no disappointment at seeing a poor child being nursed by his mother.

They prostrate themselves before him (Matt 2:11), says the gospel. They honor him as their king and adore him as their God. Behold the faith that profoundly filled their spirit and caused them to respond in this way.

Recognize Jesus beneath the poor rags of the children you have to instruct. Adore him in them. Love poverty, and following the example of the Magi, honor the people who are poor, for poverty should be dear to you who are responsible for their instruction. May faith lead you to do this with affection and zeal because these children are the members of Jesus Christ (1 Cor 12:27). This divine Savior will thus be pleased with you, and you will find him, for he always loved poor people and poverty.

29 June
Saint Peter

Editors' Introduction: The feasts of Saint Peter and Saint Paul are now celebrated as one in Protestant and Catholic churches of the West. In De La Salle's time the two feasts were celebrated separately. He designed these two meditations to treat the themes of faith on the feast of Saint Peter and of zeal on the feast of Saint Paul. No distinction should be made between the development of the interior life of faith and zeal for the educational service of the poor in the world.

139.1 First Point

It should not be surprising that Saint Peter was so dearly loved by Jesus Christ and that our Lord established him as the head of his church (Matt 16:15–19). His great faith won him this honor, the faith that led him to renounce all things to follow Jesus Christ (Matt 19:27) and to give himself completely to him. It is true, as Saint Jerome says, that Saint Peter gave up little when we consider what he possessed; he left only a fishing boat and some nets. But if we pay attention to the fact that at the same time he gave up the desire to possess anything, he did indeed give up much, as this saint observes, because he renounced what is most important in this world, what is most capable of attracting and absorbing a person's heart.

The faith with which he was already filled enabled him to make this generous act. Because Jesus Christ was then just a common man in the eyes of the world, without any acclaim, nothing but a strong faith could have enabled anyone to leave everything to follow him, for to all appearances there was nothing to be hoped for from him.

Have you truly renounced everything with all your heart's desire? Have you put yourself under the protection of God alone with an entire abandonment to his providence? Make this generous act in imitation of Saint Peter and through his intercession.

139.2 Second Point

His great faith led this holy apostle to follow Jesus Christ always. Of the three who were with Jesus Christ in the principal occurrences of his life, he is named first in the holy gospel (Matt 17:1). He is also the first of all the apostles to go to the sepulchre looking for the body of his beloved Master (John 20:3–8), which illustrates the great attachment he felt for him. His faith shone out above all the other apostles so strongly that when Jesus questioned them to learn what people were thinking about him and then asked them what they thought of him, Saint Peter, enlightened as he was from above, as Jesus Christ declared, by a light incomprehensible to the human mind that could come to him only from heaven, replied,

"You are the Christ, the Son of the living God!" (Matt 16:16). This led Jesus Christ to entrust him with the care of his church.

Be convinced that you will contribute to the good of the church in your ministry only insofar as you have the fullness of faith and are guided by the spirit of faith, which is the spirit of your state by which you should be inspired.

139.3 Third Point

Another effect of Saint Peter's extraordinary faith is that as soon as all the apostles had received the Holy Spirit on Pentecost, he preached with so much energy and power that an innumerable multitude of those present from all kinds of nations, each hearing him speak in his own native tongue (Acts 2:5–7), were so amazed by what he told them (although he spoke in very simple terms) that three thousand of them were converted on the spot (Acts 2:41) and embraced the faith of Jesus Christ. A few days later, five thousand more (Acts 4:4) did the same. This great faith of Saint Peter also enabled him to perform a large number of miracles, which made his words effective and caused even his shadow to heal the sick (Acts 15:15).

Do you have such faith that it is able to touch the hearts of your students and inspire them with the Christian spirit? This is the greatest miracle you can perform and the one that God asks of you, for this is the purpose of your work.

30 JUNE
SAINT PAUL

140.1 First Point

The most admirable trait in Saint Paul is his ardent and all-embracing zeal, which he showed initially by defending the faith of Moses, in which he had been thoroughly instructed (Acts 22:3). Because he was very knowledgeable and saw that the Christian religion was beginning to spread throughout Judea by the preaching of the apostles, he took every possible step to oppose and destroy it. It was also a consequence of his zeal that he took part in the stoning of Saint Stephen (Acts 7:58), although he was his relative. Then, having done all he could against the faithful in Jerusalem, he took steps to secure authorization to persecute those in the city of Damascus (Acts 9:1–2).

His zeal for the law of God made him undertake all these travels and all these persecutions against the Christians (Acts 26:11), but he did all this out of ignorance (1 Tim 1:13), as he states. This is why God did not leave him in error but enlightened him in a completely miraculous manner.

You have the advantage of knowing the truth and the happiness of having been born and brought up in the Christian religion. You must necessarily consider it your first duty to uphold it. Are you as zealous in this respect as Saint Paul was to preserve the Jewish law? You have an easy means of doing so by instructing children, teaching them the truths and the holy maxims of the gospel, and strongly opposing everything that the spirit of immorality is able to inspire in them to the contrary.

140.2 Second Point

After Jesus Christ had personally converted Saint Paul and taught him his religion without the help of any man (Gal 1:11), this saint preached with so much zeal and success that he labored more to spread faith in Jesus Christ, as he says, than all the other apostles did (1 Cor 15:10). His whole effort was to procure the conversion of souls, especially the Gentiles, for whom God, he says, by his power had established him as their apostle (Gal 2:8).

His efforts brought about important results, for he preached in many provinces and performed all sorts of prodigies and miracles to establish Christianity. This made the people want on one occasion to offer a sacrifice to him as though he were a god who had come down from heaven and taken the form of a man (Acts 14:11–13). Indeed he led a life more heavenly than human, for he thought only of drawing souls to God and of instructing, strengthening, and consoling them.

God, by his power and very special goodness, has called you to give the knowledge of the gospel to those who have not yet received it. Do you look upon yourselves, then, as ministers of God? Do you fulfill the duties of your work with all possible zeal and as having to give an account of it to him?

140.3 Third Point

Zeal cannot be more genuine and more firm than when it continues in the midst of the greatest sufferings and the most cruel persecutions. In this way Saint Paul's zeal was put to the test. Several times he was thrown into prison; he was wounded frequently; often he was almost at death's door because of the beatings given him. Five times he was cruelly scourged and three times beaten with rods; once he was stoned. He was shipwrecked three times, and he spent a day and a night adrift on the sea; he was in danger of falling into the hands of robbers. Those of his own nation laid ambush for him, as did the Gentiles also. He endured afflictions and sorrow, lengthy nights of prayer, hunger, thirst, and cold (2 Cor 11:23–27); in the midst of all these ordeals, his zeal never slackened (1 Cor 4:11–13).

In your ministry you need much zeal. Imitate the zeal of this holy apostle so that neither insults nor injuries, neither calumnies nor persecutions of whatever kind may be able to diminish your zeal in the slightest or force from you a single complaint, considering yourselves to be very happy to suffer for Jesus Christ (2 Cor 12:10; Acts 21:13).

3 NOVEMBER
SAINT MARCELLINUS, BISHOP OF PARIS

EDITORS' INTRODUCTION: *This fifth-century saint, popular in France, provides De La Salle with an opportunity to extol the vocation of the educator and to emphasize the dignity of lay ministry. In a period when the episcopacy was not always noted for its pastoral dedication to education and the poor, this meditation compares the function of the lay educator with this high office in the church. The holiness of the teacher emerges from zealous attention to the needs and discipline of the students entrusted to his or her care.*

186.1 First Point

This saint's virtuous parents took great care of his education; consequently, because he was endowed with good qualities, he soon acquired such piety that he was esteemed and honored by everyone. This also won him a high reputation. What a great blessing it is to be brought up well, for in this way we acquire many virtues with great ease because the tendencies of the young are easily guided; they accept without great difficulty the impressions we seek to give them.

Consider, therefore, how important it is for you to apply yourselves as well as you will be able to educate well those who are under your guidance and to procure piety for them. This is the principal object and the purpose of your work.

Be assured that you will succeed in this only if you make yourselves pleasing to God, and that he will pour out on you and your work his abundant blessing only insofar as you make their education your principal concern.

The trouble you take to do this will in the end make your students docile and solidly submissive to their parents and to those to whom their parents confide them, self-controlled and well-behaved in public, and pious in church and in all that refers to God, to holy things, and to religion.

186.2 Second Point

This saint was so humble, reserved, and serious that the bishop of Paris at the time admitted him into the ranks of the clergy on the sole consideration of the virtues that distinguished him. He was a source of edification and an example for all the other members of the clergy, even when he was just beginning his career as an ecclesiastic. Because all considered him their model, his bishop resolved to ordain him a priest even though Saint Marcellinus, for his part, expressed a reluctance because he considered himself unworthy of this honor and of the dignity of this sacred office.

You are in a work that by its ministry resembles that of priests more than it does any other work. Because the rare and extraordinary virtue of Saint Marcellinus led to his being raised to that ministry, you, on entering your state, ought to bring and to preserve in the exercise of your ministry a piety that is more than ordinary. It should distinguish you from other people; otherwise, it will be difficult for you to carry out your ministry successfully. Because your vocation has not been instituted except to procure the spirit of religion and of Christianity for those whom you instruct, it cannot achieve its purpose and enable those who are in this work to achieve their purpose unless beforehand they have worked seriously to sanctify themselves.

186.3 Third Point

When the bishop of Paris died, the holy life of Saint Marcellinus caused him to be chosen to replace him. In this exalted responsibility, so difficult to carry out well, he showed how great was his zeal for the salvation of souls. Besides using all the natural and supernatural talents God had given him to procure their sanctification, he did not cease to pray and keep watch to help the ones who needed conversion and to draw down on others the graces needed for them to be strong in the practice of good and to advance in virtue.

In some sense it can be said that each of you is a bishop, that is, the vigilant guardian of the flock God has entrusted to you (Acts 20:28); consequently, you are obliged to keep watch over all those who belong to it, for as Saint Paul says, you have to give an account to God for their souls (Heb 13:17). Do you sometimes reflect before God how fearful this account is? The soul of each one of those you guide is infinitely dear to God, and if any one of them is lost through your fault, God has said it, and he will do it: he will require from you soul for soul (Deut 19:21; Ezek 22:14).

You have two kinds of children to instruct: some are disorderly and inclined to evil; others are good or at least inclined to good. Pray continually for both, following the example of Saint Marcellinus, especially for the conversion of those who have evil inclinations. Work to preserve and strengthen the good ones in the practice of good; nevertheless, direct your care and your most fervent prayers to win over to God the hearts of those who are prone to evil.

Chapter 3

Rule and Memoranda

✠

1718 RULE

EDITORS' INTRODUCTION: On Pentecost Sunday of 1717 the principal Brothers gathered in the second legislative meeting or chapter of the Institute of the Brothers of the Christian Schools. At this meeting sixteen Brothers represented the 102 Brothers of the Society. They elected Brother Barthélemy the second superior of the Institute (De La Salle being considered the first). Prior to this meeting, at the request of the Brothers, De La Salle put the Society's rule in a final form. In this, the final format of the Rule from the hand of De La Salle, the almost lyrical passages give voice to the life force, the spirit, of the Society. The Society is to be made up of men who see with the eyes of the provident God who wills the salvation of all, especially abandoned and poor children. These men of faith-vision will burn with the desire for God and, as a community, dedicate their every action to accomplishing this provident plan of salvation. Thus, the life force of this Society is to be one of faith, which expresses itself in zeal and is lived in community with like-graced men. Those who do not have this life force must consider themselves as dead members.[1]

CHAPTER 2
The Spirit of This Institute

That which is of the utmost importance and to which the greatest attention ought to be given in a community is that all who compose it possess the spirit peculiar to it, that the novices apply themselves to acquire it, and that those who are already members make it their first care to preserve and increase it in themselves. For it is this spirit that ought to animate all their actions and be the motive of their whole conduct. Those who do not possess it and those who

106

have lost it ought to be looked upon as dead members, and they ought to look upon themselves as such, because they are deprived of the life and grace of their state, and they ought to be convinced that it will be very difficult for them to preserve the grace of God.

The spirit of this Institute is, first, a spirit of faith, which ought to induce those who compose it not to look upon anything but with the eyes of faith, not to do anything but in view of God, and to attribute everything to God, always entering into these sentiments of Job, "The Lord gave me everything, and the Lord has taken everything away from me; nothing has happened to me except what pleases him," and into other similar sentiments so often expressed in Holy Scripture and uttered by the patriarchs of old.

To enter into this spirit and to live up to it, first, the Brothers of this Society will have a most profound respect for Holy Scripture; in proof of this, they will always carry with them the New Testament and pass no day without reading some of it through a sentiment of faith, respect, and veneration for the divine words contained in it, looking upon it as their first and principal rule.

Second, the Brothers of this Society will animate all their actions with sentiments of faith, and in performing them, they will always have in view the orders and the will of God, which they will adore in all things and by which they will be careful to guide and govern themselves.

For this purpose they will apply themselves to have great control over their senses and to use them only as needed, not wishing to use them except according to the order and the will of God.

They will make it their study to exercise continual watchfulness over themselves so as not to perform, if possible, a single action from natural impulse, through custom, or from any human motive, but they will act so as to perform them all by the guidance of God, through the movement of his Spirit, and with the intention of pleasing him.

They will pay as much attention as they can to the holy presence of God and take care to renew this from time to time, being well convinced that they ought to think only of him and of what he ordains, that is, of what concerns their duty and employment.

They will banish from their minds all vain ideas and thoughts that could withdraw them from these practices, which are very important for them and without which they can neither acquire nor preserve the spirit of their Institute.

The spirit of this Institute consists, secondly, in an ardent zeal for the instruction of children and for bringing them up in the fear of God, inducing them to preserve their innocence if they have not lost it, and inspiring them with a great aversion and a very great horror for sin and for all that could cause them to lose purity.

To enter into this spirit, the Brothers of the Society will strive by prayer, instruction, and their vigilance and good conduct in school to procure the salvation of the children confided to them, bringing them up in piety and in a truly Christian spirit, that is, according to the rules and maxims of the gospel.

The Rule will be read entirely and consecutively, a chapter at a time, on Sundays and feasts during dinner, except on feasts of the mysteries, when it will be read in the evening.

FORMULA OF VOWS

EDITORS' INTRODUCTION: *The archives of the Brothers of the Christian Schools in Rome, Italy, preserve a handwritten original of the signed vow formula used by De La Salle and twelve Brothers to make the first final vows in the Society in 1694. Each participant vows to maintain schools by association, to remain in the Society, and to be willing to beg alms and live on bread alone should that become necessary. They also vow to obey the "body of the society" and the superiors it appoints. The vow formula names all of the members participating and each participant signed his own copy.[2]*

Most Holy Trinity, Father, Son and Holy Spirit, prostrate with the most profound respect before your infinite and adorable majesty, I consecrate myself entirely to you to procure your glory as far as I will be able and as you will require of me.

And for this purpose, I, John Baptist de La Salle, priest, promise and vow to unite myself and to remain in Society with Brothers Nicolas Vuyart, Gabriel Drolin, Jean Partois, Gabriel Charles Rasigade, Jean Henry, Jacques Compain, Jean Jacquot, Jean Louis de Marcheville, Michel Barthélemy Jacquinot, Edme Leguillon, Gilles

Pierre, and Claude Roussel to keep together and by association gratuitous schools wherever they may be, even if I were obliged to beg for alms and to live on bread alone, and to do anything in the said Society at which I will be employed, whether by the body of the Society or by the superiors who will have the government thereof.

Wherefore, I promise and vow obedience to the body of the Society as well as to the superiors, which vows of association as well as of stability in the said Society and of obedience I promise to keep inviolably all my life.

In testimony of which I have signed. Done at Vaugirard on this sixth day of June, feast of the Most Holy Trinity, 1694.

MEMORANDUM ON THE BEGINNINGS

EDITORS' INTRODUCTION: This memorandum consists of remarks of De La Salle's reported by his biographer, Jean-Baptiste Blain. It provides us with one of De La Salle's few personal reflections on his role and the role of Providence in the founding of the Christian Schools. In this memorandum, the God he is coming to know is "gentle" and "wise," leading him where he would not choose to go as he passes from one commitment to another.[3]

"In vain," he told Nyel, "would you have come so far to open Christian and Gratuitous Schools in Reims if your steps took you to the house of the brother of your benefactress. If you go there, you declare your intentions, and if you do so, you will cause the entire project to fail. Will not your stay in that house lead everyone to guess why you have come?

"Your social rank, your state in life, and your type of work are entirely different from those of your host. People will ask what brings you to him and what can be the reason for your coming. They will talk about it and try to find out. The curious will investigate; the idle will gossip. Sooner or later, they will discover the truth or at least get an inkling of it. No matter how reserved you are, they will worm something out of you. They will follow you around and thus learn where you go. Once they find out your business here, they will block you at every turn. The past vouches for the future.

Just recently, a well-known canon and theological preacher, respected and revered in the city, founded a society of women teachers for the schools, which was almost ruined before it really got started.

"So close to destruction was it that only the authority of Archbishop Le Tellier was able to save it. He had to throw all his influence into the balance, and even this was scarcely enough to offset the ill will of the city officials, still less to win them over and get them to agree. Do you think they will approve a second institution for boys? No doubt the poor people of the city need this foundation, but the interests of God and of the poor so often must take second place to politics. To make the latter give way to the former, the archbishop will have to exert all his influence again. Will he be willing to do this, to make use of it a second time, perhaps at the risk of failure?"[4]

"Come," he said with a gracious air; "Stay with me. My home is a residence where parish priests from the country and other priests who are my friends often stay. It is just the place for you to reside, so as to veil your project from public scrutiny. You look somewhat like a parish priest from the country, and people will think that you are one of them. Furthermore, I certainly have the right to offer the hospitality of my home to whomsoever I please. What the world may think about it is of no concern to me; the least of my worries is what people will say. In my house, quiet and unrecognized and without being a burden to anyone, you can easily spend a week or so. This will give you time for further consideration, for refining your plans and deciding on the best way of implementing them successfully. Once this time has elapsed, you can leave for Notre Dame de Liesse, where your piety is calling you, and when you come back, you can attempt to open the schools."[5]

"The best and perhaps the only way to get these Christian and Gratuitous Schools off to a good start," he said to them, "is to safeguard them from all opposition by placing them under the protection of a pastor zealous enough to assume responsibility for them, discreet enough to avoid publicity, and generous enough to support them. Since as pastor he has a right to provide for the religious instruction of his parishioners and since his position as pastor authorizes him to appoint teachers to instruct them in Christian doctrine, nobody would venture to interfere with him or with the schools."[6]

"The pastor of Saint Symphorien," said De La Salle of the first of the four pastors proposed, "would be the man we are looking for, if only he were well thought of by his superiors, but unfortunately they do not like him, and so we had better not consider him further. The second man does not have much judgment. The third is the nephew and toady of the diocesan *officialis*, owes him everything he has become, and is devoted to him. It would take only a word from his uncle and benefactor, and he would send all of the schoolmasters away. We cannot pick him either."[7]

"All we are asking you," added De La Salle, "is to present yourself as the founder of this school and to lend it your name. Your parishioners are mostly poor people; it is your duty to provide instruction for them, since they cannot secure it for themselves. You will give it to them through Monsieur Nyel and his companion, whom we are proposing to you as teachers in your school. Take them in. If questions are asked, let it be understood that you are employing them to instruct the children of your parish."[8]

"I had thought that the care which I took of the schools and of the teachers would only be external, something which would not involve me any further than to provide for their subsistence and to see to it that they carried out their duties with piety and assiduity."[9]

"It was by these two events, namely, by my meeting Monsieur Nyel and by the proposal made to me by this woman, that I began to take an interest in the schools for boys. Prior to this, I had never given them a thought. The suggestion, of course, had been made to me before. Several of Monsieur Roland's friends had tried to motivate me to accept, but the proposal had never made any impression on my mind, and I had never considered carrying it out.

"Indeed, if I had ever thought that the care I was taking of the schoolmasters out of pure charity would ever have made it my duty to live with them, I would have dropped the whole project. For since, naturally speaking, I considered the men whom I was obliged to employ in the schools at the beginning as being inferior to my valet, the mere thought that I would have to live with them would have been insupportable to me. In fact, I experienced a great deal of unpleasantness when I first had them come to my house. This lasted for two years. It was undoubtedly for this reason that God, who guides all things with wisdom and serenity, whose way it is not to force the inclinations of persons, willed to commit me entirely to the development of the schools. God did this in an imperceptible way and over a long period of time, so that one commitment led to another in a way that I did not foresee in the beginning."[10]

"Men of little faith, by your lack of trust you set limits to a Goodness that has no limits in itself. If that Goodness is indeed infinite, universal, and continual—as you do not doubt—it will always take care of you and never fail you. You seek assurance, but does not the gospel provide it? The words of Jesus Christ are your insurance contract; there is no compact more reliable, because God has signed it with blood and has affixed to it the seal of infallible truth. Why then do you grow distrustful? If the positive promises of God cannot calm your uneasiness and your concern for the future, what is the point of looking for an investment that will produce a comparable income?

"Consider the lilies of the field, for it is Jesus Christ himself who urges you to reflect on them and on the wild flowers of the countryside and to see how richly God has adorned them and made them beautiful. They lack nothing, yet Solomon himself in all his glory was less splendidly attired. Open your eyes and see the birds that fly through the air or the little animals which creep upon the ground: not a single one of them lacks what is needed. God provides for their necessities. Possessing neither cellars nor barns, they find everywhere the food that Providence has prepared for them. They do not sow or reap, yet they find their sustenance. The heavenly Father takes care of them. If his generous and kindly concern extends to even the least insects which men trample underfoot and even to the grass that dries out and serves as fuel for the fire, how can you believe, you men of little faith, that he to whom you consecrate your labor will abandon you in your old age and leave you to finish in misery a life spent in his service?

"Therefore, stir up your trust in the Lord's infinite goodness, and honor God by leaving in the divine hands the care of your persons. Be not troubled about the present or disquieted about the future, but be concerned only about the moment you must now live. Do not let anticipation of tomorrow be a burden on the day that is passing. What you lack in the evening, the morrow will bring you, if you know how to hope in God. God will work miracles rather than let you suffer want. In addition to the words of Jesus Christ, I offer you as proof the universal experience of the saints. Providence performs miracles daily, and they cease only for those who have no trust."[11]

Tired of simply thinking these thoughts, one day the schoolmasters summoned up their courage to the point of expressing their grievance and gave De La Salle one of those blunt, direct replies that the heart feels is unanswerable: "You speak with inspiration amidst your ease, for you lack nothing. You have a rich canonry and an equally fine inheritance; you enjoy security and protection against indigence. If our work fails, you risk nothing. The ruin of our enterprise would not affect you. We own nothing. We are men without possessions or income or even a trade to fall back on. Where can we go, and what can we do if the schools fail or if people tire of us? Destitution will be our only portion, and begging our only means to relieve it."[12]

[The reasons that motivated De La Salle to resign his canonry.]

"1) I have been reduced to silence. As long as I am not poor myself, I have no right to speak the language of perfection, as I once did on the subject of poverty. I cannot speak of abandonment to Providence, so long as I am comfortably insured against penury, nor about perfect confidence in God, if my sound investments leave me no reason for worry.

"2) If I remain what I am and the schoolmasters remain what they are, their temptation will persist, because its source will continue to be there. I will not be able to remedy it, because they will always

113

find in my wealth an obvious and even plausible argument to justify their doubts about the present and their concerns for the future.

"3) Sooner or later, such a temptation, so justifiable in appearance, will not fail to produce the effect that the devil hopes it will achieve. The teachers, whether in a group or one by one, will forsake me, leaving my house empty for the second time and the schools without anyone capable of conducting them.

"4) This desertion will make a good deal of noise in the city. It will frighten off any who might have entertained the idea of becoming schoolmasters. Their vocation will wither; even before they enter, they will be seized by the same misgivings as those who have just left.

"5) Without a dependable staff of teachers, the schools will fail. In this case, the heirs of the foundations will claim the funds contributed for their maintenance.

"6) Thus, little by little, the Institution of Christian and Gratuitous Schools will be buried beneath its ruins, and it will be useless ever to think of reviving it.

"7) Even supposing that all these results do not follow, must I— can I, even—act as the superior of these schoolmasters without giving up my canonry? How can I combine my assiduous presence in the house, so as to be at their head during the exercises of piety and to keep watch over them, with attendance in the choir for the canonical Office? Are these two positions compatible? If not, I must give up one or the other.

"8) True, a canon's prebend is not in itself an obstacle to good works, and sedulous attendance at the Office to chant God's praises does not prevent him from rendering other services to the church or from devoting himself to the salvation of souls. He can divide his time between these two noble functions and prove that a canon does not have to be idle outside the choir. He does not need to seek in this title a plausible pretext to leave the choir, only to enter upon a rest that lasts all day, to grow stout in sweet indolence, and to do no work in the Lord's vineyard. But can I at the same time be a good canon and a faithful superior of a community that requires my presence constantly? If I fulfill the function of superior properly, I will have to omit all the duties of a canon, since if I must always be in the house, I can never be in the choir. If these two duties cannot be reconciled, I must choose between them. Five or six hours a day spent in reciting the Divine Office would make too great an inroad on the assiduous presence that I owe to the house I direct.

"9) Now, in the choice I must make, what should be my determining consideration? What should tip the balance? The greater glory of God, the fuller service of the church, my own higher perfection, and the salvation of souls: these are the ends I must propose to myself and the aims that must govern my choice. If I consider only these exalted motives, I must resign my canonry and devote myself to the care of the schools and to the training of the schoolmasters who direct them.

"10) Finally, since I no longer feel any attraction to the vocation of a canon, it would seem that it has already left me, even before I have given it up. This calling is no longer for me. While I entered it through the right gate, indeed, it seems to me that God is opening another door before me today so that I may leave it. The same voice that called me to it seems to be calling me elsewhere. I hear this in the depths of my conscience; this voice speaks when I consult my conscience. True, since the hand of God put me in the state in which I now am, his hand must take me out of it. But is he not showing me clearly enough today another state that deserves the preference and toward which he is leading me by the hand?"[13]

Finally, after much reflection in God's presence, after much prayer and consultation, it seemed evident to him, "toward the end of the year 1682, that God was calling him to take charge of the schools, and since he had to be the first at all the exercises of the community, he could not assist at the [Divine] Office as assiduously as his director required him to."[14]

"My God, I do not know whether I should endow the schools or not. It is not up to me to establish communities; I do not even know how they should be established. You alone know this, and it is for you to do it in whatever way you please. I do not dare to establish or endow, because I do not know what you want. So I will not contribute in any way to endowing the schools. If you endow the schools, they will be well endowed; if you do not, they will be without endowment. I beseech you to make your holy will known to me."[15]

After discussing with his director the resolution he had taken of divesting himself of his wealth and after asking for his approval, he added, "I will not do it, if you do not want me to. I will do it in whatever measure you desire; if you tell me to keep something—even only five sous—I will do so."[16]

"Do not forget, my dear Brothers, the sad times we have just come through. You have seen with your own eyes all the calamities that famine brings down upon the poor and all the ravages it can occasion to the fortunes of the rich. This whole city was like one vast hospice where the poor in their destitution gathered and spent the last days of a life which hunger would soon close. During all this time, when the wealthiest were not always sure of finding bread at any price—bread that had become as rare as it was expensive—what did you lack? Thanks be to God, although we have had neither money nor income, during these two terrible years we have lacked nothing. We owe no one anything in any of our houses, while some of our well-established neighbors have been ruined, despite their resources, since they have been obliged to sell their property and to borrow to keep alive."[17]

"Your heart will recognize your own work in the legislation that will be laid down, and the details it prescribes will seem agreeable to you because you yourselves will have been the lawgivers. Now that you have reached the point where I wished to lead you and I can testify to your fervor and pious dispositions, I wish to undertake measures with you to stabilize your state of life, to strengthen you in your vocation, to consolidate your union with one another, and to begin building the edifice of which you are the foundation stones."

He then reminded them of the ideas and suggestions that they themselves had often put forward, namely, of binding themselves to their vocation by vows. It was up to them, he said, to consider whether the time had come to impose on themselves such blessed chains which, while restraining their liberty, would bind them to God. He asked them whether, after remaining up to the present unattached to their vocation and free to come or go, they now felt that they should join themselves to it by some type of vow. He concluded by saying that on this point, as on all the rest, he wanted them to feel entirely free to declare how they felt and even freer to do whatever they wished. All he planned to do was to listen to them and to follow whatever the majority might decide. What he did recommend to them was to pray much and by a fervent retreat to place themselves in a position to know God's will.[18]

"Ever since I gave up everything, I have never met a single candidate tempted to leave us on the grounds that our community was not endowed."[19]

Among other things, he told them: "Since Providence had now joined them in a body through the perpetual vows they had pronounced the previous day, it would be wise to seek means to make this union so strong and so permanent that neither the world nor the devil could alter it. The first such means was to place all their trust in God alone, remembering that those who rely on mortal man are leaning on a frail reed which, as scripture says, when it breaks pierces the hand that holds it. As for himself, they should consider him only as a poor priest who lacked both the power and the prestige to uphold them and their Society. It was the height of folly to count on any man and to base their hopes on human resources. They should recall that although he had recovered from a mortal illness three years previously, he might find himself again at death's door any day, and in that case, they would be obliged to elect someone else as superior. Hence, it was better to provide for this eventuality ahead of time rather than wait for it to happen and be forced to make a choice. Strong reasons demanded that they do this without further delay, for if they kept on putting it off until his death, this could bring about very serious consequences for their Society."

He added that "the second means of rendering their union indissoluble would be to have as their head one of themselves, someone who was not a priest. The sacerdotal character would place a vast gulf between them and such a superior. This would weaken their union, and inferiors not closely united to the one who governs them are like a body in which the head and the members are badly joined and which consequently remains either lifeless or languishing. It was time—and high time—to take away from him the government of the Institute, and if they delayed in doing so, they would come to regret it.

"The first result of neglecting this advice of his would be that if he happened to die, there would spring up as many superiors as there were schools. This diversity of leaders would infallibly cause divisions in the flock. Once the sheep were dispersed, they would lose contact among themselves and all subordination to a common shepherd. Then, not following the same line of conduct, they would cease to have the same spirit, convictions, and sentiments. These diverse groups, no longer constituting a single organism, would adopt differing ideas and modify their doctrine, their way of life, and their habit. Very soon this division would cause their ruin. These Brothers, going their separate ways, could not be replaced save by men having different talents, customs, and views. Before long, they would see hired teachers taking over the schools, which—once they ceased to be gratuitous—would cease to be Christian and would no longer prove effective in the education of poor children.

"Suppose, for the sake of argument," he continued, "that the various ecclesiastical superiors of the localities where the Brothers are established should agree on giving you, after my death, only one priest as your superior (a highly improbable supposition). Would he be the right man to lead you? Would he understand the spirit of a community? Of yours in particular? Would he follow its rules?

Would he be willing to adopt your manner of living? Could he sympathize with you or you with him? Would you be prepared to give him your confidence? Would he be prepared to live with you as one of you? Even supposing that he were a saint, a man filled with the Spirit of God, zealous for the salvation of his neighbor, full of charity and tenderness in your regard, would he be the right man for you, not having been brought up like you and with you? In addition, his dignity as a priest would always create a gap between you and him, and with his being unacquainted with your customs, traditions, principles, and practices, how could you have but one heart and one soul with him? Would he not wish to change your rules? In a word, would he be the right sort of person to direct you? How long would it take him to acquire the experience needed to govern you according to the spirit of your Institute? Would it not call for a miracle to find a man really apt to govern you? Can you expect such a miracle? If not, why delay in doing away with your present priest-superior and in making it a law for yourselves never to give this title to anyone clothed in this dignity?"[20]

"Fear nothing. God has never failed to help those who hope in him. Everything is granted to a lively faith and perfect trust, even miracles if they are needed. Jesus Christ has obliged himself to provide those who seek the kingdom of God and his justice with everything they need. Never has he refused it to those who serve him. Every page of scripture bears witness to this truth. After all, nothing happens in this world save what God permits or ordains. Good and evil, poverty and wealth, come from his hand. It is he who distributes them with constant goodness and wisdom. If we have received so many benefits from his liberality, why should we refuse to accept from his justice the chastisement he sends us? He is the Lord; let him do what he pleases. If we conform our desires to his good pleasure, we shall find relief in our pains, put an end to our worries, and draw a treasure of merit from the depths of our poverty. Even if we have to die of hunger, if God finds us submissive, he will at least crown our virtue in heaven and admit us to the ranks of the martyrs of patience."[21]

MEMORANDUM ON THE HABIT

EDITORS' INTRODUCTION: The document deals with an attempt on the part of the pastor of the parish of Saint Sulpice to take more control over the Brothers. In the document, the Brothers together are referred to as the "Community of the Christian Schools," and they are described as a group similar to "religious communities" with an agreed-upon rule and regulated life. While it defends the dress of the community, its real significance would seem to be its declaration of independence for this small community of laymen. They were self-discerning and self-determinant.[22]

1. Whether it is appropriate to change or to keep the habit that the Brothers of the Community of the Christian Schools are currently wearing. What this community is and who compose it.

2. This Community is commonly called the Community of the Christian Schools and at present rests upon—indeed, is rooted in—Providence alone. Those who live in it follow a Rule and are dependent for everything, having no personal possessions, and treat one another as equals.

3. The members of this community devote themselves to teaching in tuition-free schools, in towns only, and to giving basic religious instruction every day, including Sundays and holidays.

4. Provision is also made for training schoolmasters for rural districts in a house, separate from the community, that we call a normal school.[23] Those who are trained there remain for only a few years, until they are well prepared in religious spirit as well as for their work.

5. They dress just like ordinary secular people except for the black, or at least dark brown, color of their clothing, and they cannot be distinguished from them except by the split white collar[24] they wear and their close-cropped hair.

6. They are taught to become proficient in singing, reading, and writing. Their room, board, and laundry are all free. In due course they are placed in a hamlet or a village as a parish assistant. Having secured a position, they maintain no further contact with the

community except for what is appropriate and courteous. However, they are welcomed back for a periodic retreat.

7. In this community we also provide training for young boys who possess basic intelligence and some religious disposition. When we judge them suitable and they themselves apply for admission, we accept them into the community from the age of fourteen and over. We introduce them to the practice of interior prayer and other religious observances. We also instruct them in religious doctrine and teach them to read and write competently.

8. The young men who are formed and trained in this community live in a separate house with their own oratory, schedule, meals, and recreation periods. Their religious observances are different and adapted to their level of mental development and to the needs of their future work.

9. Those who make up this community are all laymen without a classical education and possessing but average intelligence. As God would have it, some of those who joined after either receiving the tonsure or studying did not remain.

10. However, we will not refuse admission to young men who have studied, but we will accept them only on condition that they never again pursue advanced studies—first, because such knowledge is unnecessary for them; second, because it might subsequently lure them away from their state in life, and third, because community observances and classroom work require their total commitment.

11. What kind of habit do we wear in this community? The habit of this community is a kind of shortened cassock that reaches to the calf of the leg. It is without buttons and is fastened on the inside with little black hooks from the collar to just below the waist. From there downward it is sewn. The sleeves reach to the wrists, and the tips are fastened with concealed hooks.

12. We call this habit a robe to distinguish it from a clerical cassock, from which it differs slightly in shape.

13. A cloak or a peasant's overcoat,[25] without a collar and without buttons in front, serves as a mantle. It is fastened at the neck with a large hook on the inside. Rather long, this cloak reaches an inch or so below the robe, completely covering it.

14. The cloaks or overcoats that the Brothers of the Christian Schools wear were given to them to guard against the cold before they adopted the distinctive short cassock they now have and when they were outfitted with a pocketless but serviceable jacket.

15. At that time, cloaks were widely worn, and we judged them to be proper, useful, and comfortable attire for schoolmasters, particularly those who must leave their community residence and go to schools in distant districts for the convenience of their students. Besides wearing this cloak as a mantle in the streets, these masters used it in winter as an indoors coat when they reached their school or community residence.

16. There was considerable hesitation at the time as to whether we should give them mantles in preference to these peasant overcoats, which in the future, we realized, would come to be regarded as a distinctive sort of attire.

17. But four considerations settled the matter. In the first place, mantles would not guard against the cold in classrooms and would get in the way. Second, we feared that with these short mantles, the masters might take on the airs of court clergy if they looked outwardly just like them. Third, dressed according to current fashion, they would appear to be members of the clergy when they are nothing of the sort. Fourth, they might abscond with the mantle, as well as the jacket, as soon as the thought crossed their mind, returning home dressed like a gentleman although they had brought with them only the clothes of a peasant or a poor laborer.

18. These various drawbacks led to the conclusion that it would be better for them to use a habit that is neither clerical nor secular.

19. The disadvantage of changing this habit. The question of change in general.

20. There are few changes that are not harmful to a community, particularly in matters that might be the least bit important.

21. Changes are always a mark of vacillation and of little stability; however, constancy in practices, customs, and points of Rule appears to be one of the mainstays of community life.

22. One change within a community opens the door to others and ordinarily leaves an unfavorable impression on the mind of all, or at least some, members.

23. Most disorders and deviations in a community arise from admitting changes too readily. Hence, it is a maxim accepted by all who have had some experience with community life that

24. before introducing any change in a community, it is essential to give much serious thought to the matter and to calculate carefully the good and the evil effects that may result from it. But once a practice has been put into place, it is necessary to be extremely careful not to overturn it except for an unavoidable necessity.

25. It is apparent that the reverend Jesuit fathers have observed this practice. After the death of Saint Ignatius, when they encountered some difficulty in observing their Constitutions, they discussed the situation at their first general chapter, seeking some kind of remedy. Finally, they unanimously decided not to change any point but simply to clarify any murky question by adding marginal notes of explanation.

26. Objections to this habit in particular.

27. Changing the religious habit is a matter of importance in a community; hence, most religious communities take great care to avoid all circumstances that might lead to its alteration. In several communities the habit is prescribed not only as to its shape and the quality of the material but also with respect to its length and breadth. All the dimensions are exactly indicated so that the habit will never be altered. The communities of religious priests that adopted at their foundation the clothing then in fashion among other clerics have

steadfastly retained the original habit and have thereby ended up making it distinctive.

28. For the past five years, this habit has been worn in five different towns, both in the diocese of Reims and in that of Laon.

29. There it is regarded as a decent and appropriate habit designed both to keep the teachers true to the diligence and reserve proper to their state and profession and to invite the respect of their students and the esteem of other people, far more than the jacket they formerly wore.

30. People have grown accustomed to this habit, and changing it now would give rise to gossip, invite criticism for being faddish and frivolous, and induce superiors to bring back secular dress.

31. The Brothers of the Christian Schools have been teaching in Paris for nearly two years in this same habit, and during that time no one has lodged any complaints about it except the parish priest of Saint Sulpice, who recently has spoken rather strongly on the matter.

32. If this habit were objectionable, this should have been pointed out, it would seem, when the Brothers of the Christian Schools came to Paris and before they were employed in the schools there. They should have been told then that they would not be permitted to teach in this distinctive habit and that they would have to adopt one more commonly used. Then they would have had to decide what measures to take.

33. Reasons for adopting a distinctive habit and for keeping it.

34. In every community where the members share all their goods and live a common life, as in that of the Christian Schools, the habit either is distinctive from its foundation or becomes so eventually.

35. It seems more suitable for the welfare of a community that the habit be distinctive from its foundation rather than become so later. It will then be more difficult to change it, and a permanently distinctive habit will remove every chance of adopting the worldly fashions of ordinary people.

36.   The members of this community, being for the most part rough, unrefined, and uneducated men who ordinarily respond to feelings and impressions, need some tangible token of membership in the community to draw them to it, to retain their allegiance once they join, and to lead them to observe its Rule.

37.   Nothing is more effective in achieving these ends than a distinctive habit, which can be the hallmark of a community whose custom it may be to wear one.

38.   Monsieur Vincent judged that a distinctive habit was essential, in a sense, to hold the allegiance of the members of his congregation.[26] With how much more reason does this seem necessary in a community whose members lack any formal education or enlightenment!

39.   For most of those entering the community, having a distinctive habit effectively removes any concern about its stability and endowment.

40.   This distinctive habit encourages laypeople to look upon those who belong to this community as persons separated and withdrawn from worldly concerns. It seems appropriate that they have this notion about them so that the members themselves will not mingle too freely or converse too frequently with secular people and will maintain more reserve in their relations with them.

41.   Before the adoption of this special habit, whenever the obligation to observe the Rule was brought up, several said that they had no more reason to do so than ordinary people because they appeared to be no different from them.

42.   Since the adoption of this distinctive garb, it does not seem that anyone has raised any trouble on this score, for all regard themselves as belonging to a community.

43.   Before the adoption of this special habit, those applying for admission to this community regarded it merely as an employment agency for schoolmasters or servants and had no idea of joining a religious community. Several came to be trained so that they could

earn a living afterward. Some asked for a salary, and others thought we ought to be grateful for their conforming to our way of life and manner of dress.

44. Since the adoption of this habit, no one has applied for admission with any thought other than of joining a community and remaining in it for the rest of his life. Salaries are unheard of, and acceptance is regarded as a great honor. The habit alone produces these results.

45. Before the adoption of this habit, most of those who left the community took away with them the clothing they had received. Now the habit helps to restrain the Brothers in their temptations. Some of them have even admitted that several times they had considered leaving and would have done so had it not been for the habit.

46. Objections to wearing the ecclesiastical habit.

47. It does not seem right to give a purely clerical garb to laymen, such as the members of this community of the Christian Schools, who have not pursued a classical education—and never will—and who neither can nor do perform priestly functions or wear a surplice in church.

48. We cannot expect that their excellencies the bishops who have or may have them in their diocese will accept and tolerate persons of this sort wearing clerical garb.

49. It does not seem possible that the head of this community could give a satisfactory answer when asked why, on his own authority, he had given clerical garb to persons not of that calling. How could he justify his action?

50. There has been some talk of making them receive the tonsure, but a number of persons, including Monsieur Baudrand,[27] disagree with this notion. It is certainly difficult to believe that our lord bishops would agree to tonsure men who have never begun, and never will begin, classical studies and who never will exercise any function in the church. Yet that is what people propose for members of this community.

51.   It seems important to distinguish the members of this community from clerics by their habit.

52.   They are in the parish churches every day, and their schools are usually located nearby. They take their students to these churches to attend holy Mass and the Divine Office.

53.   Parish priests would not be satisfied with their wearing a long mantle but would insist that they also put on a surplice, and they would make use of the Brothers in religious services, at least when they needed their help.

54.   This situation would happen frequently because there are few priests in most urban parishes; often there is only the pastor and, at most, one assistant.

55.   The schoolmasters would feel honored to wear the surplice in the parishes, to rank with the clergy, and to take part in church services.

56.   As a consequence, they would readily abandon the care of their students in church, the only reason they go there and an onerous responsibility.

57.   The observations contained herein are all based on experience at Saint Jacques, Laon, and Château-Porcien.

58.   If the Brothers of this community wore clerical garb, they might be easily tempted to begin classical studies, to be tonsured, to receive holy orders, and to seek a position in the parishes.

59.   They would freely communicate and make friends with parish priests and other clerics, seeing them every day. As a result, this too frequent interaction could raise many temptations against their vocation and cause them to be less diligent in their school duties.

60.   The long mantle would get in the way of their work.

61.   With this garb, they could not easily move among their students, line them up, or keep them in order when they escort them to the parish church and remain with them there.

62.   People have mentioned that with this mantle there is a danger of knocking over most of the small children on one side or the other while trying to place them in order.

63.   In most towns we will have to staff schools in various districts where the teachers must remain every day for three and a half hours in the morning and as long in the afternoon.

64.   In these schools in winter they will require other clothes than their normal attire to guard against the cold. A long mantle would be of no use for this purpose, whereas their peasants' overcoat can serve as an indoors coat in their schools.

MEMORANDUM ON NOT USING LATIN TO TEACH READING

EDITORS' INTRODUCTION: *In 1699 the bishop of Chartres M. Godet des Marais opened two Christian Schools run by De La Salle's Brothers. A friend of De La Salle from seminary days at Saint Sulpice, the bishop was delighted with the work of the Brothers and the changes he noted in the young men who attended the Schools. In 1702 he suggested that the Brothers relax their personal discipline somewhat. More specifically, he was not in favor of abandoning Latin in the Schools for learning to read in French. In response to these suggestions, De La Salle explains the reasons for preferring the teaching of French before the reading of Latin. The reasons focus on the needs of the children.*[28]

The established practice in the Christian Schools is to begin by teaching children how to read French before teaching them to read Latin. This unaccustomed procedure did not seem to Bishop Godet Desmarets the most natural one; he wished to have it changed. De La Salle, who had introduced this modification in what was commonly practiced only because he had serious reasons for doing so, asked to be allowed to explain them and proceeded to justify the practice by such cogent arguments that the prelate agreed with him. Here, in substance, are his arguments:

"1) Knowing how to read French is far more useful to all children than knowing how to read Latin.

"2) Since French is their native language, it is incomparably easier for them to learn how to read it than to read Latin, given that they know the one and do not know the other.

"3) Consequently, it takes far less time to teach children to read French than to teach them to read Latin.

"4) Ability to read French facilitates learning how to read Latin; the reverse is not true, as experience shows. The reason for this is that to read Latin properly, all one needs to do is to articulate each syllable and enunciate each word correctly. This is easy when the child knows how to spell and to read French; it follows that anyone who knows how to read French well can easily learn to read Latin; on the contrary, when much time has been spent learning to read Latin first, still more is required to learn how to read French.

"5) Why does it take so long to learn to read Latin? As already mentioned, Latin words are just sounds to people who do not understand them; hence, it is difficult for them not to omit some of the syllables or to spell out words whose meaning escapes them.

"6) Why should people learn to read Latin, when they will never make any use of this language during their lives? What use do the children of either sex who come to the Christian Schools have for the Latin language? Nuns who must recite the Divine Office in Latin need to know how to read it well, but of a hundred girls who frequent the Gratuitous Schools, scarcely one might become a choir nun in a monastery. So, too, of a hundred boys in the Brothers' Schools, how many will later on wish to study the Latin language? Even if there were several of them, should they be favored at the expense of the rest?

"7) Experience shows that those children who frequent the Christian Schools do not stay there very long; they do not attend classes long enough to learn how to read both Latin and French well. As soon as they are old enough to start working, their parents withdraw them or else they stop coming because they have to earn a living. Under these circumstances, if we start by teaching them how to read Latin, the following inconveniences will result: they will quit school before learning how to read French or at least to read it well; when they leave, they will know how to read Latin only imperfectly; in a short time, they will have forgotten what they learned, with the result that they will never really know how to read at all, either French or Latin.

"8) The most serious drawback is that they almost never learn Christian doctrine. In fact, when children begin by learning to read French, they know how to read fairly well by the time they leave school. Knowing how to read easily, they can learn Christian doctrine by themselves and can study it in the printed catechisms; they can sanctify Sundays and feasts by reading good books and reciting well-written prayers in French. Whereas when they leave the Christian and Gratuitous Schools, if they know how to read Latin only, and that badly, all their lives they will remain ignorant of their duties as Christians.

"9) Finally, experience shows that those who do not understand Latin, who have not pursued further studies and acquired familiarity with the Latin tongue—especially the common people and, a fortiori, the poor who come to the Christian Schools—never succeed in reading Latin well and make fools of themselves when they try to read it in the hearing of those who understand that language. It is, therefore, completely useless to waste time teaching people to read a language that they will never use."

Chapter 4

The Conduct of the Christian Schools

————————— ✠ —————————

EDITORS' INTRODUCTION: *De La Salle was an innovator, but he learned from many educators before him. His genius was how he adapted what he learned to make education accessible to poor children. The Conduct offers clear, thorough directions for teachers, especially new teachers, confronted with fifty or sixty urchins off the streets of the cities of France. Step-by-step, as these excerpts illustrate, the Conduct shows how Lasallian cooperative learning is implemented, how French is to be taught, and how religious practices are to be woven throughout the school day. The first part of the volume offers specific directions about daily lesson plans, maintaining order, and religious practices so that a new teacher could "make it through the day." The second part shows teachers how to create community and how to minister to difficult children so that a teacher could "make it through the year." The final section of the book instructs the inspectors and supervisors of new teachers so that they could help teachers have "a successful career." Above all, everything done in the schools should be motivated by the gospels and done for the salvation of the children.[1]*

BREAKFAST AND AFTERNOON SNACK

ARTICLE 1:
Teacher Attention During Breakfast and Afternoon Snack

Teachers should take care that the students bring their breakfast and afternoon snack with them every day. A little basket will be set in an appointed place in the classroom, into which the children when they are so piously inclined may put what bread they have left over to be distributed among those of them who are poor. Teachers will see that they do not give away any of their bread unless they have enough left for themselves. Those who have bread to give will raise their hands, showing at the same time the piece of bread that they have to give, and a student who has been appointed to receive these alms will collect them. At the end of the meal the teacher will distribute the bread to the poorest and will exhort them to pray to God for their benefactors.

Teachers will also take care that students do not throw either nuts or shells on the floor but will have them put them into their pockets or into their bags.

Students must be made to understand that it is desirable that they eat in school in order to teach them to eat with propriety, with decorum, and in a polite manner, and to invoke God before and after eating.

Teachers will see that the students do not play during breakfast and the afternoon snack but that they be very attentive to what is being done in school during this time. In order to discover whether they are exact in this, teachers will from time to time make one of them repeat what has been said, with the exception of those who are occupied in writing.

Students will not be permitted either to give anything whatsoever to one another, not even any part of their breakfast, or to exchange it.

Teachers will see to it that the students finish breakfast by 8:30, or as near as possible.

Article 2:
What Is Done During Breakfast and Afternoon Snack

On the first two days of the week upon which school is held all day, the students who read but do not spell will recite the morning prayers during breakfast and the evening prayers during the afternoon snack. For those who are in the writing classes, on Mondays and Tuesdays one student will occupy an appointed place and say all the prayers in an audible tone: during breakfast, the morning prayers; in the afternoon, the evening ones, the commandments of God and of the church, and the Act of Contrition. Students will recite in turn, one after the other. They must learn these prayers by heart and will recite them during breakfast and the afternoon snack on these two days. The inspector will reprove them when they fail. On the last two days of the week upon which school is held throughout the whole day, they will recite during breakfast and the afternoon snack what they have learned in the diocesan catechism during the week. The teacher will see that they recite everything on these two days without a single exception. What they are to learn in each class during the week will be indicated by the director or the head teacher.

On Wednesdays when there is a whole holiday on Thursday or on those days when there is a half holiday because of a holy day of obligation during the week, those who read Latin will recite the responses of holy Mass during breakfast. This will likewise be done during the first half hour of the catechism in the afternoon.

If there are in the class in which the responses of holy Mass are recited any students who already know them or are capable of learning them even though they are not yet able to read Latin, the teacher will take care that they know them well and will make them recite them also.

The students who recite all the above-mentioned items should have learned them by heart at home or during the time that they assemble for school. They do not recite them in order to learn but only to show that they do know them, and, as for the prayers and responses of holy Mass, to learn how to say them properly. Those who do not know them, although they have already been a long time in the writing class, will also be made to learn them and to recite them.

All students who recite the prayers and responses of holy Mass will recite them in turn, one after the other, in an order different from that of the other prayers.

In the lower classes the prayers will be recited in the following manner. One of two students will announce the titles of the prayers, and the other will recite the acts or the articles all in order and in succession from the beginning of the prayers to the end. All students will take turns in doing each of these things in turn.

The student who announces the titles of the prayers and the questions of the catechism will correct the other in case a mistake is made in anything. In case the first one does not do this, the teacher will give the signal for a correction. If the student does not know what has been said incorrectly, the teacher whose duty at the time is to attend both to those who are reciting and to the order of the whole class will signal another student to make the correction in the same manner as in the lessons.

In the writing class, while the teacher is occupied with writing, a student who has been appointed inspector will do what the teacher should do but only for this recitation. Teachers shall in no way exempt themselves from watching over the general order of the class during this time.

The responses of holy Mass will be recited in the following manner. Throughout the whole recitation one student will do what the priest does and will say what the priest says as is indicated in the liturgy. Another student, who will be at his side, will reply as the server should reply and do what the server should do.

The server will do accurately all that is indicated in *The Book of Prayers for the Christian Schools*. Those who are reciting the prayers and responses of holy Mass will maintain throughout this time a very decorous and pious attitude. They should hold their hands and their exterior demeanor in the greatest control. They should be obliged to recite these prayers and responses with the same decorum, with the same respect, with the same demeanor, and in the same manner that would be expected if they were serving holy Mass or saying their prayers at home.

Teachers will take care that those who are reciting the prayers and the responses of holy Mass or the catechism speak during this time very distinctly and in a moderately loud tone in order that all may hear them. Nevertheless, they should speak low enough so that the other students must keep silent, listen, and be attentive to those who are reciting.

During this time, teachers will observe very carefully everything that happens in their classes, and make sure that all are attentive. From time to time, a teacher will stop those who are reciting in order to question those who appear to be not sufficiently attentive. If the latter are unable to answer, the teacher will impose some penance upon them or will punish them as may be judged necessary.

During this recitation, the teacher will hold either *The Book of Prayers for the Christian Schools* or the catechism and will take care that the students repeat very exactly and very well.

On the first two days of the week and on the two days upon which the catechism is to be recited, those who are learning their letters from the alphabet chart will learn and repeat only the Our Father, the Hail Mary, the Creed, and the Act of Contrition in Latin and in French as they are in *The Book of Prayers for the Christian Schools.*

Those who are studying the chart of syllables will learn and repeat the acts of the presence of God, of invocation of the Holy Spirit, of adoration, and of thanksgiving, which come in sequence at the beginning of the morning prayers as well as of the evening prayers.

Those who are spelling from the syllable chart will learn and repeat in turn, in the following order, the acts of offering and of petition, which are in the morning prayers; the act of presenting ourselves to God; the confession of sins; the Act of Contrition and the act of offering of sleep, which are in the evening prayers; the prayer to the guardian angel; and those that follow in the morning as well as in the evening prayers.

If any of those who are studying the last two of these three lessons do not know any of the prayers that they should have learned in this lesson or in the preceding ones, the teacher will make them learn and practice these prayers that they do not know with those students who are studying the lesson in which such prayers should be learned. For instance, with those who are studying the alphabet, the Our Father, the Hail Mary, the Creed, and the Act of Contrition, if they do not yet know them. When they know them well or assuming they know them well, they will learn with those who are studying the chart of syllables those acts that should be memorized by the students who are studying this lesson.

Those who are spelling or reading in the second book will learn and recite all the prayers, the morning prayers as well as the evening prayers. If the teacher notices that anyone who is reciting these prayers does not know them well, that student will be obliged to learn them privately from *The Book of Prayers for the Christian*

Schools. The teacher will fix a time for the student to recite them either entirely or in part as will seem fit.

If there are in the same class any students who should recite the catechism, they will do so on Saturday or only on the last school day of the week. If during breakfast and the afternoon snack on this day there is more time than is needed to have all of them recite it, the time that remains will be employed in having the prayers recited.[2]

Introductory Remarks on Corrections

EDITORS' INTRODUCTION: Schoolmasters in De La Salle's time whipped students regularly as the preferred method of discipline. While some use of the ferule and rod were allowed, these were last resorts in the Christian Schools and only administered under strict guidelines and supervision. If a Brother had discipline problems, he was first to examine his own behavior to see how he contributed to the problems. De La Salle's approach to discipline reflects a profound understanding of children but also a profound commitment inspired by the gospels to compassionate care of children.[3]

The correction of the students is one of the most important tasks to be done in the schools. The greatest care must be taken to make correction timely and beneficial both for those who receive it and for those who witness it. For this reason many things are to be considered with regard to the use of the corrections that may be administered in the schools and that will be discussed in the following articles. This will be done after the necessity of joining gentleness to firmness in the guidance of children has been explained.

Experience founded on the unvarying teachings of the saints and on the example they have set us affords sufficient proof that to perfect those entrusted to our care, we must act toward them in a manner at the same time both gentle and firm. Many, however, are obliged to admit—or they show by their behavior toward those confided to their care—that they do not see how these two things can easily be joined in practice. If, for example, a teacher assumes absolute authority and an overbearing attitude in dealing with children, the teacher will likely find it difficult to keep this way of acting from becoming harsh and unbearable. Although this course of action may begin as great zeal, it is not wise, as Saint Paul says, for it overlooks human weakness.

At the same time, if too much consideration is had for human weakness and if, under the pretext of showing compassion, children are allowed to do as they will, the result will be wayward, idle, and unruly students.

What then must be done so that firmness does not degenerate into harshness and that gentleness does not degenerate into languor and weakness?

To throw some light on this matter, which appears to be of no little importance, it seems opportune to set forth in a few words some principal ways in which teachers express the severity and harshness in guiding and educating children that become unbearable to them. Then the text will describe how a contrary weakness by the teacher can lead to all laxness, disorder, and so forth among the students.

The following are examples of a teacher's conduct that becomes unbearable to those in the teacher's charge.

First, the teacher's penances are too rigorous, and the yoke the teacher imposes upon the students is too heavy. This state of affairs is frequently due to the lack of discretion and judgment on the part of the teacher. It often happens that students lack sufficient strength of body or of mind to bear the burdens that many times overwhelm them.

Second, the teacher enjoins, commands, or exacts something of the children with words too harsh and in a manner too domineering. Above all, the teacher's conduct is unbearable when it arises from unrestrained impatience or anger.

Third, the teacher is too insistent in urging upon a child some performance that the child is not disposed to do, and the teacher does not permit the child the leisure or the time to reflect.

Fourth, the teacher exacts little things and big things alike with the same ardor.

Fifth, the teacher immediately rejects the reasons and excuses of children and is not at all willing to listen to them.

Sixth, and finally, the teacher, not mindful enough of personal faults and not knowing how to sympathize with the weaknesses of children, exaggerates their faults. This is the situation when a teacher reprimands them or punishes them and acts as though dealing with an insensible instrument rather than with a creature capable of reason.

At the other extreme, the following are examples of the teacher's weakness, which leads to negligent and lax conduct by the students.

First, the teacher cares only about matters that are important and that cause disorder; other less important matters are imperceptibly neglected.

Second, not enough insistence is placed on the performance and observance of school practices and on what constitutes the duties of the children.

Third, children are easily permitted to neglect what has been prescribed.

Fourth, to preserve the friendship of the children, the teacher shows them too much affection and tenderness. This involves granting something special or giving too much liberty to the more intimate. This conduct does not edify the others, and it causes disorder.

Fifth, on account of the teacher's natural timidity, the children are addressed or reprimanded so weakly or so coldly that they do not pay any attention or the correction makes no impression on them.

Sixth, and finally, the teacher easily forgets that a teacher's own proper deportment consists principally in maintaining a gravity that encourages respect and restraint on the part of the children. This lack of deportment manifests itself either in speaking to the students too often and too familiarly or in doing some undignified act.

It is easy to recognize by these examples what constitutes too much harshness and too much gentleness. Both these extremes must be avoided if the teacher is to be neither too harsh nor too weak, firm in attaining a purpose, gentle in the means of attaining it, and in all showing great charity accompanied by zeal. A teacher must be constant in persevering; however, children must not be permitted to expect impunity or to do whatever they wish, and the like. Gentleness is not proper in such cases.

We must know that gentleness consists in never allowing any harshness or anything whatsoever that savors of anger or passion to appear in reprimands. Instead, being gentle means showing the gravity of a father, a compassion full of tenderness, and a certain ease, which is, however, lively and effective. The teacher who rebukes or punishes must make it quite clear that such punishment arises from necessity and is administered out of zeal for the common good.

ARTICLE 2:
Frequent Corrections and How to Avoid Them

Correction must be rare if a school is to be well regulated and in excellent order.

The ferule[4] must be used only when necessary, and matters must be so ordered that this is a rare necessity. Because of the different circumstances that may render the more or less frequent use of the ferule obligatory, it is impossible to determine precisely the number of times that it may be used each day. Nevertheless, steps should be taken to guarantee that its use will not exceed three times in a half day. To make use of it more than these three times, the circumstances must be truly extraordinary.

Correction by use of the rod should be much rarer than that with the ferule. It should, at most, be inflicted only three or four times in a month.

Extraordinary correction should, consequently and for the same reasons, be very rare.

To avoid frequent correction, which is a source of great disorder in a school, it is necessary to note well that silence, restraint, and watchfulness on the part of the teacher establish and maintain good order in a class. It is not harshness and blows that establish and maintain good order. Teachers must make a constant effort to act with skill and ingenuity to keep students in order while making almost no use of correction.

To be effective, the same means of correction must not always be used; otherwise, the students will grow accustomed to them. Rather, a teacher must sometimes threaten, sometimes correct, sometimes pardon, and sometimes make use of various other means that the ingenuity of a skillful and thoughtful teacher will easily suggest on the appropriate occasion. If, however, a teacher should happen to think of some other particular means and believes these could be adopted to keep the students at their duties and forestall correction, they should be proposed to the director. The teacher will not make use of them until having received permission.

Teachers will not administer any extraordinary correction without having first consulted with the director. For this reason they will postpone them, which is at the same time a very proper thing to do to have adequate time for some reflection beforehand, to give more weight to what they intend to do, and to leave a greater impression on the minds of the students.

ARTICLE 3:
Qualities That Corrections Should Possess

Correction, to be beneficial to the students, should be accompanied by the following ten qualities.

First, it must be pure and disinterested. That is to say, correction must be administered purely for the glory of God and for the fulfillment of God's holy will. It must be administered without any desire for personal vengeance, the teachers giving no thought to themselves.

Second, correction must be charitable. That is to say, correction must be administered out of a motive of true charity toward the student who receives it and for the salvation of the student's soul.

Third, correction must be just. For this reason it is necessary to examine carefully beforehand whether the matter for which the teacher is considering correcting the student is effectively a fault and whether this fault deserves correction.

Fourth, correction must be proper and suitable to the fault for which it is administered. That is to say, it must be proportionate to the fault both in nature and in degree. Just as there is a difference between faults committed through malice and obstinacy and those committed through weakness, there should also be a difference between the chastisements with which they are punished.

Fifth, correction must be moderate. That is to say, it should be less rigorous rather than more rigorous. It should be of a just medium, and punishment should not be administered precipitously.

Sixth, correction must be peaceable. Those who administer it should not be moved to anger and should be totally self-controlled. Those to whom it is administered should receive it in a peaceable manner with great tranquility of mind and outward restraint. It is especially necessary that those who inflict a punishment should take great care that nothing appear in their demeanor that might indicate that they are angry. For this reason it would be more proper to defer a correction until a time when the teacher no longer feels agitated than to do anything that the teacher might later regret.

Seventh, it must be prudent on the part of the teacher, who should pay great attention to what is done so as to do nothing that is inappropriate or that could have evil consequences.

Eighth, it must be willingly accepted by the students. Every effort must be made to make the students accept it. The seriousness of their fault and the obligation under which the teacher is to remedy it must be made clear to them. They must be helped to understand the great harm that they can do to themselves and, by their bad example, to their companions.

Ninth, those punished must be respectful. They should receive punishment with submission and respect, as they would receive a chastisement with which God would punish them.

Tenth, it must be silent. In the first place, the teacher must be silent and should not speak, at least not aloud, during this time. In the second place, the student must be silent and ought not to say a single word, cry out, or make any noise whatsoever.

ARTICLE 4:
Faults That Must Be Avoided in Corrections

There are many faults to be avoided in corrections, and it is important that teachers pay very particular attention to them. The principal ones that must be avoided are described in what follows.

No correction should be administered unless it is considered useful and advantageous. Thus, it is unwise to administer correction without having previously considered whether it will be of some use either to the student to whom it is to be administered or to the others who are to witness it.

When a correction is considered useful only to give an example to the others and not to the recipient, it should not be administered unless necessary to maintain order in class. When delay is possible, the advice of the director should be asked. If the case concerns a teacher of one of the lower classes, that teacher will ask the advice of the head teacher. If the head teacher has the problem and at the same time must resolve it, action will be taken only with much precaution and under an evident necessity.

No correction that could be harmful to the one who is to receive it must ever be administered. This would be to act directly contrary to the purpose of correction, which has been instituted only to do good.

No correction should be made that could cause any disorder in the class or in the school. Examples of this would be those that would only serve to make the child cry out, be repelled or embittered, or want to leave the school. Such action would lead the student to hold the school in aversion. The complaints that the child or the child's parents would make would repel others and prevent children from coming to school. The teacher should endeavor to foresee these possible consequences before administering any correction, for it is important not to fall into them.

A student should never be corrected because of feelings of aversion or annoyance that a teacher may have for a student who causes trouble or because the teacher has no liking for the student. All these motives, which are either bad or merely worldly, are very far from those that should inspire people who ought to act and to conduct themselves only according to the spirit of faith.

Nor should students be corrected because of some displeasure caused either by themselves or by their parents. Students who lack respect for their teachers or commit some fault against them should instead be urged by words to recognize this fault and to correct it themselves. This is preferable to punishing them for it. Even if it should be necessary to punish them on account of the bad example they have given, it would be well to assign some other motive for the correction, such as having caused disorder or having been obstinate.

When administering corrections, familiar forms of address must not be used. Instead of *tu, toi, ton, va, viens*, the teacher should say *vous, vôtre, vos, allez, venez*, and so on.[5]

It is also important never to use insulting words or words that are even in the slightest degree unseemly, for example, *rascal, knave*, or *sniveler*. None of these words should ever be in the mouth of a teacher in the Christian Schools.

No other means of correction should be used than those approved for the Christian Schools. Thus, students should never be slapped or kicked, nor should they be struck with the pointer. It is altogether contrary to the decorum and the seriousness of a teacher to pull the children's noses, ears, or hair. It is even more unseemly for a teacher to strike them, to push them roughly, or to pull them by the arms.

The ferule must not be thrown at a student who is then to bring it back. That is highly unbecoming behavior. A student must not be struck with the handle of the ferule on the head, on the back, or on the back of the hand, nor must two slaps in succession be given with it on the same hand.

In using the ferule great care must be taken not to strike either the head or the body. The ferule is used only on the palm of the hand.

In punishing students, teachers must be very careful not to strike them any place where they may have a sore or an injury, lest it worsen, and not to strike so hard that marks may appear.

Teachers should neither leave their place to administer the ferule nor speak while administering it. They should not allow the student who is receiving it to speak, much less to cry aloud, either when being punished or afterward.

Teachers will also be careful not to assume any improper posture when administering correction, such as stretching the arms or contorting the body, or to make any other unseemly motions contrary to modesty.

Teachers will, finally, be very careful not to administer any correction impulsively or when agitated. They will watch so carefully over themselves that neither angry passions nor the least touch of impatience will have any part when administering correction. Such behavior can prevent the benefit and place an obstacle to the blessing God would give.

Here is the practice to follow concerning who should or should not administer correction.

Every teacher may, in the teacher's own class, use the ferule as often as necessary. Teachers who have not yet reached the age of twenty-one will not administer correction with the rod unless they have consulted the director or the one whom the director has put in charge of such matters and have taken that person's advice upon the subject. The teacher in charge of such matters will also watch very carefully over the punishments these younger teachers administer either with the ferule or otherwise and will report twice each week to the director on all that has been done in the classes.

The same line of conduct will be followed with respect to teachers who will reach the age of twenty-one during the six months of trial they will spend in the schools or during the first year after their novitiate.

ARTICLE 5:
The Children Who Must and Who Must Not Be Corrected

Five vices must ordinarily never be excused: (1) lying, (2) fighting, (3) theft, (4) impurity, and (5) indecorum in church.

Liars must be punished for their lies, even the least, to make students understand that there are no little lies in the sight of God, for the devil is the father of lies, as our Lord tells us in the holy gospel. Let them rather be pardoned or punished less severely when they frankly acknowledge their faults. They may be led afterward to conceive the horror they ought to have of lies, and they will be persuaded to ask pardon humbly of God while kneeling in the middle of the classroom.

Those who have been fighting will be corrected in the same way. If two or more were involved, they will be punished together. If it was a student and another child who is not of the school, the teacher will ascertain exactly who was at fault. The student will not be corrected unless the teacher is very certain that the student was at fault. Teachers will act in exactly the same way with all other faults committed outside of the school. If students have been fighting in the school, they are to be punished as an example, and they must be made to understand that this fault is one of the gravest they can commit.

Those who have taken and concealed anything, however small its value may be, even if it be only a pen, will be similarly punished. If they are found to be subject to this vice, they will be expelled from the school.

Those who have been guilty of any impure act or have used obscene words will be punished by the same correction.

Those who have been playing with persons of the opposite sex or who have been frequently in their company will be seriously warned the first time. If they persist in this fault they will likewise be severely punished. Teachers will often seek to instill in their students a great disinclination for the company of these people and will urge them never to mingle with them. Even if they are their relatives and even if they are sometimes obliged to converse with them, however young they may be, let it be very rarely and always in the presence of their parents or of some sensible elderly people.

Those who have been disorderly in church will be severely punished, and they will be made to understand the great respect they must have for God in this holy place. Furthermore, they must understand that it is to be lacking in faith to be in church without piety and without both inner and outer self-control.

For this last fault, teachers must not punish all kinds of students, large and small alike, in the same manner. Unless the little ones are very carefully watched while they are in church, and unless the teacher has acquired great authority and control, it will be difficult for the young ones to observe the moderation and control required of them. It is necessary, however, to pay great attention to this matter. Nothing should be omitted to prevent any student from behaving in a disorderly way in church.

If a teacher is not sufficiently vigilant and does not possess sufficient authority to keep order in church, another teacher must be appointed to do so. The one who is appointed on this occasion will do what the other cannot.

Section 1: Ill-bred, Self-willed, or Delinquent Children

There are some children to whose conduct their parents pay very little attention, sometimes none at all. From morning until evening they do only what they please. They have no respect for their parents. They are disobedient. They grumble at the least thing. Sometimes these faults do not come from an evil disposition of heart or mind; they come from their having been left to themselves. Unless they are naturally of a bold and haughty temperament, they must be frequently admonished. They must also be corrected for their bad disposition. When they let some of their faults appear in school, they must be subdued and rendered submissive. If they are of a bold and haughty spirit, they should be given some charge or responsibility in the school, such as monitor, if they are considered qualified, or collector of papers. They should be promoted in something such as writing, arithmetic, or spelling to inspire them with a liking for school. But along with this they must be corrected and brought into line, never allowed in anything whatsoever to act as they please. If such students are young, there are fewer measures to be taken. They must be corrected while they are young so that they may not continue in their bad conduct.

As for those who are bold and insolent, teachers must speak with them little and always only seriously. When they have committed some fault, they should be told and corrected, if it appears that it would help them to confuse and humble their disposition. They must be held in check and not allowed to reply to anything that is said to them. It would be a good thing to admonish and reprimand them sometimes in private for their faults. Such admonishment must always be administered with great seriousness and in a manner that will keep them respectful.

Those who are heedless and frivolous must be corrected a little. Ordinarily, they do not reflect much, and a short time after having been corrected, they sometimes fall again into the same fault or into another fault that deserves the same punishment. Their faults arise not from pure malice but from thoughtlessness. They must be treated in a way that may prevent them from misbehaving. They can be shown affection, but they should not be given any charge or responsibility. They should be seated as near the teacher as possible, under the pretext of helping them, but in reality to watch over them. They should also be placed between two students of a sedate disposition who do not ordinarily commit faults. They should also be given some rewards from time to time to make them diligent and fond of school, for it is these who are absent most frequently, and to induce them while there to remain in order and silent.

Section 2: Stubborn Students

The stubborn must always be corrected, especially those who resist and are not willing to accept correction. However, two precautions must always be taken in regard to this kind of children. (1) No attempt to correct them is to be made without having thoroughly examined the faults they have committed and unless it is clear that they deserve correction. (2) When such children resist, either because they do not want to submit to correction or because they do not want to leave their seats, it will often be much more to the purpose to let their bad attitude pass. In this case it is best not to let it appear that there is any intention of making the correction. Some time later the teacher will call them and speak with them gently, making them realize and admit their fault, both originally and in resisting. The teacher will then correct the student as an example. In case the student is not yet willing to accept the correction, the student must be forced to do so, for only a single example of resistance would be needed to produce several others afterward. Some time later, when it seems that the bad mood has passed, the teacher will gently make the student draw near to reflect on the incident. The teacher will lead the student afterward to admit the fault and to ask pardon while kneeling.

However, the school should be so ordered as to forestall this sort of resistance and to make it happen very rarely; otherwise, it would cause a very bad effect.

There is another kind of stubborn children who mutter after they have been corrected. When they have returned to their seats, they lean their heads on their arms or maintain some other unseemly posture. Such manners must never be permitted. These students should be obliged to study or to follow the lesson. If the teacher cannot prevent a student who has been corrected from grumbling, muttering, weeping, or disturbing the school in some other manner because of youth, low intelligence, or some other reason, and if it has been observed that punishments not only do not bring a sense of duty but perhaps even render the student more stubborn, it would ordinarily be more to the purpose not to make the correction. It would be better to pretend not to notice it when such a student does not study or fails to do some other duty. It might be better even to send the student home.

In these situations the teachers will take care to obtain clarification or permission from the director concerning what they should do. Silence during correction and a proper manner of administering it will ordinarily prevent most of these failures.

One of the most effective means for avoiding many of these problems is not to send students back to their places immediately after administering the ferule or the rod. They should be left kneeling in full view of the teacher.

Section 3: Gentle Children, Newcomers, Special Cases

There are some parents whose manner of bringing up their children is to give them all that they ask. They never contradict or oppose them in anything, and they almost never correct them for their faults. It seems that they fear to cause them pain, and so they cannot suffer that the least correction be administered to them.

Because such children are almost always of a gentle and peaceable nature, it is ordinarily better not to correct them. It is usually more prudent to correct their faults by some other means, such as giving them a penance that is easy to perform, preventing their faults in some skillful manner, pretending not to see them, or admonishing them gently in private.

If teachers sometimes judge it necessary to correct them, it should not be done without consulting the director or the head teacher. In such cases correction should be light and very rare.

If the means that are used to prevent their faults or to correct them are of no avail, it is often better to send them away than to correct them. An exception to this might be made after speaking with the parents and making them agree that it will be well to correct the child.

Those who have a gentle and timid disposition should not ordinarily be corrected. The example of students who do well, the fear they naturally have of the chastisements they see inflicted, and some penances will suffice to make them do their duty. They do not often commit faults, and they easily keep still. Furthermore, their faults are not considerable, and they should sometimes be tolerated. At times, a warning will suffice for them; at other times, a penance. Thus there will be no need of corrections and chastisements to keep them in good order.

Much the same can be done in the case of slow-witted children, who create a disturbance only when it becomes necessary to correct them. Ordinarily, this should not be done. If they are troublesome in school, it is better to send them away. If they cause no trouble and create no disturbance, they should be let alone.

The faults children like these commit ordinarily include not following the lesson, not reading well, not remembering or reciting catechism well, and learning nothing or very little. What is beyond their capacity must not be required of them. Nor should teachers let them become discouraged; they should manage somehow to advance them, encourage them from time to time, and be satisfied with whatever little progress they make.

With respect to those who are sickly, it is important that they should not be corrected. This is especially the case when the correction might increase their ailment. Some other means of correction should be used with them or a penance be imposed on them.

There are also many little children who likewise must not be corrected or only very rarely. They have not attained the use of reason and are not capable of profiting from correction. Deal with them in much the same manner as with children of a gentle and timid disposition.

Finally, teachers must abstain from correcting children who are just beginning school. It is necessary, first, to know their minds, their natures, and their inclinations. They should be told from time to time what they are to do. They should be placed near some students who acquit themselves well of their duties. In this way they may learn by practice and by example. They should ordinarily be in school about two weeks before being corrected, for correcting newcomers can only repel them and alienate them from school. However, if it is important to act thus to new students, it is no less important that a teacher who is new in a class refrain from administering any correction until the students are understood.

CAUSES OF ABSENCES AND MEANS OF PREVENTING THEM

When students are frequently absent from school, it is either through their own fault, through that of their parents, or through the fault of the teachers. The first cause of absences of students proceeds from the students themselves. It is because they are frivolous or undisciplined, because of their wildness, because they have a distaste for school, or because they have little affection for or a dislike of their teacher.

Those who stay away through frivolity are those who follow the first idea that comes into their minds, who go to play with the first child they meet, and who ordinarily act without paying attention to what they do.

It is very difficult for students of this sort not to absent themselves from time to time. All that can be done is to deal with them in such a way that their absences are rare and of short duration.

Such students should be corrected only a little for their absences. This is because they will again absent themselves on the next day or on the first occasion afterward. They will reflect neither upon what has been said to them nor upon the correction they have received. They will be induced to come to school more by gentleness and by winning them than by correction and harshness.

The teachers will take care from time to time to stimulate children with this type of mind and to encourage them by some reward or by some outside employment if they are capable of undertaking it. Above all, they will never threaten them with correction.

The second reason students absent themselves is lack of discipline. This is either because they cannot be subjected to remaining a whole day in the same place, attentive and with their minds busy, or because they love to run about and play. Such children are ordinarily inclined to evil, and viciousness follows lack of discipline. For this reason it is necessary to seek a remedy for their absence with great care. Everything should be done to anticipate and to prevent it. It will be very useful to assign them some office in the class. This will give them a liking for school and will sometimes even cause them to become an example to the others. Much must be done to win them and to attract them, at times being firm with them and correcting them when they do wrong or absent themselves, always showing them much affection for the good they do and rewarding them for small matters.

The third reason students absent themselves is because they acquire a distaste for school. This may be due to the fact that they have a new teacher who is not yet sufficiently trained. Such teachers do not know how to conduct themselves in school. They at once resort to corrections, or they are too lax and have no order or silence in the classroom.

The remedy for absences of this sort is to leave a teacher neither alone in a classroom nor placed solely in charge until thoroughly trained by a teacher of great experience in the schools.

This is very important for the welfare both of the teachers and of the students. It is important in preventing frequent absences and various other disorders.

The remedy for teachers who are lax and who have no order in their classrooms will be for the director or the head teacher to watch over them and require them to account for all that takes place in the classes. They will particularly be required to account for their actions when they have neglected to look after the absent or have been remiss in any of their duties, however small and of however little consequence it may appear.

The fourth reason why students absent themselves is that they have little affection for their teacher. This is due to the fact that the teacher is not pleasant and in almost every situation does not know how to win the students. This kind of teacher resorts only to severity and punishments; consequently, the children are unwilling to come to school.

The remedies for this sort of absence will be for the teachers to endeavor to be very pleasant and to acquire a polite, affable, and frank appearance without, however, assuming an undignified or familiar manner. Let them do everything for all their students to win them all to our Lord Jesus Christ. They should all be convinced that authority is acquired and maintained in a school more by firmness, gravity, and silence than by blows and harshness and that the principal cause of frequent absences is the frequency of the punishments.

Parents are the fifth principal reason for absence. Parents either neglect to send their children to school or do not take much trouble to make them come or to be diligent. This difficulty is quite common among poor people, whether because they are indifferent to school, persuaded that their children learn very little, or for some other trifling objection.

The means of remedying the negligence of parents, especially of the poor, is to speak to them and make them understand their obligation to have their children instructed. They should understand the wrong they do to their children by not making them learn to read and write and how much this can harm their children because lack of this knowledge will leave the children incapable of any employment. Then they must be made to realize the harm that may be done to their children by lack of instruction in matters related to their salvation, with which poor people are often little concerned.

Second, because these kinds of poor people are ordinarily those who receive alms, a list should be given to the parish priests of all those who do not come to school, their ages, and their addresses. This is done so that no alms be given their parents and so that the parents may be urged and obliged to send their children to school.

Third, an effort must be made to attract the children of people like this and to win them over by every possible means, which can often be done with success. Ordinarily, children from poor families do as they wish. Their parents often take no care of them and even idolize them. What their children want, they also want. Thus it is enough that their children should want to come to school for their parents to be content to send them there.

When parents withdraw their children from school to make them work while they are too young and not yet sufficiently instructed, they must be made to understand that they are harming them a great deal. To have their children earn a little, they will make them lose a far greater advantage. It should be explained to them how important it is for a worker to know how to read and to write well. It should be emphasized that however limited the child's intelligence, the child who knows how to read and write will be capable of anything.

Parents must be urged to send their children to school if not for the whole day, at least for the entire afternoon. It will be necessary to watch very carefully over children of this sort and take care of them. To obviate the problem of having parents complain because their children learn only little or nothing and so wish to withdraw them from school, directors or the inspectors of Schools must watch with great care over all the teachers under their direction. They must particularly watch those of lesser ability. They must see to it that they instruct as diligently as possible all the students entrusted to them; that they neglect none and apply themselves equally to them all, even more to the more ignorant and more negligent; that they keep order in the schools, and that the students do not absent themselves frequently. The freedom children have to be absent is often the cause of their learning nothing.

The sixth principal reason why students absent themselves frequently is either because the teachers are too complacent in bearing with those who are absent from school without permission or because they too readily give permission to be absent.

To provide a remedy for this problem, every teacher must be very exact in watching over those who go to visit the absentees. Every teacher must make sure that these visitors go to the homes of all the absentees, that they do not let themselves be deceived by false reasons, and that they afterward report to the teacher the reasons that have been given them. Second, the teacher who receives the absentees and excuses their absences is to require their parents to bring the children back and to receive no student back in the school who has been absent without first knowing and investigating well the reason given for the absence.

The reasons ordinarily are that their parents needed them or that they have been ill. Others are absent because they are delinquents.

For the first reason to be good and valid, the need must be great and also be very rare. The inspector or the teacher will not accept the second reason if the student has been seen outside the house or playing with other children. Every teacher will be sure that those who visit the homes of the absentees see all the ill students and report on the condition in which they find them.

As for the delinquents, the inspector or the teacher will observe what has been said above in the article on students who must or must not be corrected. They will not correct them in school, but before permitting them to return to school, they will oblige the parents to correct them at home.

Children who have been absent without permission under the pretext that their parents needed them must not be easily excused. It is ordinarily the same ones who are guilty of this fault. If they repeat it three or four times without troubling themselves about it, they must be sent home and not received at the school again until they, as well as their parents, are ready to ask permission for every absence from school.

When a student asks permission to be absent, teachers must always appear reluctant to grant permission. They are to investigate the reasons well, and when they find these good and necessary, they will always send the student to the head teacher to obtain the permission. The head teacher will, however, grant the permission only after great difficulty. The head teacher will never listen to a student who asks for a permission that has already been refused.

Absences for trivial reasons will be rare. This is a matter about which the teachers must be very careful. It is better to send students home than to permit them to absent themselves frequently, for this sets a very bad example. Three or four students will be found in every school who always ask permission to absent themselves. If it is granted, they will easily lead others to absent themselves without reason. It is better to send students of this sort home and to have fifty who are very diligent than to have a hundred who are absent at every moment.

However, before sending students home for these or other reasons, the teacher will speak with their parents several times and explain to them how important it is that their children come to school regularly and how it is otherwise almost impossible for them to learn anything, for they forget in one day what they have learned in several. Students will not be sent away from school unless it appears that both they and their parents are not concerned about it and do not profit in the least by everything that could have been said to them in this matter.

Finally, before sending away students on account of absences or for anything else, it is well to make use of the following means to remedy the situation: (1) deny any rewards for diligence gained by a student who has been absent, even with permission; (2) do not promote the student to another level or to another lesson the next month, even though the student knows how to read perfectly or is capable of being promoted; (3) make the student stand for several days in school, or apply some other penance that will embarrass the student, be unpleasant for the parents, and incite the student to come punctually and thus oblige the parents to force the child to be diligent.[6]

SCHOOL OFFICERS

EDITORS' INTRODUCTION: *The sample job descriptions of school officers provide a glimpse into the life of the Christian Schools. With classes of fifty or more boys, the Brother needed assistance, and appointing school officers gave boys responsibility and ownership of the school. The practice was both practical and part of religious instruction. In addition, it assisted students who often lived in chaotic circumstances to create a sense of order and purpose in their lives.[7]*

There will be several officers in the school charged with a number of different functions that teachers cannot or should not do themselves.

These officers will be appointed by the teachers of each class on one of the first three school days after the vacation.

Each teacher will submit the names of those chosen as class officers to the director or to the head teacher. The teacher will not have them begin to exercise their duties until they have been approved. If it later becomes necessary to change them or to change one of them, the nomination of another or others will be made in the same manner. These officers and their obligations will be discussed below.

The Reciters of Prayers

There will be two officers in each school to whom will be assigned the duty of reciting the prayers. One of them will recite the prayers in the morning; the other will recite the prayers in the afternoon. They will alternate between reciting morning and evening prayers.

The one who says the prayers in the morning during one week will say them in the afternoon during the following week. The other one will change in the corresponding way. They will recite sedately, attentively, and decorously all the prayers that are said in school. They will recite all the prayers in such a manner that they can be easily heard by all the students.

No students will be appointed to this office unless they know all the prayers perfectly, recite them distinctly, and are reserved and well behaved so as not to cause the distraction of the other students.

Two reciters of prayers will be appointed each month and will be chosen from among the class of writers. They may be continued in this office in case there are no others who can acquit themselves as well as they do of this duty, but for no other reason, for this appointment contributes much to making students recite the prayers well in private and to making them like to say their prayers at home with deliberation and attention.

The Bell Ringer

There will be in each school a student whose function will be to ring the bell for the beginning of school and of prayer exercises.

At the beginning of school and at every hour, this attendant will ring five separate strokes of the bell. On every half hour, five or six strokes of the bell will be tolled.

At the end of school, the bell will be rung and then also tolled five or six strokes. This will announce that it is the end of school and that the prayers are to begin.

Care must be taken to ring the bell exactly on time. About the time for a *Miserere* before the beginning of the prayers in the morning and before catechism in the afternoon, the bell ringer will toll two or three strokes to notify the students to put their books away, the collectors to gather up all papers, and all to prepare themselves and be ready to begin the prayers without a moment's delay and as soon as the bell has ceased ringing. This officer should be very diligent in attending school and careful, vigilant, exact, and very punctual in ringing the bell on time.

Monitors and Supervisors

There will be monitors in all the classes during the absence of the teachers but at no other times. The exception is in the classes of the writers. In those classes there will be a monitor during breakfast and the afternoon snack. The monitor will supervise those who are repeating the prayers, the catechism, and the responses of holy Mass.

All the care and attention of the monitor will be directed to observing everything that takes place in the classroom. The monitor will do this without saying a single word, no matter what happens, and without leaving the assigned place. Monitors will not permit any student to speak to them or to approach them during the entire time they are fulfilling their duties.

The monitor will not threaten any student either by signs or otherwise, no matter what fault is committed, and will never use the ferule or anything whatsoever to strike the students.

The monitor will always remain seated at the assigned place and will report faithfully to the teacher everything just as it has happened, without adding or concealing anything, noting those who keep silent and those who make the least noise, and above all, being careful to give a good example to the others. Students who have been appointed to this class office must be convinced that they have been put there not merely to watch all that takes place in the school but also, even more important, to be the model for the others.

Teachers will examine carefully the things that the monitor reports, in a low tone and privately, before determining whether to punish those who have been reported for having committed faults. To find out more easily whether the monitor has told the truth, a teacher will ask privately the most trustworthy students who have witnessed the faults whether the matter took place in the manner and under the circumstances that the monitor has declared. The teacher will punish the students who have committed the faults only in case the teacher finds that what the others say agrees with what the monitor has reported.

Teachers will listen to any complaints made against the monitor, especially if those who make them are disinterested and among the more sensible and trustworthy students. Should the monitor be found guilty, the punishment will be much more severe than for another student committing the same fault. Furthermore, this monitor will at once be deprived of the office.

The monitor must be very punctual and among the first to come to school. The monitor must be vigilant so as to observe all that takes place in the school. The monitor must be neither frivolous nor a liar and must not be prone to partiality for anyone. In other words, students who have this office must be prepared to accuse their siblings, their friends, and their companions, that is to say, those with whom they associate, as well as they are prepared to accuse others. Above all, the monitor must not receive any gift from anyone. If detected in this fault, the monitor will be very severely corrected and deprived of office.

Supervisors

There will be two students in each class appointed to watch the conduct of the monitor while the latter is exercising the functions of that office. Their responsibility is to see whether students who hold the office of monitor allow themselves to be corrupted by gifts; whether they demand anything from the others for not declaring their faults; whether they are always among the first to come to school; whether they speak when they should be silent; whether they leave their place; whether they see to it that no others leave their place; in short, whether they fulfill their duties with very great exactitude. It will be best if these supervisors are not known to the monitor. For this reason, they will not be appointed like the other class officers and will not even be called officers. These supervisors will be among the most sensible, the most pious, and the most punctual students. They will be privately instructed to pay attention to the conduct of the monitor and will render an account of that conduct as soon as possible whenever anything extraordinary happens.

There will also be certain monitors or supervisors for the streets, especially for those where many students live. They will observe how the students of the neighborhood to which they have been assigned behave when returning from school.

There will be supervisors in each neighborhood or important street. They will watch everything that takes place and will at once notify the teacher of it in private.

Distributors and Collectors of Papers

There will be in the class of writers one or two students to distribute the papers to the writers at the beginning of the writing period, to collect them at the end of it, and to put them back in the proper place.

If all the students in the class are learning to write, there will be two charged with this function. If only some of the students in the class are learning to write and if they are not too numerous, there will be only one student assigned to this class office.

The distributors and collectors of papers will be careful to place all the papers in the proper order, one upon another, in the same order as the students are seated to whom they belong. In this way they can return all the papers properly.

They will go from table to table, both to give the papers out and to take them back. If any students are absent, they will nevertheless leave the papers at their places. They must distribute and collect all the papers promptly and silently.

If the teacher finds it useful, these officers will go to each writer a short time before collecting the papers to see what each has written. They will note whether students have written as much as they should have, whether the paper is rumpled, and the like. If they find that anyone has been remiss in anything, they will at once inform the teacher.

Collectors will make sure that all the students dry what they have written and fold their papers before returning them.

Sweepers

There will be one student in each classroom whose duty will be to sweep it and keep it clean and neat. This student will sweep the classroom once daily without fail at the end of the morning school session. If the students go to holy Mass, the sweeper will return to the school for this purpose.

Before beginning to sweep, this student will put the benches near the wall, some on one side and some on the other. When there is need of it, the two sweepers from two adjoining classrooms will help each other to remove and replace the benches but in nothing else.

After having removed the benches, the sweeper will, if necessary, sprinkle the floor of the classroom. The student will then sweep the room and carry all the rubbish in a basket to the designated place in the street. The sweeper will then replace the broom, the basket, and the other things that have been used back in the place where they are ordinarily kept.

The teachers will see that the sweepers always keep the classrooms of which they have charge very clean.

The sweepers should not be slow but very active so that they do not take too much time in acquitting themselves of their duties.

They should be distinguished by a great care for neatness and cleanliness. They must, however, also be sensible and not given to quarreling or trifling.

The Doorkeeper

In each school there will be only one entrance door. If there is more than one door, the others, which the director will select, will be closed and always kept locked.

A student from one of the classrooms, ordinarily the one at the entrance, will be appointed to open and shut this entrance door each time anyone enters the school. This student will be called the doorkeeper.

The doorkeeper will be placed near the door to open it promptly. The doorkeeper will not leave the door open and will always bolt it.

The doorkeeper will allow no one to enter except teachers, students, and the priest of the parish in which the school is situated.

When someone knocks at the door of the school, the doorkeeper will at once open it quietly and with the least possible delay answer the person who is knocking. After having again bolted the door, the doorkeeper will notify the teacher who has been designated as the one to speak with visitors.

While the teacher is speaking with someone, the doorkeeper will leave the door sufficiently open for it to be possible to see from within the classroom both the teacher and the person with whom the teacher is speaking.

The doorkeeper will guard the door from the time when it is first opened until the time when the students begin to leave the school. For this reason this student must always be the first to arrive at school. The doorkeeper will always keep silent and will never speak to any student who is entering the school or going out of it.

The doorkeeper will be exact in reading in turn like the others, and as far as possible, he will pay attention to and follow the lesson during all the time when not busy at the door. Doorkeepers must be frequently changed, and care should be taken that they do not lose time for reading. This can be done by making the student read at the end of school or by having another act as doorkeeper during the lesson.

This officer will also have charge of a piece of wood given to the students when they go outside, giving it to the one going out and taking care that no student goes out without it. In this way and as far as possible, no two will go out together for this reason. The doorkeeper will put the item away every day after school, both morning and afternoon, and will let no student go out without it.

The doorkeeper will be chosen from among the most diligent and the most regular in attendance at school. The student should be sensible, reserved, well behaved, silent, and capable of edifying the people who come and knock at the door.

The Keeper of the School Key

The keeper of the school key will be at the door of the school punctually every day, mornings before 7:30 and afternoons before 1:00. This class officer will be forbidden to give the key to any other student without the permission of the teacher who is in charge of this school. When the students do not return to the school after holy Mass, the keeper of the school key will return with the rosary carrier, the holy water bearer, and the sweepers and will see that the latter make no noise while they are sweeping. The keeper of the school key will not leave before the others do.

This student will also be responsible for everything in the school and must take care that nothing is carried away. This class officer should be chosen from among those who are the most diligent and who never miss school.

PROMOTING STUDENTS FROM ONE LESSON TO ANOTHER

One of the most important things in a school is to promote the students from one lesson to another at the proper time. The inspector of schools will pay much attention to this process. Promoting students will be carried out with regularity and order. To achieve this, each teacher will prepare the students for promotion according to what is indicated in part one. The inspector of schools will make these promotions with due preparation and care. The inspector should make sure that the students fulfill the conditions and qualifications for promotion. Finally, these promotions will be made at the time and in the manner that have been established.

Article 1:
What Is to Be Done Before Promoting Students

Toward the end of every month, the inspector of schools will inform the teachers of the day on which they should examine the students who might be ready for promotion. The inspector and the teachers will then confer on those who should not be promoted because of inability, absenteeism, or lack of piety or modesty; because of laziness, negligence, or youthfulness, or finally, because of the need to sustain the lesson and keep it in proper order.

The inspector of schools will, however, take care not to let a student remain in the same lesson or in the same order of lesson when the student is capable of doing more advanced work or is content to remain back. This case calls for diplomacy and concerted action among the teachers and may be accomplished either by use of rewards or by giving the student some class office. This does not apply, however, if the child is being held back because of absenteeism, negligence, laziness, or some other considerable fault. The inspector of schools can use these reasons as justification for the decision, should the occasion warrant it.

The inspector of schools, if the inspector is also the director, will then set the deadline for the teachers to make their report so that they can give it to the inspector before the promotions are to take place. An inspector who is not also the director will request the latter to fix the day. The inspector, after receiving the reports from the teachers, will ask them for further explanations and information needed to avoid mistakes in promotions.

The inspector will then inform the students in each school of the day on which the promotions will be made, so that all of them can be present, and warn them that any who are not present on the promotion day will not be promoted until the end of the following month.

In promoting students the inspector of schools will neither be influenced by any personal considerations nor give weight to any extraneous influences. The inspector will not promote any students from one lesson or level to another unless they have the ability and fulfill all the conditions laid down in the following article. The inspector will also very carefully insist that the teachers not propose any students for promotion who are not quite capable of doing the required work.

The inspector will always follow the same procedure in making the promotions in all the schools and classes, beginning every time with the same level and the same class and always finishing with the same ones. In each school the inspector will begin with the lowest class and end with the highest, and in each class, with the lowest lesson and at the level of the beginners in each lesson.

ARTICLE 2:
Requirements for Promotion

It is most important never to place any student in a lesson that the student is not yet capable of following; otherwise, the student will find it impossible to learn anything and will risk being kept in lifelong ignorance. Therefore, teachers should not take into consideration the age, the size, or the length of time a student has been in a lesson but only ability when promoting to a more advanced lesson. Thus, for instance, a student must spell perfectly and read by syllables before learning to read fluently.

Smaller children, who are usually quick-witted and have good memories, do not always need to be promoted even when they could go on to more difficult work. It may not be good if they do not stay in school long enough. It is desirable, without displeasing the parents, to help extend their stay in school as much as possible. The two extremes must be avoided. It is not good to keep a student too long in the same lesson, for fear that the student and the parents may lose interest. However, for the reasons already given, it is not good either to advance too rapidly those who are very small, very young, or lack the necessary ability.

There are certain conditions and requirements for promoting or not promoting a student.

Those who lack modesty and piety or who show themselves lazy and neglectful in studying and in following the lesson will be promoted only with great hesitancy; they will be examined with greater rigor and exactness than the others. If in the succeeding month they fall back into their old faults, they will not be promoted on the next occasion, no matter how capable they may be.

Those who have been absent for five full days during the month, even with permission, will not be promoted to a higher lesson at the end of the month, even though they might be capable of doing the work.

Those who have been absent without permission for two full days during the month will be promoted neither from one lesson to another nor from one level to another. Those who have been tardy six times during the month will not be promoted.

No student will be moved from one lesson to another unless the student has gone through the three levels of beginner, intermediate, and advanced, nor will any student be moved to a higher lesson or level of a lesson without spending all the time prescribed in the lower one.

Students will not be moved up from the alphabet chart unless they have been reading from it for at least two months. In other words, they should have read each line of it for at least a week and the entire alphabet for the rest of the two months. They will not be moved up from the syllable chart until they have read from it for at least a month.

Those who read from the spelling book will not be promoted until they have spent at least five months on it, two months in each of the first two levels and one month in the third.

Those who are learning spelling from the first book will not be promoted until they have spent at least three months on it, one month in each level of this lesson.

Those who spell and read from the second book will not be promoted unless they have spent the same amount of time on it. Those who only read from the second book and are not learning spelling will not be promoted unless they have spent an equal amount of time reading from it.

Those reading from the third book will do so for at least six months, two months on each level, before they can be promoted to another lesson. Those who read Latin will not read in sentences until they have read by syllables for at least two months. They will not be promoted until they have been reading in sentences for at least four months, two months at the intermediate level and two months at the proficiency level.

Those who are reading from *The Rules of Christian Decorum and Civility* will not be promoted from the first to the second level unless they have been reading on the former level for at least two months. They will then remain at the second level for as long as they continue coming to school. Those who are reading from documents will not be promoted from the first to the second level unless they have spent at least three months reading on the former level. The same rule will also be followed in promoting students in the subsequent four levels. When they reach the last level, they will remain there for as long as they continue coming to school.

Students will not be promoted from the first level of writing, where they learn how to sit correctly, hold the pen properly, and make straight and circular strokes, until they have spent at least a month in this level. Those in the second level of writing, who are writing the five letters *c, o, i, f,* and *m,* will not be promoted until they have written these letters for at least three months.

Those who are in the third and fourth levels, who are writing the alphabet with linked characters, one page or one line for each letter, will not be promoted until they have written them for at least six months, one page of each letter for four months and then a line of each letter for two months.

Those who write the alphabet entirely in linked characters on each line will not be promoted until they have done so for three months. Those who write lines of large commercial characters will not be promoted until they have done so for at least three months.

Those in the seventh level, who write in financial characters, will not be promoted to writing in small hand and rapid script until they have written at the sixth level for at least six months.

Those in the first and second levels of arithmetic, who are doing addition and subtraction, will not be promoted until they have mastered both over a period of at least two months.

Those in the third level, who are doing multiplication, will not be promoted until they have spent at least three months on this operation. Those in the fourth level, who are learning how to divide, will not be promoted to doing the rule of three until they have spent at least four months doing simple division.[8]

Chapter 5

The Rules of Christian Decorum and Civility

— ✠ —

EDITORS' INTRODUCTION: De La Salle wrote this text to be used in the class-room. He offers instruction on everything from care of the body, to the manner of dressing and undressing, to amusements that are not permitted, to "the sword, the stick, the cane, and staff." As may be seen in the excerpts included here, he believed that decorum and civility were manifestations of Christian charity. Indeed, acting with decorum and civility were charity in action, the lifeblood of the body of Christ. Acting politely and civilly were "a practical expression of a life lived in the Spirit of Jesus Christ....[The Rules] proposes Christian love as the foundation of cultured refinement." From 1730 to 1875, the Rules went through over 45 editions and 120 reprintings, making it one of the most popular of all French texts.[1]

PREFACE

It is surprising that most Christians look upon decorum and politeness as merely human and worldly qualities and do not think of raising their minds to any higher views by considering them as virtues that have reference to God, to their neighbor, and to them-selves. This illustrates very well how little true Christianity is found in the world and how few among those who live in the world are guided by the Spirit of Jesus Christ (Gal 5:25). Nevertheless, this Spirit alone should inspire all our actions, making them holy and agreeable to God. Saint Paul points out this obligation to us when he tells us in the person of the early Christians that because we should live by the Spirit of Jesus Christ, we must also act in all things by that Spirit (Gal 5:25).

According to the same apostle, because all our actions should be holy, there are none that should not be done through purely

Christian motives. Thus, all our external actions, the only ones that can be guided by the rules of decorum, should always through faith possess and display the characteristics of virtue.

Fathers and mothers ought to pay attention to this truth while educating their children. Teachers entrusted with the instruction of these children should also be especially concerned.

While teaching children the rules of decorum, parents and teachers should never fail to remind them that they should observe these rules only through purely Christian motives, which concern the glory of God and their own salvation. Parents and teachers should avoid telling the children in their care that if they fail to act in a certain way, people will blame, have no respect for, or ridicule them. Such remarks can only inspire children with the spirit of the world and turn them away from the spirit of the gospel.

Rather, when they wish to train children in practices pertaining to bodily care and simple modesty, they should carefully lead them to be motivated by the presence of God, as Saint Paul does when he makes the same point with the faithful of his time, saying that their modesty should be known to all because the Lord is near to them. In other words, children should do these things out of respect for God, in whose presence they are. When teaching children and training them to observe the practices of decorum that refer to their neighbor, teachers should urge them to show others the signs of consideration, honor, and respect appropriate to members of Jesus Christ and living temples of God, enlivened by the Holy Spirit.

In the same way, Saint Peter exhorts the early faithful to love their brethren and to pay everyone the honor due to him, thereby showing themselves true servants of God and making known in this way that they honor God in the person of their neighbor.

If all Christians make it a practice to display goodwill, esteem, and respect for others only from considerations of this kind and from motives of this nature, they will sanctify all their actions and make it possible to distinguish, as they must, between Christian decorum and civility, and what is merely worldly or almost pagan. Thus they will live like true Christians, for their exterior behavior will be conformable to that of Jesus Christ and will correspond with their Christian profession. They will thereby show themselves to be different than infidels and those who are Christians only in name, as Tertullian remarks when he says that in his time people could know and recognize Christians by their exterior conduct and their modesty.

Christian decorum is, then, the wise and well-regulated conduct that governs what we do and say. It arises from sentiments of modesty, respect, union, and charity toward our neighbor. It leads us to give due regard to appropriate times and places and to the people with whom we must deal. Decorum practiced toward our neighbor is properly called civility.

In the practices of decorum and civility, we must give due consideration to the times in which we are living, for many practices that were in use in past centuries or even in rather recent years are no longer accepted. Whoever follows them will be considered eccentric and far from being regarded as a polite and courteous person.

We must also conduct ourselves in matters of decorum according to what is acceptable in the country where we live or where we happen to be, for each nation has its own particular customs of decorum and civility. It happens often enough that what is considered improper in one country is regarded as polite and courteous in another.

The same is true regarding matters required by decorum in certain special places but entirely forbidden in others. What must be observed in the presence of the king as well as in the royal apartments must not be done elsewhere. The respect we must have for the person of the king demands that certain signs of reverence be shown when in his residence that would be out of place in a private home.

We ought to behave in our own home differently than the way we act in the homes of others, and so too in the homes of people we know as opposed to those we scarcely know.

We are expected by politeness to have and to show special respect for certain people that we do not owe to others. Showing the same kind of respect to everyone would also violate decorum; therefore, whenever we meet or converse with anyone of some social standing, we must pay attention to the person's rank so as to deal with and to treat that person according to what this rank requires.

We must likewise consider ourselves and who we are, for whoever is inferior to others is obliged to show submission to those who are superior whether by birth, official position, or social rank. We should pay them much greater respect than we would someone who is our equal.

A peasant, for example, should show more exterior respect for a lord than should a worker who does not depend upon the lord. Similarly, the worker should show far greater respect for the lord than should another gentleman who happens to be visiting that lord.

Strictly speaking, decorum and civility consist only in the practices of modesty and of respect for our neighbor. Because modesty is especially shown in our deportment and because respect for our neighbor is shown in the ordinary acts we usually perform in the presence of others, we intend to treat these two topics separately in this book. In the first part we examine the modesty that should be shown in the deportment and the care of the various parts of the body. In the second part we examine the external marks of respect or special consideration that should be manifested in the various actions of life with regard to all the people in whose presence we may be and with whom we may have to deal.

Part One
THE MODESTY YOU SHOULD SHOW IN YOUR DEPORTMENT AND IN THE CARE OF THE VARIOUS PARTS OF THE BODY

1. Deportment and Care of Your Body

If you wish to have a distinguished appearance and to be esteemed because of the modesty that marks you as a wise and well-behaved person, you must learn to control your body in the way prescribed by nature or by custom.

You ought to avoid, for this reason, several defects in the way you carry yourself. The first of these defects, which is affectation and constraint, makes you appear awkward. This is entirely opposed to decorum and the norms of modesty.

You must also avoid the kind of negligent attitude that betrays slovenliness and indolence in your conduct and that would expose you to contempt because it indicates a meanness of spirit as well as low birth and poor education.

You ought also to be very careful not to let anything flighty appear in your bearing, for this may indicate that you are frivolous. If your mind is naturally flighty and heedless and if you wish to avoid falling into this defect or to correct yourself of it, you must pay attention not to move a single part of your body without attention to what you are doing and to move only with due restraint. If your temperament is fiery and hasty, you must watch over yourself carefully. Never act without great moderation; always think before doing anything, and keep your body as tranquil and steady as possible.

Although you should not cultivate any artificial poses, you must, nonetheless, learn to control all your movements and regulate properly the deportment of all the parts of your body. This behavior must be carefully taught to children; people whose parents were so negligent as not to have trained them from their earliest years must still apply themselves in a special way until they have mastered these habits, which will have become easy and almost natural.

A person's deportment must always be somewhat sedate, even majestic. You should take care, however, that there be nothing to suggest pride or arrogance of spirit, for such attitudes greatly displease everyone. The simple modesty and wisdom that you, as a Christian, display in all your conduct will produce this sedateness. You are truly of noble birth because you belong to Jesus Christ and are a child of God, the Supreme Being; therefore, in your exterior there should be nothing vulgar. Everything in you should denote a certain air of nobility and greatness, a reflection of the power and the majesty of God, whom you serve and who gave you being. This dignified appearance should not flow from arrogance or lead you to prefer yourself to others, for every Christian wishing to act according to the laws of the gospel ought to show honor and respect to all others, considering them as children of God and brothers of Jesus Christ and regarding himself as one burdened with sin, for which he should constantly humble himself by placing himself beneath everyone else.

When standing, you must hold your body erect without leaning to one side or the other. Do not bend forward like an old man who no longer can hold his body erect. It is also very unbecoming to assume a haughty posture, to lean against a wall or anything else, to make bodily contortions, or to lounge about in an unseemly manner.

When seated, do not sprawl out in a slovenly way or lean too noticeably against the back of your chair. It is unbecoming to be seated in a chair that is too low or too high unless you cannot do otherwise. Ordinarily, it is better to be seated too high than too low; however, in company you should always make it a special point to give women the lower chairs because these are usually more comfortable.

Neither cold weather nor any other type of pain or discomfort should induce you to assume an unbecoming posture. It is also against decorum to show in your demeanor that you are suffering from something uncomfortable unless you truly cannot do otherwise.

It is a sign of exaggerated fastidiousness and delicacy if you cannot endure the least disagreeable thing without showing it exteriorly.

2. The Head and the Ears

To hold your head in a proper manner, you should keep it erect without bending it forward or letting it lean to the right or to the left. You must be especially careful not to hunch your shoulders or to turn your head repeatedly from side to side, for this indicates a flighty mind. Furthermore, making frequent gestures with your head is the sign of a disturbed and confused person. It is also a sign of arrogance if you hold your head in an affected manner. It is entirely against the respect due to another person to lift your head high, to shake it, or to wag it from side to side while someone is speaking to you. This indicates that you are not showing the respect the speaker deserves and that you are not prepared to believe or to do what you are being told.

A liberty you should never allow yourself is to support your head on your hands as if you could not otherwise sustain its weight.

To scratch your head while speaking or, when in company, even when not speaking, is very unbecoming and unworthy of a person who has been well brought up. This is also a sign of great negligence and of lack of cleanliness because such behavior ordinarily happens when you have neglected to comb your hair and to keep your head clean. Any person who does not wear a wig should attend to these matters. Such people should be very careful not to leave any dirt or greasy spots on their hair, for only people poorly brought up fall into such negligent ways. You should consider the cleanliness of the body, especially of the head, as an outward mark and indication of the soul's purity.

Because modesty and refinement require that you not let your ears become full of dirt, from time to time you should clean them with a specially designed instrument called an ear swab. It is extremely unbecoming to use your fingers, or even a pin, for this purpose, and it is against the respect you should have for the people you are with to do this in their presence. It is also contrary to the respect you owe if you are in a holy place.

It is not appropriate to wear a feather behind your ear, to put flowers in your ear, or to have pierced ears with earrings. This is most inappropriate for a man, for it is a sign of slavery, which is not at all becoming.

The most beautiful finery for your ears is to keep them unadorned and very clean. Ordinarily, men keep their ears covered by their hair; women more frequently have their ears uncovered. It is sometimes the custom, particularly for women of rank, to wear earrings of pearls, diamonds, or other precious stones. It is, however, more modest and more Christian not to have any accessories attached to your ears, for through them God's word reaches the mind and the heart. The respect you ought to profess for that divine word should lead you to avoid anything that suggests vanity.

The finest adornment for the ears of a Christian is to be well disposed and ever ready to hear attentively and to receive submissively any instructions concerning religion and the maxims of the holy gospel. For this reason laws of the church bade all ecclesiastics to keep their ears entirely uncovered, thus giving them to understand that they should always be attentive to God's law, to the doctrine of truth, and to the science of salvation of which they are the repositories and the dispensers.

3. The Hair

You should not fail to adopt faithfully the rule and the practice of combing your hair daily; you must never appear before anyone at all with tangled and dirty hair. Take particular care that the hair be free of lice and nits. This precaution is particularly important for children.

Although it is not advisable to use much powder on your hair, which suggests effeminacy, you should avoid leaving your hair greasy. If your hair is naturally oily, you can use some bran to remove the excess oil or comb your hair with a little powder on the comb to dry off some of the oil. This process will also remove some of the natural dampness that could soil your linen and clothes.

It is highly unbecoming to comb your hair in public, but the offense becomes quite intolerable if you do so in church, a place where you should be very neat and clean out of the respect you have toward God. This respect makes it imperative that you already be very clean when you enter the church.

Saint Peter and Saint Paul forbid women to curl their hair, but they condemn with even greater reason this sort of behavior in men, who, having naturally far less inclination than women to such vanities, should reject them all the more resolutely and be much less inclined to yield to them.

Just as it is not proper to wear your hair too short, which would contribute to disfiguring your appearance, it is also inadvisable to wear it too long. In particular, it should not hang over the eyes; therefore, it is good to trim your hair neatly from time to time.

Some people, for their own convenience when they feel too hot or have something to do, push their hair behind their ears or under their hat. This is very rude. You should always let your hair hang down naturally. Self-control and refinement also require that you not touch your hair unnecessarily, and the respect due to others demands that you not put your hand on your hair in their presence.

You should, therefore, avoid smoothing your hair by repeatedly pressing down on it with the palm of your hand. You should not allow strands of hair to spread loosely, curl them with your finger on either side, run your fingers through your hair as if combing it, or shake out your hair by tossing your head. All these are ways of acting that people adopt for convenience or simply through a lack of manners, but that refinement, self-control, and respect for others do not permit.

Because it is an even greater violation of decorum to have a wig poorly combed than to have your hair poorly combed, those who wear wigs should take particular care to keep them clean, for the hair with which wigs are made lacks natural consistency and must be combed and arranged much more carefully than natural hair.

A wig is much more fitting and appropriate for a man when it matches the color of his hair rather than when it is lighter or darker in shade. Some men, however, wear wigs so curled and of such a light blond color that they seem more appropriate for women than for men.

Although you should not completely neglect these kinds of adornments when they are in common use, it is against decorum and good judgment for a man to spend much time or to go to great lengths to keep them neat and well fitted.

4. The Face

The wise man says that you can tell a person of good judgment by the look on his face (Sir 19:29). By their facial expression, people should try to show that they are agreeable, and at the same time, their exterior appearance will edify their neighbor.

To be agreeable to others, you should not assume a stern, forbidding countenance or let anything unsociable, shocking, too giddy, or resembling a schoolboy appear. The entire face should reflect an air of seriousness and wisdom. Nor is it according to decorum to have a melancholy or peevish countenance, and your face should never reflect any passion or ill-regulated affection.

Your face should be happy and show no sign of either dissolution or dissipation. It should be serene but not too easygoing. It should be open, without giving signs of too great a familiarity. It should be gentle, without softness, and never suggest anything vulgar. To all it should manifest either respect or at least affection and goodwill.

It is, however, proper to allow the expression on your face to reflect the different business matters and circumstances that arise. Because you should sympathize with your neighbor and show by your appearance that you share what afflicts him, you should not put on a happy and cheerful countenance when a person brings sad news or when misfortune has befallen someone. Nor should you exhibit a somber countenance when something agreeable is said or some happy event has occurred.

As a person of good judgment, you should always try in your own concerns to be even tempered and to display a serene countenance. Just as adversity should not cast you into dejection, prosperity should not make you unduly elated. You should maintain a tranquil countenance that does not readily change its disposition or expression no matter what happens, agreeable or disagreeable.

People whose countenance changes at every occasion that comes along are extremely disagreeable, and it is very hard to put up with them. Sometimes they appear with a happy look on their face; at other times, with a melancholy air and countenance. Sometimes they show plainly that they are upset; at other times, that they are in a great hurry. All this serves to reveal people who have little virtue and do not strive to keep their passions in check. This way of acting is entirely human and natural and shows little of the Christian spirit.

You should not adopt too happy and easygoing a countenance in your dealings with people generally.

Refinement demands that you show on your countenance a great deal of circumspection when you find yourself with people to whom much respect is due, and it is always a sign of decorum to assume an air both serious and grave in their presence. It is also prudent not to have too open an expression on your face when dealing with inferiors, especially servants, for although you are obliged to treat them with kindness and consideration, it is also important not to be familiar with them.

Toward people with whom you are more at ease and meet regularly, it is proper to show a happy countenance to give a greater ease and pleasure to the conversation.

Neatness demands that to clean your face, you wipe it every morning with a white cloth. It is not good to wash with water, for this makes the countenance more sensitive to the cold in winter and to sunburn in summer.

You would be lacking in refinement to rub or to touch any part of your face with your bare hands, especially when there is no need to do so. If it does become necessary to remove some dirt, do so gently with a fingertip. If you are obliged to wipe your face in very hot weather, use a handkerchief for this purpose, and do not rub too hard or with both hands.

It is a lack of decorum to allow any filth or dirt to remain on your face, but you should never clean your face in the presence of others. If it happens that you notice something of this sort when you are already in company, you should cover your face somewhat with your hat while you remove the dirt.

It is something very improper, showing great vanity and not at all becoming in a Christian, to apply beauty spots and paint to your face, covering it with powder and rouge.

Part Two
DECORUM IN COMMON ACTIVITIES AND IN ORDINARY SITUATIONS

7. Meetings and Conversations

Article 1: Qualities That Decorum Dictates Should Accompany Your Speech

Section 1: The Truth and Sincerity That Decorum Requires in Speech

Refinement cannot abide that you should ever say anything false. On the contrary, it exacts that, as Saint Paul advises, everyone should speak the truth to his neighbor (Eph 5:6). According to the wise man, refinement regards falsehood as a shameful flaw and the life of a liar as a life deprived of honor and always threatened by embarrassment (Sir 20:24–25). Also according to the wise man, it is in accord with refinement that lies, even if told out of weakness or ignorance, should not fail to bring shame upon the liar (Sir 20:26).

In the same vein, the royal prophet, instructed in the rules of decorum as he was in true piety, says that if you wish to live a life of happiness, you should keep watch over your tongue so that you speak no falsehood (Ps 34:12–13). The wise man wishes you to look upon lying as something so detestable that even a thief is preferable to the habitual liar, for the lie is always found in the mouths of vicious people (Sir 20:24–26). You might say that even if you fall into no other vice, frequent lying is enough to push you quickly into a vicious life. Jesus Christ explains why this is so when he tells us that the devil is the father of lies (John 8:44).

Because lying is so shameful, whoever yields to it even slightly is acting totally contrary to decorum. Thus, when someone questions you or when you are speaking to a person, it is not courteous to use equivocation or words with a double meaning. Rather than trying to equivocate, it is ordinarily more appropriate to excuse yourself politely from answering when it is clear that you cannot say plainly what the truth requires or what you think. The wise man says that a devious tongue draws down embarrassment (Sir 20:26), and Saint Paul also condemns this behavior in clerics when he says that equivocation is not to be tolerated in them.

You must be particularly circumspect in your words when someone has entrusted you with a secret. It would be very imprudent to divulge it, even if you urge the one to whom you repeat the matter to keep it to himself and if the one who confided the secret to you has not asked you to refrain from mentioning it to others. As the wise man says so correctly, if you reveal the secrets of a friend, you lose all credibility and will soon be unable to find any close friends (Sir 27:16). He considers this fault as being much worse than speaking injuriously to your friend, for as he says, even after harsh words reconciliation is possible, but if you have been base enough to betray a friend's secrets, there can remain no hope of reconciliation, and you will try in vain to recover the lost friendship (Sir 27:19–21).

It is also a great act of incivility to try to mislead a person whom you should respect. This indicates a lack of the confidence and consideration you should show to a friend. It is not at all courteous for you to play the hypocrite with anyone and for this purpose

179

to use some manner of speaking or some terms that he cannot grasp unless you explain them to him.

It is most uncouth in company for you to speak to one person in particular and then to make use of expressions that the others cannot understand. You should always speak openly to the whole group, and if you have something to tell someone in private, you should wait until that person is apart from the rest. If the matter is urgent, you should withdraw together to some place more isolated after asking leave of the group to do so.

Because it often happens that people relate incidents that are not true, be extremely careful not to repeat these tales too readily unless you know or have it on good authority that they are true. Never tell from whom you received this information if you have reason to think that the author would not be pleased to have this known.

You should make an effort to be so sincere in what you say that you will earn the reputation of being entirely truthful, a person whose word can be counted on, a person people can rely on. The wise man also considers this piece of advice very important; he urges us to keep our word and to deal faithfully with our neighbor. Nothing is more honorable for you than the sincerity and the fidelity you show in keeping your promises, just as nothing makes you more worthy of contempt than breaking your word.

Just as it is a matter of honor to be faithful in your words, so it is very imprudent to speak lightly without having seriously considered whether you will be able to keep your promises. Therefore, never make a promise without carefully weighing the consequences to make sure that you will not have to regret it later on.

If it happens that others do not believe what you say, you should not take it too much to heart; still less should you allow yourself to fall into fits of exaggerated impatience leading to harsh words and reproaches. People who are not convinced by your reasons will certainly not be persuaded by outbursts of passion.

It is shameful for you to make use of fraud and deceit in your words. People who do this will soon find that they are no longer believed by others and that they have won for themselves an infamous reputation for dishonesty.

Because dreams, as the wise man says, are nothing but the products of our imagination, it is never appropriate to tell others your dreams, however beautiful and edifying you think they are (Sir 34:1–7). Only a person with a weak mind would want to do this.

Chapter 6

The Duties of a Christian to God

✠

EDITORS' INTRODUCTION: *The catechisms included under the title* The Duties of a Christian to God *provide a comprehensive compendium of the Tridentine theology of the time. The longer catechism that the Brothers studied is in prose and attempts to provide a full exposition of the doctrinal and moral teachings of the church. The smaller catechisms for the children reproduce the question-and-answer format of similar Tridentine and diocesan catechisms. The final catechism focuses on the liturgical and ritual expressions of the faith of the church. The selections excerpted here come from the first catechism, which speaks of a living faith. In the first selection De La Salle describes the poor man, Jesus. The next selections present De La Salle's exposition of prayer and its importance in living in the spirit of Jesus as poor disciples.*[1]

VOLUME 1, PART 1, TREATISE 1

CHAPTER 4

Section 3—The vocation and mission of the apostles; the preaching, miracles, and life of poverty of Jesus Christ

Jesus Christ came to bring us the new law. For thirty years he prepared himself to proclaim it, and as soon as he left the desert, he began doing so. One of the first things he did was to select twelve of his disciples, whom he called apostles, a name that means *envoys*, for he destined them to preach his gospel alongside him. This gospel is the new law that he had come to announce to all humanity.

These apostles are Simon, also called Peter, and his brother Andrew; James and John, the sons of Zebedee; Philip and Bartholomew; Matthew and Thomas; James, son of Alpheus, and

182

his brother Jude, or Thaddeus; Simon the Canaanite; and Judas Iscariot, who betrayed Jesus.

Simon and his brother Andrew were the first ones Jesus Christ chose to be his apostles. On the same day he summoned James and John, the sons of Zebedee, to follow him. He called Philip the next day. They left everything and followed him as soon as he called them. Some time later, passing by the tax gatherer's stall, he called Matthew, a publican (meaning a collector of revenue) and told him, "Follow me!" (Matt 9:9). This he did at once, leaving everything behind. Later, Matthew gave a great feast for Jesus and his disciples and invited several other publicans, with whom Jesus Christ gladly associated, for as he said, he had come to convert sinners and encourage them to do penance. In like manner he selected all the other apostles. Next, he sent them from town to town and village to village to preach. He also went on the same mission.

For three years, he traversed all Judea, instructing the people. With him went the apostles and seventy-two disciples, whom he dispatched two by two into all the towns where he intended to go. They were to dispose the people so that they would profit by his preaching. He spoke everywhere and performed a great number of miracles to confirm his teaching. He restored health to the sick and sight to the blind, and he cured the lame and the paralyzed. He also raised three dead persons to life: the son of a widow at Nain; the daughter of the chief of the synagogue at Capernaum; and Lazarus, the brother of Martha and Mary. In all these miracles his single purpose was the conversion of souls. While curing bodily infirmities, he also pardoned sins and urged sinners to sin no more.

From all over Judea and also from Syria, people brought him those who suffered from various maladies and cruel afflictions: the possessed, the insane, the paralytic. All these he cured. This great number of miracles caused him to be followed in a short time by a huge multitude drawn from Galilee, the Decapolis, Jerusalem, and beyond the Jordan.

He strove to instruct all these people and to teach them his new doctrine, making known to them by lengthy discourses how much more excellent and perfect this new law was than the old law and what sort of perfection this new law required of them. The people were so surprised and touched by his teaching that five thousand men, not counting women and children, followed him and remained with him for days on end without eating or showing any concern about their welfare. This obliged Jesus to perform another miracle: feeding them all by multiplying five loaves of bread. All ate their fill. Just as Jesus lived frugally, so too did he feed them sparingly with some barley bread and a little bit of fish.

Although Jesus could have lived without lacking anything and have had whatever he desired, he always lived in such a poor manner that he sometimes had nothing to eat. He did not possess a home to call his own or even, as he said, a stone on which to lay his head. He was accompanied by his twelve apostles, who were almost all of lowly origin. He required them also to experience severe poverty. On one occasion they were forced to rub heads of grain in their hands to eat the kernels within.

On a number of other occasions he showed how little he esteemed the rich and how much he loved poor people. To give public proof of this, he felt obliged to go to cure a centurion's servant but not to visit the home of a royal official whose son lay sick at Capernaum, even though the father had begged him to come to heal the boy. For the same reason, he told the parable of the heartless rich man, emphasizing the torments this man endured, to show that those who are attached to wealth will be punished in hell and that poor people who have suffered the miseries of this life patiently for the love of God will be happy and filled with consolation in heaven.

During the time Jesus Christ was preaching his gospel, about a year before his death, he resolved to manifest the glory he enjoyed also in his sacred humanity. His body, although a natural, mortal body, had been from the moment of his conception as glorious as it now is in heaven. Although the splendor of his glory had never appeared outwardly, he retired one day to a high mountain with three of his disciples, Peter, James, and John. While he was in prayer, he was transfigured before them: His face became as bright as the sun, and his clothes as white as snow. Suddenly the three disciples saw Moses and Elijah in glory as they conversed with Jesus about what was going to happen to him and what he would suffer in Jerusalem. Peter, astounded by what he beheld, said to Jesus that he wished they could remain in this spot and that if Jesus so desired, they would build three booths, one for Jesus, one for Moses, and one for Elijah.

While Peter spoke, a luminous cloud surrounded Jesus, Moses, and Elijah, from the depths of which a voice was heard saying, "This is my Son, the Beloved; with him I am well pleased; listen to him" (Matt 17:5). The three disciples were so overawed on hearing this voice that they fell to the ground with their faces in the dust. But Jesus immediately told them to get up, and they saw nothing but Jesus alone. As they all came down from the mountain, he forbade them to relate what they had seen until after he had risen. The transfiguration of Jesus Christ took place in the presence of these three apostles so that they could give testimony to this mystery in which Jesus gave them an assurance of his own resurrection and imparted to them the hope that each one's body would also rise again some day, along with the body of the ever blessed One and destined to share in his glory.

TREATISE 2
PRAYER, THE SECOND MEANS TO OBTAIN THE GRACE WE NEED TO FULFILL OUR DUTIES TO GOD PROPERLY

CHAPTER 1
Prayer

Section 1—What prayer is

Our Lord Jesus Christ instituted the sacraments as the ordinary means for imparting habitual grace to us, but we still needed another means to help us preserve this grace and to obtain the necessary actual graces. Receiving the sacraments provides us with many of these graces and enables us to preserve and augment habitual grace when we possess it; nevertheless, we do not receive the sacraments every day, although we need grace constantly to help us perform our actions properly, to resist the temptations that assail us, and to keep us on the right path. Therefore it was important for God to give us a means other than the sacraments to make it possible for us to enjoy all the advantages that we can easily secure by means of prayer. For this purpose God established prayer as a special help, constantly at our disposal, which we can make use of at every moment to obtain from God everything needed in this world to ensure our salvation and to acquire eternal life.

Prayer is the application of our mind and the elevation of our heart to God to give him due reverence and to ask for everything we need for our salvation. We say that prayer is an application of our mind because no matter what words we repeat and what gestures we perform, God does not consider them as prayers addressed to him unless we apply our mind to the subject of these prayers.

We also say that prayer is a raising of our heart to God because in prayer we lift ourselves above sensible things and are concerned only with God and with what brings us closer to God, for when we pray, we address God more with the heart than with the lips. Prayer disposes us to reach out to God, to elevate ourselves to him, and to unite ourselves intimately with him by conforming our affections with his so that we want and desire nothing but God or what refers to God.

We fulfill our duties to God when we adore him, thank him, and offer ourselves to him with all we have.

To adore God means to recognize his infinite greatness, his sovereignty over all creatures, and his independence from anyone and anything whatsoever. While considering these aspects, we humble ourselves deeply and express sentiments of profound respect regarding his divine majesty.

To thank God means to express our gratitude to him for all the natural benefits we do and can enjoy only because of him: He created us; he preserves us day by day, and he gives us all we need for our body and the preservation of our life. All these gifts are the effects of God's infinite goodness to us, and we certainly ought to show gratitude for them.

Giving thanks also means expressing to God how much we are indebted for all the graces he gives us in general, such as redeeming us, delivering us from our sins, letting us be born in a Christian and

Catholic country, giving us our faith, and preserving it. We should also thank God for the special graces we have received since birth, such as the opportunity to receive the sacraments, the deliverance from a great number of temptations, the frequent gifts of inspiration to do good, and the help to put these inspirations into practice. We should also thank God for special favors, such as pardoning an enemy, overcoming a temptation to pride or impurity, and so on.

Offering ourselves and all we have to God means to present ourselves to him and to dedicate to him all our thoughts, words, actions, and goods, whether spiritual or temporal—in a word, everything we possess in this world. We assure God that because we are wholly dependent on him, we also wish to consecrate ourselves to him and his service and to abandon ourselves entirely to what he may choose for us, not wishing to follow our own will. We beg him not to permit us to entertain a single thought, utter a single word, or accomplish the slightest action that is not in conformity with his holy will and with what he asks of us. We should also remind God of all the graces we have received from him and tell him that far from abusing any of them, we wish to act in such a way that none of them may prove useless but that all may attain their full effect. Finally, we should offer and consecrate to God in particular all the natural advantages and temporal goods we may possess, declaring that just as we have received them all from God, we wish to make use of them only for his sake.

This offering of ourselves, all we possess, and everything we have received from God forms part of our prayer of adoration in which we recognize and profess our dependence on God. For if we offer all these things to God, it is because we count on him to provide or to preserve them for us and because he has given them to us only so that we may render him honor and glory because of them.

We ask God for the things we need to achieve our salvation when we beg him both to give us the graces necessary for us to do good and avoid evil and to grant us pardon for our sins.

Asking God for the graces needed to do good means asking him to give us the opportunity and the facility to perform some good action that we find difficult, such as pardoning a person who has wronged us or who is ill-disposed to us, doing all the good we

can for that person, or, more particularly, greeting that person, salut-
ing when we meet, and speaking with much charity even if we feel
great repugnance in doing this, or accomplishing some other good
action that we may have an opportunity of doing either now or soon.

To ask God for the graces we need to avoid evil means praying
to him to grant us all the help required to avoid committing any sin
or to keep from falling into some particular fault when an occasion
for doing so is present to us or could turn up in the future. It means
asking God, for instance, to help us not to succumb to a temptation
of pride or impurity, not to give in to anger or impatience when we
feel inclined to yield to these passions, or not to swear or lie on the
occasions we foresee as times when we might allow ourselves to fall
into one of these defects.

Although prayer in general includes all these elements, what
we specifically and properly call prayer is what we address to God to
ask some grace of him; the word *prayer* means a request we present
to God with humility and insistence. This is the kind of prayer we
will discuss in this treatise.

Section 2—The necessity of prayer

Because we are created solely for God, we undoubtedly have
an obligation to pay God the homage due to him. Because we constantly need God's help, we must also frequently address him in
prayer to obtain graces for ourselves and to beg the infinite bounty
to grant them to us.

Because God has given us all we have, we should often do him
homage for all these benefits. As God's creatures we are also bound
to pay him respect and adoration by humbling and prostrating ourselves interiorly and exteriorly before our Creator, keeping in mind
our own lowliness and nothingness and the grandeur and infinite
excellence of God's majesty, which shines forth in all his creatures
and before which they are all less than mere atoms.

The great number of graces that we have received from God
and continue to receive from him every day also obliges us to have
recourse to God and to thank him for them, for ingratitude is one of
the things God finds most displeasing. God wants those who serve

him to recognize that all they possess comes from him, and he does not ordinarily grant them any increase of grace unless they show themselves grateful for what they have already received from him.

Our privilege of being children of God, members of Jesus Christ, and living temples of the Holy Spirit should persuade us to offer our soul to God every day so that he may fill it with the fullness of his Spirit. We should also offer our body as an object that should be entirely consecrated to him and therefore no longer be used for anything profane, much less for anything as shameful as sin. This offering is so vital for us that unless we are faithful in making it, we will not draw down God's blessings on us.

Without doubt we need light to know and to see the path that will lead us to heaven and the virtues we must practice to get there. Without such light we would grope about like blind people and would most likely lose our way. This is what Saint John Chrysostom declares will happen to us without fail if we do not apply ourselves faithfully to prayer, which he says is the light that illumines our soul like the sun enlightens our body. He goes even further, stating that it is impossible for us to live a Christian life unless we spend much time in prayer, which he asserts is the life of our soul. Whoever does not pray to God assiduously is dead, miserable, and inanimate, even as a body separated from the soul is thereby bereft of life. He proves this by citing the example of Daniel, who preferred to die rather than omit his accustomed prayers for three days (Dan 6:10). If God does not come to our help in need, the soul will prove incapable of accomplishing anything good; God will not come to our assistance and bring us relief except insofar as we love prayer.

As the same saint assures us, God made this a commandment when he enjoined us, by the lips of Jesus Christ, to pray often. We should be more concerned about the worship of God than about our own life because, as the saint says, without prayer we cannot obtain for ourselves the benefit of living in a Christian manner, grow in piety, or fill our heart with it as with a precious treasure. Indeed, one person may have a strong attraction for purity; another may want to keep chastity easily; a third may wish to control anger and practice the virtue of meekness; a fourth would like to be free of avarice; and another may wish to live a life of piety. All of them will find all this possible by means of prayer.

It cannot happen that those who ask God for purity, justice, meekness, liberality, and the other virtues will not obtain them readily, for our Lord assures us that if we ask anything of God, he will give it to us because "the one who asks receives" (Matt 21:22). If even those who are wicked give good things to their children, how much more willingly will our heavenly Father give his Holy Spirit to those who ask him? Saint John Chrysostom makes this point and concludes by saying that it is easy to understand how impossible it is to live in the practice of virtue without having recourse to prayer.

Saint Augustine says that there are virtues we cannot obtain except by prayer, for instance, chastity, wisdom, and perseverance in good; his proof is by examples from Holy Scripture. The wise man tells us that we cannot be chaste unless God gives us this grace (Prov 20:9), and Saint James declares that if we want wisdom, we should ask for it with faith and confidence, and God will bestow it on us (Jas 1:5). Saint Augustine does not imply that we can obtain some virtues without prayer; what he means is that prayer is necessary in a special way for the above-mentioned virtues, because to possess them we must more frequently and continually implore God to give them to us.

If we need prayer so urgently to do good, prayer is no less necessary to deliver us from sin. Saint John Chrysostom admirably expresses this thought by saying that no matter how many sins we may have committed, if we love prayer, we will soon be freed and entirely purified of them. Prayer, he claims, is a divine medicine for the soul that is sick and infected by sin, and once prayer reaches down into the inner recesses of the heart, it drives out all the malice found there and fills it with justice. Jesus Christ assures us in the holy gospel that the demon, that is, the sin of impurity, which is the most difficult to eradicate from a person's heart once it has taken possession of it, cannot be driven out except by prayer and fasting.

From all this it is easy to conclude that just as light is necessary in this world, just as we need life in our body to preserve it, and just as a sick person needs medicine to get well, so too prayer is necessary for the soul that wishes to serve God and not allow itself to be corrupted by sin.

Section 3—The advantages of prayer

Even if prayer were not necessary for us to be saved, its utility and the advantages it offers should still induce us to apply ourselves to it. Because these advantages cannot be better expressed than in the words of Saint John Chrysostom in two works he composed to make known the excellence, necessity, and utility of prayer, we will merely summarize here what the saint says on this topic.

The first and most notable advantage to which he calls our attention is that the person who prays has the honor of conversing with God. This privilege is so stupendous, says the saint, and so far beyond what we might conceive, that it makes us join the ranks of the angels, for prayer is their special occupation. Indeed, would it not seem that God has created the angels only so that they might devote themselves to prayer? Humbling themselves before God, they honor him and do him homage; they pray to him for those who are entrusted to their care, and they present our prayers to God. Thus when we pray, we are doing what the holy angels do, and although there is a great difference between angels and ourselves, prayer is something common to us both.

Saint John Chrysostom goes further by saying that prayer even lifts us far above the dignity of the angels. They appear before the infinite majesty of God to give him their due homage only with sentiments of awe mingled with fear and trembling, but when we pray, we enjoy the privilege of conversing familiarly with God. We should experience great satisfaction of mind and be joyful when we reflect on the honor that God does us, mortals as we are, by conversing with us. This honor is all the more exalted, says the saint, because by this happy communing with God, we cease to be mere mortal, perishable beings; by our perseverance in prayer, we enter life immortal.

By prayer, adds the saint, we become temples of Jesus Christ. Just as marble, gold, and precious stones are used to build and ornament the houses of kings, prayer shapes souls into temples of Jesus Christ and adorns them by giving them so much beauty and splendor that they seem to be quite transformed from what they were before. In this way Saint Paul brought Jesus Christ to dwell in the hearts of the faithful through his prayers. Prayer so changed the city of Nineveh in a short time that anyone who had known it previously and returned after the people had given up their unregulated life and embraced a life of piety would not have recognized it.

The saint further declares that prayer is for our soul what the foundation is for a house and that it establishes and fortifies piety within us. He again assures us that when a soul applies itself regularly to prayer, all the virtues enter it at the same time. Who, he asks, is more just and holy than those who have familiar dealings with God? It is hard to describe their wisdom, prudence, goodness, and sobriety—in short, all their virtues and the purity of their life. Prayer has this wonderful power of filling with justice those in whose hearts it has established its dwelling place. It cannot coexist with any evil and easily makes pure again the soul that had withered in the toils of sin.

We have, says Saint John Chrysostom, an example of this in the gospel story of the publican, who obtained from God the forgiveness of his sins as soon as he begged for it, and another instance in the case of the woman taken in adultery. She who had spent her life in sensuality and impurity obtained salvation and the healing of her soul as soon as she prostrated herself at Christ's feet.

Although prayer obtains considerable benefits for a soul by making it practice virtue, by driving out of the heart all the malice contained there, and by purifying it from all its sins, its beneficial action is not limited to these effects. Prayer delivers those who apply themselves to it from all kinds of spiritual and temporal perils.

As for spiritual dangers, namely, temptations, if they arise from within us and from our natural inclination to sin, prayer so strengthens the soul against all evil thoughts that it suppresses them or makes them powerless. If they come from the devil's suggestions, says Saint John Chrysostom, no sooner do these malignant spirits notice that a soul has taken refuge in prayer than they fall back. On the contrary, if they find the soul bereft of the force and stamina resulting from prayer, they tempt it to many sins and soon reduce it to a most wretched state. They so greatly fear the courage and strength drawn from prayer that they dare not approach a soul that applies itself thereto. This thought makes Saint John Chrysostom say that prayer is a formidable fortress confronting the demons.

As for temporal and passing dangers found in this world, it is enough to pray, and they will be turned away from us. Saint John Chrysostom proves this by the example of Moses and David, reminding us that the kings of earth usually put their expectation of victory in the number and skill of their warriors and in their own military prowess, but Moses and David made sure of the defeat of their enemies only through prayer, which became for them a rampart surrounding their troops. This happened when the Israelites assailed the inhabitants of the Promised Land. Moses used no arms other than prayer against their numerous enemies. From this we learn that the prayers of the just are more powerful than weapons to overcome the mightiest and bravest foes. While Moses was praying, the Israelites were victorious, whereas when he stopped praying, his men lost the advantage. Saint Peter was delivered from prison, and its gates were opened for him, thanks only to the prayers offered by the church. Prayer often helps cure bodily illnesses, such as happened to the leper who was instantly cured as soon as he prostrated himself at Jesus' feet. This caused Saint John Chrysostom to ask that if God so promptly restored a body devoured by a dreadful malady, will he not with greater reason heal our souls infected by the illness and leprosy of sin?

Prayer also often succeeds in appeasing God's anger aroused against us, which is what happened to Moses when God was angered by the Israelites. Moses prayed to God so fervently that he obliged God, as if in spite of himself, to give up the idea of exterminating his people as he had determined to do. Holy Scripture testifies that God said to Moses, "Let me alone; do not prevent me from allowing my anger to flame up against this people" (Exod 32:10).

Prayer also gives us special strength to endure patiently everything that we find most difficult. Prayer made it possible for Saint Paul, after he had spent half the night in prayer, to suffer the most painful torments, such as the blows of whips on his body, as though he were a statue. Prayer also helps us to renounce the pleasures of the world, and it establishes in a soul a total disregard for the things of earth.

Such are the principal effects of prayer, as we learn from Saint John Chrysostom, which teach us clearly enough the benefits we can derive from it and how useful it is for us to apply ourselves to it.

CHAPTER 2
The Circumstances That Should Accompany Prayer

By the circumstances that should accompany prayer, we mean the conditions it must have to be useful to us and agreeable to God, the places and times for engaging in prayer, and the posture we should assume during prayer. All these points will be treated in the following two sections.

Section 1—The conditions required for prayer

It is not enough to pronounce words or to seem to be praying exteriorly if we wish to pray in fact and to make our prayer agreeable to God and useful for ourselves and our neighbor. Our prayer must fulfill various conditions without which it might often be displeasing to God and would be of little use, perhaps even of no use at all. The principal conditions required for prayer are purity of heart, attention, devotion, fervor, humility, resignation, confidence, and perseverance.

Purity of heart means keeping our heart entirely detached from sin, an extremely important condition for those who wish to apply themselves to prayer. God does not care about our prayers and does not answer them by his blessings if we pray to him with a heart sullied by sin. The royal prophet aptly expressed this when he said that the eyes of the Lord are on the just and his ears are open to their prayers, but he pays no attention to the supplications of sinners, who, being his enemies, cannot be heard by him or obtain what they ask of him (Ps 34:15–16). Saint John Chrysostom gives us two more reasons for this. The first is that because prayer is an activity that transcends our natural powers, the Spirit of God must be present in us to enliven and guide us in our prayer, and this Holy Spirit is in us only insofar as we distance ourselves from sin and feel a true horror for it. The second reason mentioned by the saint is that the devil does all he can to prevent us from occupying our mind with holy thoughts when we are praying. Once a soul has been sanctified by the Spirit of God, the evil one finds no easy access to it, will only with difficulty disturb it during this sacred time, and can hardly put an end to or hinder the salutary effects of its prayers.

We must also be attentive in our prayer because it displeases God unless we pray with devout concentration, thinking of God or of what we are asking of him. The reason is given to us in Saint Cyprian's treatise on the *Pater Noster*, where he says that it is not proper to expect God to hear us when we do not even listen to our own words in prayer. It is, he adds, criminal negligence to allow ourselves, when we are praying to God, to be overcome by profane thoughts suggesting that there are things other than God about which we could better and more advantageously occupy our mind.

To pray without attention means to allow our mind to wander and to dwell on evil or useless thoughts. We call this being distracted in prayer. When we willingly or through negligence allow our mind to dwell on such thoughts, this sin will at least cause our prayer to produce no good effect. However, when these distractions are not willed, rather than being sinful they are often a source of merit for us before God. We must not only do nothing to give rise to them but also strive to put them aside as far as we are able. For this purpose we should concern ourselves during the day only with what refers to our duties and our salvation.

True, it is difficult to keep our mind so constantly applied to prayer that it is entirely exempt from distractions. Because we are not always the master of our thoughts, we must watch closely over ourselves during our prayer so as to enter often into ourselves and not allow our mind to be filled with all sorts of thoughts and thus prevent those that sometimes enter in spite of our best efforts from leading to any evil effects.

Just as attention gives our prayer its value and merit, devotion sustains it, obtains for those who pray an abundance of graces, and explains why God readily and willingly grants what they ask of him. We pray with devotion when we experience a tender affection for God and for everything that concerns his service or can procure his glory. This affection and desire cause us to present him our respectful homage and worshipful service.

Prayer will hardly be agreeable to God unless devotion has some part in it; however, it is not necessary that this devotion be of a sensible kind or that it be perceived externally. On the contrary, it is often more useful for it to remain completely interior. Provided that our heart is fully penetrated by it, God usually is better satisfied with our prayer if we do not let our devotion show itself by signs or transports of mind or heart that might do nothing but inspire us with pride or some vain satisfaction.

Because the most precious result of our prayer is either knowledge and love of God or some grace that will help us acquire the one or the other, we should beg these two things of God with all the more fervor, for they are God's most precious gifts, the ones most beneficial to us. God also wishes us to show a vehement desire for possessing them; the more ardent this desire becomes, the more promptly God grants what we ask of him. We see this in God's behavior with Daniel, when he had the angel tell him that his prayer had been heard because he was a man of desire.

Although fervor should accompany all our prayers, we should not display an equally urgent desire of obtaining everything we ask of God. Because we can—and should—ardently desire the spiritual goods we lack and everything that has to do with the salvation of our soul, all of us are obliged to ask God fervently for a horror of sin, affection for what is right, victory over temptation, deliverance from the defects to which we are subject, acquisition of solid virtue, and perseverance in piety. We should desire all these things.

It is also important to show extra fervor in our prayer on certain special occasions, such as when we are assailed by some violent temptation that makes us fear we might fall into sin, when we find it difficult to overcome ourselves and to perform some good action, or when we must put up with something for which we feel great repugnance.

As for what concerns temporal benefits, we are not allowed to be overly eager to possess them. Because we never know whether they will be advantageous for our salvation, we cannot desire such things absolutely. Hence, if we display some fervor in asking for them, it should only be because we are paying our due homage to God and are praying to him, not showing how much we desire what we are asking of him.

Humility, no doubt, is one of the main conditions required in prayer. It is essential because it is humility that obtains from God with great readiness what we beg of him. Abraham made use of the humblest terms imaginable when he asked God not to destroy the cities of Sodom and Gomorrah. "Will I dare speak to my Lord," he said, "when I am but dust and ashes?" (Gen 18:27). Likewise, it was humility that gave Judith confidence that she would by herself win victory over the enemy of the Jewish people, for she remembered that God had always been favorably impressed by the prayers of the humble. This is the meaning of what we read in Ecclesiasticus, "The prayer of the humble pierces the heavens" (Sir 3:18).

Saint John Chrysostom says the reason for this is that humility lifts our prayer to God. "God," says Saint Jerome, "is so good to the humble that because they are little and cannot raise themselves to him, he abases himself and comes down to them to hear their prayers and answer them." We see the same thing in the case of the publican in the gospel. Not daring to raise his eyes to heaven and standing out of humility behind the door of the Temple, he deserved to be heard on the spot because of the humility displayed in his prayer.

The humility we are obliged to manifest in our prayer should give us an entire resignation to God's will and make us desire what we ask only insofar as it will please God to grant it to us. What should especially make us take this attitude of resignation is to be convinced, as we should be, that God knows far better than we do what we need and what is good for us, and that he is always prepared to give us this; consequently, God grants it to us when we pray to him. Jesus Christ displayed this attitude throughout his life, especially in his prayer in the Garden of Olives before his passion. After imploring the eternal Father to deliver him from the bitter chalice of suffering that confronted him, he added these words: "Yet, may your will be done, Father, and not mine" (Matt 26:39).

The resignation to God's will that we ought to have when we pray should produce in us a kind of indifference as to whether we obtain from him what we ask for. This indifference, however, must not be indiscriminate with regard to everything we can ask of God. Because God has put us in this world only to save our soul, we are certain that God wishes to give us the means of doing so. Consequently, we must desire, seek, and ask God for them with insistence, persuaded that if we earnestly desire them and plead for them, we will not fail to be resigned and abandoned to God's will. According to Saint Paul, the will of God is to bring about our sanctification (1 Thess 4:3); God also wants us to ask for it and for the means to contribute to it, for as a rule God does not give them except in proportion as we beg him for them.

The same rule does not hold true with regard to temporal benefits. Not being true goods, they may jeopardize as well as favor our salvation. Although it is sometimes permitted to ask God for them, we can do this only with complete indifference, persuaded that God will be good enough to grant them to us insofar as we need them for his service, which we should make our first and principal goal, as Jesus Christ tells us in the holy gospel.

This abandonment to God's will that we should profess when we implore him should not prevent us from praying with all possible confidence, for God is more eager to grant us what we ask of him than we are to pray to him. Does he not tell us in the holy gospel, "Ask, and you will receive; why have you not asked for anything in my name?" (Matt 7:7). Does he not urge us to pray without ceasing and assure us that he will grant us all that we ask?

This kind of confidence inspired the prayer of the Canaanite woman and of the centurion in the gospel. Their trust was so great and unexpected that it elicited the admiration of Jesus Christ and was the reason he granted their request immediately.

Our confidence in prayer cannot expect to produce such startling effects unless it is based on the merits of our Lord Jesus Christ, for it is only through him, as Saint Paul says, that we have access to the eternal Father. He made satisfaction for our sins and reconciled us with God when he made himself the victim for our sins and became sin itself, as Saint Paul again says, to destroy sin in us.

Yet, no matter how great the confidence of those who turn to God in prayer may be, it would be of little use to them if it were not backed up by perseverance. Although it is true that God does not allow those who trust in him to be frustrated in their hopes, he does not often grant what they ask for in prayer unless they continue begging it of him, and it is by perseverance in prayer that he often tests whether we truly trust him. This is why our Lord, after explaining to the apostles how to pray, taught them by two parables that if they persevered in prayer, even though God would not grant their prayers just because they were his friends united to him by grace, their importunity would, so to speak, enable them to obtain everything they needed.

Let us not, therefore, be surprised if God does not grant us right away what we ask him, for when God delays to hear us, says Saint Augustine, it is not because he means to refuse our request; by so acting he only wants to teach us to esteem more highly what he gives us. Furthermore, we experience greater satisfaction in obtaining at last the favors we have so long desired. "Do not give up praying," says Saint Ephrem, "even though God delays granting your request. Do not grow discouraged because of that; remember the Canaanite woman, and imitate her perseverance. If Jesus Christ deferred for a time giving her what she begged for so insistently, he did not let her go away without hearing her prayer. This was to teach us by her example to persevere in prayer, even when we do not at once receive the graces we need."

Section 2—The place, time, and posture for praying

There is no place where we cannot pray. Saint Ambrose proves this by the words of our Lord, "When you wish to pray, go into your room" (Matt 6:6). Saint Paul, in his first epistle to Timothy, prescribes that we should worship God everywhere. We also have the example of the saints, who offered prayers everywhere because in all places we can honor God, who is present everywhere. There is no place where we should not recognize him as God and offer him our respect.

But the place where we should pray to God that is preferable to all others is the church, for of all places it is the one most especially consecrated to the worship of God. This is why Jesus Christ calls it the house of God and a house of prayer. We also have reason to believe that our prayers, when offered in church, will be more quickly and readily heard than if we prayed anywhere else. For if God promised Solomon that he would listen to the supplications of those who invoked him in the Temple of Jerusalem, which was only a figure of our churches, with how much more reason will our petitions be heard in our churches, where Jesus Christ resides constantly in the most blessed sacrament of the altar and where we thus possess in him the fullness of the divinity?

There is no inappropriate time for praying. We can offer prayers at any hour of the day or night. Although David was a king, busy with the concerns of his kingdom, he says that he rose at midnight to prostrate himself before God and that by remembering his sins every night when he had retired, he felt so contrite and humble and wept so abundantly that he bedewed his couch, so to speak, with his tears, so deeply sorry did he feel for having offended God so gravely.

Jesus Christ has given us the example of praying during the night; the gospel relates that he often spent the night in prayer. This is a very appropriate and proper time to pay homage to God, because then we are not so easily interrupted or distracted. Because the devil tempts people more ordinarily and more powerfully during the hours of darkness, we also need more grace then; hence, we are more strictly obliged to pray. No doubt for these reasons Saint John Chrysostom says that because the nights are much longer in winter, it is proper for us to spend a greater part of them in prayer, happy to be able to give more time to the worship of God. If few people do this, we at least cannot dispense ourselves from having frequent recourse to God during the day. This saint declares that in this matter we should begin before sunrise, for, says this father, how could we dare to look at this splendid orb if we had not previously adored the one who gives us its light to enjoy? He adds that we are no less obliged to pray in the evening before going to bed, for we would easily give impure spirits an opportunity to tempt us during the night if we went to sleep without having forearmed ourselves against their assaults.

The same father also urges us never to omit invoking God before we sit down at table. He implies that it would show extreme ingratitude to take the liberty of eating what is set before us without having previously paid homage to God, who does us so much good and from whom we receive our food.

This saint requires much more than this from all Christians. He orders them not to let a single hour of the day go by without offering God some prayer so that the flow of our acts of piety, as he says, may parallel the passing hours of the day. This is how ordinary Christians can put into practice what our Lord recommended to us in the holy gospel, namely, to pray without ceasing, and what Saint Paul enjoined on the early Christians in several passages of his epistles, where he tells them that the will of God is that they should invoke God not only with affection but also with assiduity. Saint Augustine, exhorting his people to pray without ceasing, says that although it is true that we cannot be on our knees, prostrate in prayer, or with our hands lifted in supplication all the time, we can pray unceasingly without much effort. To do so, it is sufficient for us not to spend a single day without praying at set times.

Praying without ceasing, according to the same father, means having in all our actions a lasting hunger and a constant desire of enjoying God's company. He says further that we can succeed in this by practicing what was common among the hermits of Egypt, who often uttered short but fervent prayers that for this reason are called ejaculations. These helped to bring their attention back to God, for prayer, as he says, is continual when this attention to God remains in all its fervor.

Finally, this saint claims that nothing can prevent those who work with their hands from meditating continually on the law of the Lord and from singing incessantly the praises of God. It is also very useful and appropriate to pray when there is no special action we need to perform. A life thus entirely spent either in good works or in the exercise of prayer should be considered as a continual prayer.

Although we can pray in any bodily position, when we address God in private, Christian piety and the respect owed to God require us to kneel on both knees, without leaning on anything or sitting on our heels, and to show ourselves very recollected and modest. According to Tertullian, it is highly irreverent to God's majesty to pray to him while sitting, unless we are working or doing some obligatory action and wish to occupy our minds with holy thoughts. This is something that Saint Augustine highly recommends, provided that at some other time we fulfill the duty we have as a Christian of praying to God daily on our knees for a certain length of time.

This is how the holy apostles prayed, and how Saint Paul tells us that he also did, imitating the example of Jesus Christ, who knelt and prostrated himself on the ground in the Garden of Olives, wishing to appear before his Father in the name of all as a criminal. The church has always observed this custom on penitential days, as Saint Ambrose testifies.

It has also been the practice of the church during the paschal season and on all the Sundays of the year, as we learn from Tertullian, Saint Ambrose, and Saint Augustine, to pray while standing to symbolize the joy that Christians feel over the resurrection of our Lord Jesus Christ, which took place on a Sunday.

Saint Paul desires that men should worship uncovered and that women should do so with their head veiled, which is what all Christians usually do when they pray.

It is also a rather common practice to pray with our hands joined. According to Tertullian, the practice of lifting our hands to heaven also goes back a long time in the church. This is what David says he did when praying. Some people hold their arms out in the form of a cross, after the example of Moses when the Israelites were warring with the Amalekites. This illustrates the advantage and the facility that all Christians enjoy of being able to overcome all the demons through prayer in virtue of the merits that Jesus Christ won for them through his passion. According to Saint Ambrose and Tertullian, this was done in the early church by all the faithful on Good Friday.

As for the eyes, some keep them lifted to heaven to show that they are addressing their prayers to God, who resides especially in heaven. Our Lord did this on some occasions when he asked certain graces from his Father. Others keep their eyes cast down like the publican out of humility and to give proof of the contrition they feel over their sins and out of respect for God.

An ancient and very common practice in the church was to face east when praying, especially in the public assemblies of the faithful. This is why churches are ordinarily built oriented toward the east. Saint Basil affirms that this was done because the earthly paradise lay toward the east and because the church wishes Christians to show by doing this the desire they feel to return to their true country, from which they have been driven, that is, to their state of primitive innocence. Saint Augustine claims that this is done because those who pray should turn to God, who is symbolized by the east. Saint John

Damascene concludes that it is because Jesus Christ was crucified facing the west and because the church wants us to have him always in view as our mediator when we pray. He says that it is for this purpose that in churches a crucifix is placed facing west and that having Jesus Christ always facing us when we enter, we may consider him as our model and redeemer.

CHAPTER 3
For What and for Whom We Can and Should Pray to God

Our prayers would be of little use unless we applied ourselves to asking God for what pleases him and to praying to God for all those for whom he wants us to pray. We will explain this in the following two sections.

Section 1—What we should ask of God in prayer

We are not allowed to ask God for everything that comes into our head; it would be most inappropriate to follow our own way of thinking in our prayers. Saint Paul says that we do not know what we should ask of God; the Holy Spirit must pray in us and inspire us to ask God only for what can further his glory and our salvation or that of our neighbor.

Tertullian teaches that Jesus Christ came into this world to renew all things and to transform what is earthly into what is spiritual. Hence, he wished to teach his disciples not to ask any longer for the goods of this world but only for the things that can lead them to heaven. For this reason in the formula he taught us called the Lord's Prayer he illustrated a new manner of praying that is so excellent that Tertullian does not hesitate to say that it sums up the whole gospel.

The church has always held this prayer in great veneration. The fathers of the first centuries were in the habit of often explaining it to the faithful, especially to the catechumens and the newly baptized. From the beginning of the church, it was also customary to recite it thrice daily. No doubt for this reason Saint Augustine says that fathers and mothers should teach it to their children and all

Christians should know it by heart. The church saw fit to prescribe this in the seventh canon of the Sixth General Council. It would be sinful to remain ignorant of this prayer out of negligence.

Saint Augustine tells us that Jesus Christ gave us this prayer only to teach us what we should and what we can piously and usefully ask of God, which is admirably expressed in the formula purposely left us by Jesus Christ as the model of all the other prayers that we may formulate for ourselves. He also adds that nothing will be found in other prayers that is not implied in this one and that although we are free to make use of other words when addressing God, we are not at liberty to ask God for things other than those contained in this prayer.

In fact, according to the same father, in the Lord's Prayer we ask for all the temporal and spiritual needs of our present life and for our eternal life, as well as the grace to be delivered from all evils—past, present, and future. Therefore, if we wish to make known to the faithful everything they ought to and can ask of God, we need merely to explain to them, as Tertullian and Saint Augustine did, what is contained in the seven petitions of the *Pater Noster*.

The first thing our Lord has us ask for in this prayer he left us is that God's name be hallowed. As Tertullian remarks, not that God's name is not holy and sanctified in itself—for it sanctifies all else—but that what we ask for in this prayer, says Saint Augustine, is that God's name be so perfectly hallowed and so fully recognized as holy that we may be convinced that nothing can be holier and that this conviction may make us fear to offend him and bring us to aim at nothing but the glory of God in everything we do.

The second thing we ask for in this prayer is that the kingdom of God may come. Saint Augustine declares that by these words we stir up in ourselves the desire for the kingdom of God and eternal life. While on earth, he says, all our wishes should tend to this. According to this same father, we can also understand by these words the reign of God over the just through his holy grace. As our Lord declared in the gospel, "The kingdom of God is within you" (Luke 17:21). We ask God that he never cease reigning in these souls and that he sanctify them more and more to make them worthy of possessing his heavenly kingdom.

Tertullian asserts that by the third petition we ask God to give us in this world the means of saving ourselves, for this is the accomplishment and the end of God's will for us. Thus we beseech God to help us obey his commandments with as much fidelity and exactness as shown by the angels in executing his orders or as we will accomplish his will in heaven when we are fortunate enough to get there. As Saint Augustine affirms, we are sure of doing God's will when we observe his commandments. We also ask God, this saint tells us, to enable us to subject our flesh to the spirit, because what is most capable of causing chagrin to a soul that seeks God is to see how the flesh continually wars against the spirit as long as we remain in this world.

Saint Augustine argues that the fourth petition, "give us this day our daily bread," means that we can pray for our bodily as well as our spiritual nourishment. If we are asking for bodily food, says the saint, this request does not reach very far; nevertheless, it is in conformity with what Saint Paul advises when he writes that we should be content as long as we have what we need to live and to be clothed.

Jesus Christ includes all the needs of the body under the word *bread,* for the scriptures often sum up all our necessities in this word. We are also to understand that we are not allowed, as Saint Augustine warns, to desire and demand temporal blessings except those that are truly necessary.

Both rich and poor people are obliged to ask God for their daily bread, for although they might not lack what is necessary, they need to acknowledge that God is the one who has given them their temporal wealth and who can take it away whenever he pleases. Those who work with their hands to earn the necessities of life must also address this prayer to God, who satisfies their needs by blessing their work. If he did not do so, their labor would remain quite useless.

If by these words we ask God for food for the soul, we mean, asserts Saint Augustine, either the sacrament of the holy Eucharist, which is called our daily bread because we can receive it every day, or God's grace, which we need not only every day but at every moment, or again the gift of meditating on the law and the word of

God. We need all these things constantly to restore the vigor of our soul and to lead us to sovereign blessedness.

By the fifth petition, "forgive us our trespasses," it is clear, says Saint Augustine, that we ask God to pardon the sins we have committed. This we implore of God alone because only he can forgive them. We must realize that to make this prayer effective and to obtain this grace from God, all of us are obliged to pardon from the heart the faults committed against us and the insults we might have endured. Those who are not so disposed when reciting this prayer bring down on themselves their own condemnation and the malediction of God. The just need to say this prayer as much as sinners because all of us stand in need of God's mercy, for no one on earth is exempt from slight faults that can readily be pardoned by the efficacy of this prayer.

Saint Augustine explains that by the sixth petition, "lead us not into temptation," we ask God not to allow us to be tempted beyond what we can bear and not to abandon us to temptation to such an extent that we might be led astray and succumb. Rather, we beg him to give us the grace to resist temptation and to draw benefit from it. We should often repeat this prayer because during this life we are always liable to be tempted, and on many occasions we can scarcely avoid it.

By the last petition, "deliver us from evil," we ask God to spare us all the punishment due to us because of our sins, the evils of the next life in hell and purgatory, and those of this present life. In addition, we beg God to help us endure our sufferings patiently and to deliver us from all those corporal and spiritual afflictions that might hinder us from saving our soul.

It is especially with regard to the tribulation and suffering of this life, observes Saint Augustine, that we do not know what we should ask of God, for these trials may be most useful as well as harmful to us. Because they are in themselves painful, irksome, and contrary to nature, we are inclined to beg God with all our will to take them away from us, but we should not believe that God has forsaken us if he does not at once deliver us from these trials. On the contrary, we should thank God for them, convinced that it is much better that his will be done than ours and that the patience we show in supporting them will obtain great benefits for us. For this reason we are not allowed to ask God to deliver us from our temporal afflictions except insofar as this may be expedient for our soul because they might also lead us to fall into sin. We are, however, obliged to beseech God simply and absolutely to save us from eternal death because this is the one evil that we must at all costs avoid.

Saint Augustine also remarks that when we ask God for temporal blessings, we should do so only with restraint and with the fear of displeasing him and only on condition that God gives us the things he judges will be to our advantage. On the contrary, if God knows that they will harm us, we should hope that he will refuse our prayer, for it is only with a kind of tolerance and condescension for our weakness that God suffers us to ask for such things. This is why, declares this saint, we should never request anything specific with regard to temporal matters but beg God to give us what he knows will be best for us, for we ourselves do not know this.

We must not, continues the saint, yearn for riches, for many have been lost through possessing wealth. Nor should we long to enjoy the pleasures and goods of this earth, for we would slight God by seeking our own satisfaction in such things. Nor should we procure or ask God to give us high and honorable positions because of the pomp and display that accompany them and the vainglory that inspires them. The saint concedes that such petitions are tolerable if we pray for them to do good to those over whom we will be placed, not because of the honors and other rewards in themselves. The safest course, says the saint, is never to pray for any temporal benefits at all.

Section 2—Those for whom we can and should pray

The first obligation God has imposed on us is to labor for our own salvation; prayer is one of the principal means we can use to obtain this favor for ourselves. Hence, when we devote ourselves to this sacred exercise, it should be for our own sake, first of all, to obtain from God all we need to enjoy the grace and love of God in this world and to secure eternal life.

However, God also requires all of us to contribute to the welfare of our neighbor, and Christian charity, the most beautiful ornament of our religion, obliges us not to think only of ourselves but to help others, insofar as we are able, to save themselves. Furthermore, because there is no one for whom this obligation is not binding, it is our duty to pray for everyone. This is what Saint Paul tells us and what he recommends to Timothy as the first thing to which we should apply ourselves in our assemblies. This is also what Saint Augustine exhorts us to do, saying that if we pray only for ourselves, we will enjoy only the efficacy of our own prayers, but if we have enough charity to pray for everyone, all of them will pray for us in return. The saint goes even further and declares that if God in his goodness and according to his accustomed mercy grants what we ask him for others, we will be doubly rewarded in heaven.

Those for whom we are especially bound to pray are all Christians, our brothers and sisters in Jesus Christ, as we learn from Saint James, who orders all the faithful to pray for one another to be saved. As Saint Jerome assures us, whoever saves a sinner, that is, another Christian, will be helped in turn by this person's prayer.

Saint Augustine does not wish us to be content with praying for those who belong to the church; he advises us to offer frequent and fervent prayers for those who are separated from her, such as schismatics, who refuse to recognize the church's head, and heretics, who contest her teachings. We should weep over them, says this father, because they are our brothers and sisters, even though they do not wish to be such any more, and we should pray to God for them so that they may come to know and love him and that there may henceforth be one flock and one shepherd. We should also pray for the Jews, he continues, even though they incurred God's curse, and for pagans, who believe neither in God nor in Jesus Christ, so that they may come to know the one true God, the Lord of the universe.

Those who are exceedingly weak in virtue and those who are enmeshed by the world and live according to its maxims are the ones who need the most help. Hence, they are likewise the ones among Christians, as Saint Augustine again teaches, for whom charity urges us to pray to God most earnestly and ardently, especially if we have taken part in their disorderly and licentious life. He tells us that we should ask God that they may become our companions in a life of piety as we were once theirs in sin.

Although the just are in the state of grace and friendship with God, they are not certain of remaining such; therefore, we are not allowed to forget them in our prayers. Saint John Chrysostom teaches us this by the example of the first Christians, who did not hesitate to pray for Saint Peter and Saint Paul even though these apostles were at the time the very pillars of the church.

We should also, Saint Jerome declares, pray constantly for God to uphold and extend the church. The persons in the church for whom we should ordinarily offer our prayers are those who govern and exercise authority over her, whether spiritual, such as the pope, bishops, and pastors, or temporal, such as kings, princes of the earth, and magistrates. This practice, Tertullian states, has been observed in the church from the beginning. It is what Saint Paul recommends Timothy to have his faithful do.

Saint Paul also wishes prayers to be offered for the preachers of the gospel, so that God may give them the light they need to announce the mysteries of Jesus Christ and to preach the word of God effectively.

Our obligations to our parents should lead us to pray for them, asking for whatever may be advantageous to them. The church also wishes us to pray for our friends and benefactors, for she has instituted special prayers for their intentions.

It would be of little merit to pray for our friends unless we also pray for our enemies. Jesus Christ ordered us to do this and presented himself as an example in the gospel to induce us to do so. He asks us what reward we can expect if we show affection only to those who love us, for then we are doing nothing more than pagans do. Realizing that this practice is something we would find difficult, he willed to give us an example in this regard by praying publicly for those who were crucifying him. If we think we cannot rise to the level of imitating our Lord Jesus Christ, remarks Saint Augustine, at least we can imitate his saints, who were his servants just as we are. Such were Saint Stephen, one of the first deacons, and Saint James the Apostle, surnamed the Just, who prayed to God on their knees for their persecutors.

Nor does it suffice, warns Saint Augustine, for us to pray to God for the living; we must also offer God our supplications for the dead, as Holy Scripture exhorts us. Such entreaties are very useful to those who have not entirely made satisfaction for their sins in this life. Saint Augustine assures us that he frequently prayed thus for his mother, and he adds that the church has always practiced this custom. She makes a general commemoration of all, without naming anyone in particular, to show that she does not forget in her intercession the dead who have no relatives or friends on earth to pray for them. As he observes, if we did not pray for the dead, it would be of little use to bury them in consecrated ground.

We are not allowed to pray for the devils or for the damned so that they may by God's mercy be delivered from the torments they deserve in all justice. Saint Augustine teaches that these persons cannot do penance to provoke the mercy of God; consequently, the church's prayers for them cannot be heard.

Nor are we permitted to pray for the saints, for they already possess sovereign beatitude, which they cannot hope or desire to increase. It would also be offensive to God were we to pray for them. All we can do for the blessed is to thank God for the graces he bestowed on them and for the glory they enjoy in heaven.

CHAPTER 5
The Different Ways of Praying

Section 1—Different kinds of prayer

Because we have both a soul and a body, it is only right that both should pay homage to God and render him their due worship. No doubt this is why the church was not satisfied with prescribing that Christians should perform interior acts of religion but also prescribed inclination, prostration, genuflection, joining our hands, extending our arms, striking our breast, and so on, either to honor God in an external way or to show God sensible signs of the sorrow we feel for our sins.

For the same reason God has willed that we should be able to pray in two different ways: in our heart or with words. Prayer that springs from the heart is ordinarily called interior prayer, that is, prayer of the mind, for the body takes no part in it. By this kind of prayer we fulfill our duties to God and ask him for what we need, speaking from the heart only. Prayer expressed in words is called vocal prayer because it utilizes our voice, and by this means we honor God and represent to him what is necessary or useful for our salvation.

David, who has admirably taught us about the different kinds of prayer, tells us in the psalms that he often had recourse to the one and to the other. Sometimes, he says, God's praises were always in his mouth; his lips rejoiced when he was praising God; his tongue was busy all day long paying honor to God's justice. He also says that he cried out to the Lord with a loud voice and that he begged God to let his ear be attentive to the sound of his prayers.

But when he speaks of the prayers that he formed in the depths of his heart without expressing them externally, he says that he sought always to apply his mind to the presence of God, that the law of God was the subject of his meditation, that he arose in the middle of the night to think of God's judgments, that he seriously reviewed his past years and often kept eternity in mind, and that he meditated on this during the night in the depths of his heart. Sometimes he informs us about the effects of his fervent meditations that often caused him to lament, watering his bed with his tears night after night.

However, this manner of praying from the heart was not much used in Old Testament times. We see this in the surprise felt by the high priest Eli when he saw Hannah, the mother of Samuel, praying in the Temple with her lips scarcely moving. He took the occasion to insult her as if she were full of wine and ordered her to leave the Temple until she had sobered up (1 Sam 1:13–14). The reason for this reaction is that the Jews were a materialistic people who made all their religion consist in external practices.

Jesus Christ came to this earth to establish a new law based mainly on interior worship. He taught us by his example and words how to pray to God more frequently and more often from the heart than from the lips, for it is said of him that he often spent the night in prayer. To encourage us to adopt this practice of addressing ourselves to God from the heart alone, he told us that because God is a spirit, we should adore him in spirit when we wish to fulfill our duties to him and that the hour had come when the true worshipers would adore the Father in spirit and truth (John 4:23).

Not that our Lord condemns vocal prayer, for he taught one to his disciples that they should say when praying to the Father. But he wished to make us understand that the best way of praying is to appeal to God from the heart, for as Saint Cyprian says, it is not the mouth but the heart that speaks to God. God also complained through one of the prophets that too often people honor him with their lips while their heart is far from him (Isa 29:13).

Prayer from the heart, or interior prayer, enjoys the advantage over vocal prayer of being good and useful in itself. No doubt this is why our Lord says that adoring God in spirit is adoring him in truth, whereas vocal prayer is of worth only when it is joined to interior prayer that springs from a heart that loves him; it draws all its power and efficacy from this source. For this reason David tells God that his tongue will meditate on God's justice (Ps 35:28), because the prayer that issues from the mouth is of no value whatever if the mind is not meditating while the tongue speaks and prays.

We also enjoy the advantage of praying to God in our heart at all times and occasions. It can happen, says Saint John Chrysostom, that we may pray with deep attention while walking through the city; while with our friends, we may keep our mind fixed on God; while doing something else, we may invoke God interiorly with great fervor and devotion. A pious and ancient author reports that this is what the anchorites of old did; they never ceased praying to God in the depths of the heart.

We can pray to God interiorly in different ways but especially in these five. We may simply keep ourselves silently in the presence of God with sentiments of respect and adoration and without expressing any thoughts or asking anything of God. Cassian appears to speak of this manner of praying in his Ninth Conference, where he says that sometimes in prayer the mind is hidden from itself in deepest silence. We can also pray by thinking without uttering a single word. Saint John Chrysostom has this kind of prayer in mind when he states that it is made perfect through the fervor of our spirit. We can also pray to God through our affections when we ask something of him by the sole movement of the heart. According to

Saint Cyprian, it was thus that Hannah, the mother of Samuel, was praying. We can pray by actions when we perform good ones with a view of rendering our duties to God or of obtaining some favor from him. But one of the best ways of praying to God in our heart is to pray by means of our sufferings, which we do when we endure patiently the afflictions that God sends us and with the intention of doing him honor or of procuring some spiritual or temporal benefit.

Vocal prayers can be made in public or in private. Public prayers are those said by Christians in common when assembled in church. Private prayers are those said by each of the faithful in private. Public prayers have the advantage over private prayers because they are ordained by the Holy Spirit, who leads the church; because by them we can obtain more easily what we ask of God on account of their number and the union of heart by those praying together; because each individual has a share in the merits of all the others who pray alongside. The most typical public prayers are the religious exercises that Christians perform in common when assembled on Sundays and feasts, such as at the parish Mass and the Divine Office. The prayers Christians say most commonly in private are those in the morning and evening, at holy Mass, and at different occasions during the day.

Chapter 7

Explanation of the Method of Interior Prayer

✠

EDITORS' INTRODUCTION: *In his final days De La Salle delighted in teaching the art of interior prayer to the novices at St. Yon in Rouen. Recalling his own training in the Sulpician Seminary of Paris, he taught a method of multiple affective acts based on a process that recalled God's presence, reflected on the gospel and how the gospel should be lived, and ended in thanksgiving. The multiple acts were centered on cultivating faith in the active presence of God. During the interior prayer members were taught to stop in "simple attention" whenever the Spirit of God prayed in them. Interior prayer was kept alive during the day by repeated acts of recollection, which remembered the pervading presence of a provident God. Interior prayer provided members with the source of the spirit of faith that gave life—zeal—to their society and its work of salvation.* [1]

THE FIRST PART OF THE METHOD OF INTERIOR PRAYER

Interior Prayer in General and the Disposition of the Soul

Interior prayer is an inner activity whereby the soul concentrates on God. We call it interior prayer to distinguish it from vocal prayer, an activity that in part the body produces with its mouth but on which the mind must simultaneously concentrate.

We call it interior prayer because the activity is not simply of the mind but of all the powers of the soul and because to be genuine and effective, it must take place in the depths of the soul, that is, in the innermost part of the soul.

If interior prayer occurred only in the mind or in the superficial part of the heart, it would easily lie open to human and material distractions that would prevent it from being fruitful. This mental

214

activity, not having penetrated the soul, would only be temporary; consequently, it would leave the soul arid and devoid of God.

We call interior prayer an inner activity because the soul concentrates therein on what is proper to it in this life, namely, to know and to love God and to take all the means necessary to achieve both these ends.

The principal activity of the soul in truly interior prayer is to fill and to unite itself interiorly with God. This activity is for the soul a kind of apprenticeship and a foretaste through vibrant faith of what the soul will experience throughout eternity. We call interior prayer, therefore, an inner activity whereby the soul concentrates on God.

Interior prayer has three parts. The first part is the disposition of the soul, properly called recollection; the second part is the concentration on the topic of interior prayer; the third part is the thanksgiving at the end of interior prayer.

We say that the first part is the disposition of the soul for interior prayer because the human mind, ordinarily attentive during the greater part of the day to things exterior and material in themselves, thereby goes outside itself in some manner and takes on, at least to some degree, the characteristics of the objects it pays attention to.

Therefore, when we wish to apply ourselves to interior prayer, we must begin by withdrawing the mind entirely from attention to exterior, material things and concentrate only on spiritual, interior things.

For this reason we must begin by being attentive to the presence of God. Throughout their duration the acts of the first part serve to support and to occupy the mind with the presence of God. In this way the first part disposes us for interior prayer, inasmuch as the attention to the presence of God to which we apply ourselves, which the acts of the first part help keep before the mind, withdraws it from exterior things only to occupy it with what alone can keep the mind within itself and thus render it interior.

Because God is a spiritual being, attention to God has the characteristic of being incompatible with attention to exterior and material things. Because God is infinitely above all created things, however perfect and detached from matter they may be, attention to

God is in no way compatible with attention even to spiritual creatures. The more the mind pays attention to God, the more this attention supplants attention to creatures.

It follows necessarily that the more a soul is attentive to God, the more it will disengage from all attention to creatures and, consequently, from whatever attachment and affection it may have had for them. Because attention to creatures produces attachment to them, the elimination of the one from the soul necessarily causes the elimination of the other.

In this way the soul, by imperceptibly filling itself with God, detaches itself from creatures and becomes what we call interior by turning away and disengaging from material, exterior objects.

We call the first part of interior prayer *recollection* also for this reason, because recollection serves to empty the mind of exterior things, to bring it back within itself, to keep it there, and, consequently, to recollect the soul through attention to God and to purely interior matters.[2]

The Different Ways of Placing Ourselves in God's Presence

The first thing to do in interior prayer is to become filled interiorly with the presence of God, which we must always do through a sentiment of faith based on a passage from Holy Scripture.

We can consider God present in three different ways: first, in the place where we are; second, within us; third, in church. Each of these three ways of considering God present can be divided into two other ways.

We can consider God present in the place where we are: first, because God is everywhere; second, because wherever two or three people gather in the name of our Lord, he is in their midst.

We can consider God present within us in two ways: first, by being in us to maintain us in existence; second, by being in us through his grace and his Spirit.

Finally, we can consider God present in church: first, because it is the house of God; second, because our Lord Jesus Christ is present there in the Most Blessed Sacrament of the altar.

The second way of placing ourselves in the presence of God in the place where we are is to consider our Lord present in the midst of those who gather in his name.

We can consider God present in the place where we are because our Lord says in Saint Matthew's gospel that where two or three gather in his name, he is in their midst (Matt 18:20).

When we are together with our Brothers to engage in interior prayer or to perform some other spiritual exercise, is it not a great blessing to know that we are in our Lord's company and that he is in the midst of the Brothers? Jesus Christ is in our midst to impart his Holy Spirit to us and to direct us by his Spirit in all our actions and in everything we do.

Jesus Christ is in our midst to unite us to one another, thus accomplishing what he asked his Father for us, before his death, in these words of Saint John: "That they may all be one, as you, Father, are in me and I in you; that they may be brought to perfection as one" (John 17:21, 23), in other words, so closely united and bound together, having but one spirit, namely, the Spirit of God, that we will never be disunited.

Jesus Christ is in the midst of the Brothers during our spiritual exercises to give us the spirit of our state and to maintain and strengthen our possession of this spirit, our source and assurance of salvation as long as we preserve it soundly and without alteration.

Jesus Christ is in the midst of the Brothers to teach us the truths and the maxims of the gospel, to implant them deeply in the heart, to inspire us to adopt them as the rule of our conduct, to help us understand them, and to make us know how to put them into practice in the manner most agreeable to God and most suitable for our state in life.

Jesus Christ is in the midst of the Brothers to lead us to practice these gospel maxims in our Society in a uniform manner so that we can always preserve entire and perfect union among us.

Jesus Christ is in the midst of the Brothers during our spiritual exercises so that by directing all our actions to him as to our center, we will become one in him by the union we will have with him, who acts in us and through us.

Jesus Christ is in the midst of the brothers during our spiritual exercises to give them completeness and perfection, for he is to us

217

like the sun, which not only bestows on plants the power to produce but also gives their fruit its goodness and perfection in greater or lesser proportion as the plants are more or less exposed to the sun's rays.

Similarly, we perform the exercises and the actions appropriate to our state with greater or lesser perfection insofar as we are in greater or lesser contact, conformity, and union with Jesus Christ.

This method of placing ourselves in God's presence by considering Jesus Christ in our midst can produce three different benefits.

The first benefit is that all our actions refer to Jesus Christ and tend toward him as their center. They draw all their efficacy from him, just as the branches of a vine draw sap from the vine. Thus, there is a continual movement of our actions to Jesus Christ and from Jesus Christ back to us, for he gives them the spirit of life.

The second benefit is that we establish a close union with Jesus Christ, who lives in us and in whom we live, as the apostle Saint Paul so admirably describes (Gal 2:20). Because of this union, he says, we can do nothing without Jesus, who does everything in us because he dwells in us and we in him. In this way, Saint Paul tells us, we will bear much fruit.

The third benefit is that Jesus, as he says by a prophet, pours out his Spirit on us. The world cannot accept this Spirit of truth, he says, because it does not know it (John 14:17). Because this same Holy Spirit enlivens our actions and becomes their life-giving spirit, these works are not dead; they are Christian but also related to our state in life and to our perfection, which requires them to have a special quality.

Here is an example of placing ourselves in God's presence in our midst:

"How happy I am, my God, to be praying with my brothers, for we have the advantage, according to your words, of having you in our midst. You are present here, O my Jesus, to pour out your Spirit upon us, as you declared through your prophet and as you did for your apostles and your first disciples when they were together in the Cenacle, persevering in prayer in intimate union of mind and heart.

"Through your presence in our midst as we gather to pray to you, give me also the grace to possess an intimate union of mind and heart with my brothers and to enter into the disposition of the holy apostles in the Cenacle.

"After receiving your divine Spirit in the fullness you have destined for me, may I be guided by the Spirit in fulfilling the duties of my state so that I can share in your zeal for the instruction of those you kindly entrust to my care."

We can make similar reflections modeled on the previous example and based on other purposes and benefits of this method of placing ourselves in God's presence by considering Jesus Christ in our midst as we pray together.[3]

The Second Part of the Method of Interior Prayer

Considering a Mystery

In the second part of interior prayer, we can take as the subject of our meditation one of the mysteries of our holy religion, especially the mysteries of our Lord.

By the mysteries of our Lord we mean the principal actions that the Son of God made man accomplished for our salvation, such as his incarnation, his nativity, his circumcision, and his passion and death. We can also meditate on one of the mysteries of the Most Blessed Virgin, such as her immaculate conception, her nativity, and the like.

We begin by filling ourselves with the spirit of the mystery by considering either what the gospel says about it or what the church teaches on the subject. We do so either by a simple view of faith— that is, by focusing on the mystery we believe in because faith teaches us—or by a reflection on the mystery or on the text of the meditation that speaks of it. These reflections should stimulate our devotion to this mystery and keep us in an attitude of interior respect as we consider it.

We must join to this respect for the mystery an interior desire to profit from it and to receive the spirit, the grace, and the benefits that our Lord wishes us to draw from it. Jesus Christ accomplished these divine mysteries of our holy religion not only to redeem us but also to instruct and to lead us by his example to practice the most profound and sanctifying virtues that he practiced while

219

accomplishing these sacred mysteries. This is what we mean by the spirit of the mysteries.

Each mystery has its own unique spirit because our Lord practiced certain evident virtues in it that we can observe with particular admiration and astonishment when we pay serious, profound attention to the mystery.

Our Lord practiced these virtues to give us an example and to lead us to practice them in imitation of him, aided by the grace he merited for us that accompanies the mystery as a component of its spirit and its reality.

For example, the spirit of the mystery of the incarnation is charity. It is by charity and by love for the human race (as our Lord says) that "the eternal Father gave his only Son" (John 3:16), that the Son became incarnated, and that the Holy Spirit accomplished this mystery. The spirit of the incarnation is also humility, for as Saint Paul says, "the Son of God emptied himself, taking the form of a slave" (Phil 2:7).

The spirit of the mystery of our Lord's nativity is the spirit of childhood. When the Son of God came into this world, as we read in Saint John's gospel, "to those who did accept him, he gave power to become children of God" (John 1:11–12). This spirit of childhood consists of simplicity, docility, purity, and contempt for worldly riches and grandeur.

The spirit of the mystery of the circumcision is humility and mortification. In undergoing circumcision our Lord willingly accepted the mark of a sinner and shed his blood in suffering and pain.

The spirit of the mystery of the transfiguration is the spirit of vocal and interior prayer, and so on with the other mysteries.[4]

Considering a Virtue

In the second part of interior prayer, we can also apply ourselves to the consideration of a particular virtue as the subject of our meditation.

Virtues are the holy actions, sentiments, motives, and affections that are contrary to vices and sins. For example, chastity is opposed to impurity; humility, to pride; penance, to sensuality, and so on.

By his example and his words, our Lord taught us the practice of virtue as necessary for salvation; as he said, he is the way (John 14:6). By practicing these virtues, we walk forward on the path to heaven and arrive at true, eternal, and blessed life, a life that makes angels and humans infinitely happy.

Our Lord communicates this life to us by sharing his grace in this world and his glory in the next. We merit a share in this blessed life to the degree we practice virtue.

We must begin by convincing ourselves interiorly of the necessity of the virtue we are considering. We can do so in two ways, first, by calling to mind with conviction and faith a passage of Holy Scripture that speaks of this virtue. For example, to convince ourselves of the need for humility, we can recall the words of Saint James, "God resists the proud but gives grace to the humble" (Jas 4:6) and then remain in an attitude of interior respect while concentrating on the virtue taught in this passage.

The second way to convince ourselves of the need for this virtue is to reflect on it on the basis of whatever Holy Scripture, especially the New Testament, says of it that can persuade our mind of the need to practice it. We might, for instance, make these reflections on humility:

"O my God, what a dreadful misfortune it is to be proud, for you resist such people and show yourself to be their enemy."

"Lord, how happy are the humble, for to such you grant your grace."

"My God, you are the friend of the humble. How powerfully this should convince me to become humble!"

Having thus based ourselves firmly on faith, we proceed to make the nine acts of the second part, which we should apply to the virtue we selected for interior prayer, considered in relation to our Lord's teaching by his words and his example.[5]

Considering a Maxim

In the second part of interior prayer, we can make the consideration of a maxim of the holy gospel the subject of our prayer.

Maxims are the sentences, or passages, from Holy Scripture that contain certain truths necessary for salvation, interior words that make us understand what we should do or avoid, esteem or despise, seek or escape, love or hate, and the like. The New Testament is full of such passages.

Some maxims, or sentences, contain truths that are precepts, which impose an obligation to practice the truth contained in the maxim. For example, "Forgive, and you will be forgiven" (Matt 6:14); "Do not judge, and you will not be judged" (Matt 7:1). They are maxims of precept because our Lord positively commands us to carry them out under pain of damnation.

Other maxims express counsels; in other words, we are not absolutely obliged to practice them to be saved. They are only suggested as necessary means to acquire greater perfection. For example, "If you wish to be perfect, go, sell what you have, and give to the poor, and you will have treasure in heaven. Then come, follow me" (Matt 19:21).

Some counsels are perfectly clear, intelligible, and easy to understand, such as this one: "Love your enemies; do good to those who hate you; bless those who curse you" (Luke 6:27–28).

Other counsels are obscure, difficult to understand, and need to be explained, such as the following: "If your right eye causes you to sin, tear it out, and throw it away" (Matt 5:29). "If anyone comes to me without hating his father and his mother, he cannot be my disciple" (Luke 14:26). A number of other similar texts should not be taken literally.

Recalling the scriptural passage that contains the maxim, we should begin by convincing ourselves interiorly, through a sentiment of faith, of the necessity or the usefulness of the maxim on which we wish to make interior prayer.

We call the *spirit* of a maxim the holy impression and the good effect that it should produce when seriously contemplated and understood, as in this subject for interior prayer: "What use is it for a person to gain the whole world if he loses his soul?" (Matt 16:26).

This maxim, if deeply pondered and relished, convinces the mind that there is no true fortune except winning eternal glory, that nothing in this life is advantageous except what can contribute to our salvation, and that true goods are found only in heaven. This maxim makes us develop a profound contempt for everything worldlings so passionately love and pursue. It detaches us from the perishable, deceptive, and fleeting goods of the earth so that we can attach ourselves only to those of heaven, which are true, permanent, and eternal.

The spirit of this next maxim, "Any who wish to follow me must deny themselves, take up their cross, and walk in my footsteps" (Matt 16:24), is to do violence to ourselves to resist the vicious inclinations leading us to sin and to overcome the repugnance and difficulties we encounter in the pursuit of virtue. This spirit makes us accept, in submission to God's holy will and as coming from God's hands, all afflictions, pains, and adversities; it encourages us to endure them patiently for the love of our Lord and in imitation of him.

The spirit of another maxim, "Whoever would save his life will lose it, but whoever loses his life for love of me will save it for eternal life" (Matt 16:25), is to despise and reject sensual pleasures, to seek no natural comfort, and to dread no suffering and mortification, at least voluntarily, much less to flee from it. This spirit leads us to do voluntary penance and to persevere in our tasks, especially when obligatory and imposed by our state in life, unconcerned about the effect on our health, which the words of the gospel inspire us to sacrifice willingly to the Lord: Whoever loses his life for love of him will find it (Matt 16:25).

The spirit of this maxim made the early Christians joyfully face martyrdom and inspired the ancient desert fathers to embrace such excessive and lengthy austerities with so much courage and constancy. Our Lord kept his promise to them, not only by rewarding them in heaven with a blessed and eternal life but also by making most of them live exempt from illness to an extremely old age in this life.

So it is with all the other maxims: each one has its own particular spirit.[6]

Chapter 8

Letters and
Personal Documents

⁜

RULES I HAVE IMPOSED ON MYSELF

EDITORS' INTRODUCTION: Of his biographers, only Blain refers to this collection of personal rules. Here we meet the De La Salle for whom the presence of God is a lived reality, especially in light of the difficulties that he and his community would face. We also see the centrality of Sacred Scripture in the life and spirituality of De La Salle.[1]

1. I will not leave the house without necessity and without spending a quarter of an hour considering before God whether the need is real or only imaginary. If it is urgent, I will take the time of a *Miserere* for that purpose and to put myself in the proper frame of mind.

2. I will take a quarter of an hour every day to renew my consecration to the Most Holy Trinity.

3. It is a good rule of life to make no distinction at all between the work of our vocation in life and the work of our salvation and perfection. We can be sure that we cannot work out our salvation better or achieve perfection more surely than by discharging our responsibilities, provided that we accomplish them in view of the will of God. We must try to keep this precept ever in mind.

4. When I pay anyone a visit, I will be careful to say only what I must and not chat about what is going on in the world or engage in any small talk. I will not stay there any longer than a half hour, at most.

5. At least twenty times a day I will unite my actions with those of our Lord and try to make his perspective and intentions my own. To keep myself on track, I will pierce a small piece of paper as often as I perform this act. For as many times as I fail to observe this practice each day, I will say the *Pater Noster*, kissing the floor after each one, before I go to bed.

6. When my Brothers come to me for advice, I will ask our Lord himself to give it to them. If the matter is serious, I will take a moment to pray about it. At least I will try to keep myself recollected during the interview while lifting my heart to God.

7. When they tell me their faults, I will hold myself blameworthy before God for my failure to prevent their occurrence, whether because of the advice I gave them or for not being attentive to them. If I impose a penance on them, I will inflict a greater one on myself. If the fault is serious, I will, in addition to the penance, spend some time in private, perhaps a half-hour or even an hour, for several days afterward, especially at night, to ask for God's forgiveness. If I consider that I am holding our Lord's place in their regard, this ought to be with the understanding that I must bear their sins as our Lord has borne ours. God has given me this kind of responsibility for them.

8. I will always regard the work of my salvation and the founding and governing of our community as the work of God. This is why I will abandon the care of both to him to bend myself only to his purposes. I will often seek his guidance to know what I must do for the one or the other. I will often repeat these words of the prophet Habakkuk: "Lord, the work is yours."

9. I must frequently remind myself that I am only an instrument, which has no value except in the hands of the Master Craftsman. For this reason I must wait for the promptings of Providence before I act but not allow them to slip by once I perceive them.

10. In whatever circumstance I find myself, I will always follow a plan and a daily schedule, relying only on the grace of God, in which I place full trust, to carry them out, because I have never been able to accomplish this on my own. As my situation changes, I will

adjust my plan and daily schedule. To make sure this happens, I will spend a day in retreat.

11. When I have to go into the countryside, I will spend a day in prayer and reflection to prepare myself and will firmly resolve to spend three hours daily at interior prayer during my trip.

12. When anyone, whether a superior or someone else, causes me pain and from a purely human point of view offends me in some way, I will be careful not to say a word. If someone asks me about it, I will excuse the persons who offended me and make it clear that they were right in doing what they did.

13. I must keep an accurate account of the time I have squandered and be careful not to do so again. Only constant watchfulness can ensure this; furthermore, only a long retreat will enable me to acquire this vigilance.

14. It is a good rule to worry less about knowing what ought to be done than about doing perfectly what is already known.

15. Every morning I will devote fifteen minutes to prepare myself for the coming day, foreseeing the business I must attend to, so that I can act prudently, and anticipating the occasions when I might commit any faults, so that I can sidestep them. Thus I will be able to spend my day well.

16. In the past I have often neglected to say the Rosary, even though it is a prescribed prayer in our community. From now on, I must not go to bed without having said it.

17. In addition, I will never let a day go by, unless I am traveling in the country, without visiting the most blessed sacrament. Even on the road, if I can pass near a village church, I will enter and kneel down to adore the most blessed sacrament. I will do this as often as the opportunity arises.

18. I will make it a point to raise my heart to God whenever I begin some new activity. Whatever I undertake will begin with a prayer.

19. The Rule of our community is not to enter the house or any room in it without saying a prayer to God and fastening our thoughts on him. I will make certain not to neglect this practice.

20. Once every day, I will recite the *Pater Noster*, with as much devotion, attention, and faith as I can summon, out of respect for our Lord, who taught us this prayer and instructed us to say it.

THE HEROIC VOW

EDITORS' INTRODUCTION: *In 1691 things looked bleak for De La Salle and his infant Institute. The poverty of the community and its rigor had caused a number of the Brothers to leave. The difficulties in Reims had caused more defections. Discouragement was everywhere. Against this backdrop De La Salle remembered the story of the founding of the great seminary of Saint Sulpice in Paris. When all had seemed to be impossible for Father Jean Jacques Olier, he invited two of his closest companions to go with him to Montmartre and make a promise to found a seminary to God's glory even if they had to resort to begging and living on bread and water. John Baptist gathered two of his trusted companions, Brother Gabriel Drolin and Brother Nicolas Vuyart around him. In private they made a vow to remain faithful to the establishment of the Society of the Christian Schools "even if they had to beg and live on bread and water." We have the text of this vow in the biography written by Canon Blain. He alone has the story, and it would seem that he received it from Brother Gabriel Drolin, who was the only one alive at the time of the biography's writing. The formula affirms the consecration of these three men to the glory of God and equates the founding of the Society of the Christian Schools with that glory. The vow is a vow of association for the mission. The text follows.*[2]

Most Holy Trinity, Father, Son, and Holy Spirit, prostrate with the most profound respect before your infinite and adorable majesty, we consecrate ourselves entirely to you to procure with all our efforts the establishment of the Society of the Christian Schools in the manner that will seem to us most agreeable to you and most advantageous to the said Society.

And for this purpose, I, John Baptist de La Salle, priest; I, Nicolas Vuyart, and I, Gabriel Drolin, from now on and forever, until the last surviving one of us or unto the complete establishment of the said Society, make the vow of association and union to bring about and maintain the said establishment, without being able to withdraw from this obligation even if only we three remained in the said Society and if we were obliged to beg for alms and to live on bread alone.

In view of which, we promise to do, all together and by common accord, everything that we shall think in conscience and regardless of any human consideration to be for the greater good of the said Society.

Done on this twenty-first day of November, feast of the Presentation of Our Lady, 1691. In testimony of which we have signed.

SELECTED LETTERS

EDITORS' INTRODUCTION: His letters to the Brothers may seem brisk, even curt, but in most cases he was responding to the points in each Brother's letter to him. And, he had to write dozens of letters in response to their monthly correspondence with him. The Brothers who wrote were mostly young men, new to the community, with little education either in religious practice or pedagogy. So the advice in these excerpted letters moves from listening to God's will, to reprimands for smacking children, to answering the bell on time, to not yelling out a window. Even when De La Salle scolds a Brother, he almost always adds encouragement. The letters show us De La Salle: a busy man trying to lead a group of roughhewn men to be "ambassadors" of Christ to poor children.[3]

Letter 4: To Brother Denis

8 July [1708]

Nothing is farther from my mind than to abandon you, my very dear Brother. If I did not answer your last letter at the same time as I did those of the Brothers at Rouen, it was because I didn't have the time. Indeed, there are two Brothers besides yourself whose letters I could not answer.

There is no need to buy material for a robe. There is one here made for you. You will not have to go without.

I am very glad that you have eased your father's anxieties.

I am annoyed with Brother Thomas for treating you as you say. I will see to it that he changes his manner of acting in this matter. It is not true that I wrote to Brother Thomas what you told me about your needs, for I complained to him that he was not supplying what the Brothers require.

You must be particularly careful not to be lax with regard to your spiritual exercises. This is not the way to draw down God's blessing. You will have no virtue unless you are hard on yourself, and it is not a question of merely appearing so; your virtue must be solid. You do not acquire virtue by taking your ease and seeking your comfort.

I am glad that you sometimes practice mortification of the mind and of the senses, but it is also important to practice them when occasions present themselves.

Be exact in observing silence out of love for God; this is one of the principal points of the Rule.

It is a very useful practice to apply yourself to the remembrance of God's presence. Be faithful to it.

Nothing will draw down on you the blessings of God as much as fidelity in carrying out small matters.

Be especially careful to recite vocal prayers thoughtfully and to see that they are said in the same manner in class, for what makes vocal prayers pleasing to God is the attention with which they are said.

Take care not to become impatient with your Brother but always speak politely to him.

Because prayer is the mainstay of piety, you must bring great attention to it.

Be careful to leave everything and everybody as soon as the bell rings.

So as not to let the pupils waste time, conclude conversations briefly with persons who come to the school door.

Be careful to correct the children, the ignorant even more than the others.

It is disgraceful to call them hurtful names. Be careful not to let human respect prevent you from doing good. It is disgraceful to call your pupils by insulting names, and it also gives them bad example.

As you are aware, we make progress in virtue only insofar as we do ourselves violence; therefore, you must be careful to do so.

Make a point of practicing mortification of the mind and the senses, which for you is an obligation of your state.

No doubt the Rule can be carried out even when there are only two of you. I am very happy that you try to be faithful to the Rule. Praise be to God for the good sentiments that he gives you in this matter!

The attitude you bring to your spiritual exercises is good; keep on with it.

It is quite wrong to make your spiritual reading out of curiosity; this is no way to benefit from it.

When you find yourself without good feelings during prayer, humble yourself.

You are right that particular friendships among the Brothers cause serious difficulty in a community.

I am delighted that you have a good number of students at present. Make sure that you keep them.

Keep an eye on that Brother who slaps the students and see to it that he stops doing it. This is most important.

I pray that God may keep you in your good disposition, and

I am, my very dear Brother,
Devotedly yours in our Lord,
De La Salle

Letter 8: To Brother Hubert

EDITORS' INTRODUCTION: *At age twenty-three, Brother Hubert was already director of two schools and a community of six in Laon. Given Brother Hubert's inexperience but heavy responsibility, De La Salle's letter is filled with specific advice.*

Paris
1 June 1706

It gives me great consolation to learn from your last letter that you are in an attitude of complete abandonment, my very dear Brother.

I don't know why you have doubts about your vocation.

With regard to the vows, it is not I but you who must decide on that; the decision to make them must be your own. But since you ask my opinion, I must say that I see nothing in your conduct that could be considered an obstacle.

On Thursdays, the day free from class, the Rule is to be observed in the mornings.

You are not to read at holy Mass when you assist at it with your students.

Don't be upset by temptations to impurity or by natural movements. Try to think of something else.

When you feel yourself giving way to impatience in class, remain still and silent for a short time until the feeling has passed.

Take care to be always serious in class; the good order of the school depends a great deal on that.

Be careful that the topics of conversation during recreation time are suitable and that useless matters are not introduced.

Always have God in view in what you do; this is important if your actions are to be done in a Christian manner.

Be faithful to follow the method of prayer.

Make sure that Brother Clément keeps well.

I urge you not to let anything be done for payment nor for anything else without permission.

You did well not to carry out those errands that Brother Cassien gave you. Visits of that sort are not appropriate for us.

When there are only a few days before the monthly letter is due, there is no need to write unless the matter is extremely urgent.

Brother Robert is not to come back to Paris.

There is to be no gardening during recreation time, unless a day is set aside for watering. Even so, a serving Brother could do it. It would be better to have a gardener do it.

Nothing must be left undone to ensure that the classes make progress, especially your own.

Take care that the Brothers do not talk together.

Rest assured that your soul is very dear to me and that I will watch over it, but as regards a general confession, the reasons you advance are not serious enough to make it necessary for you. Indeed, you can do no better than entrust yourself entirely to your superiors.

Apparently you have been talking to the Brothers about Brother Charles, for those who do not know him are speaking about him. That is very wrong.

You must not let the temptations against purity that you experience upset you. They should not keep you away from communion.

Tell me everything you feel you want to about your conduct, and I will try to help you.

You must not carry candles at Saint Martin's or anywhere else. If it was done last year, no one has spoken or written to me about it. Tell me who the director was then.

It is not true that the serving Brothers do not make novenas. If Brother Isidore didn't make one, see that he does so.

Follow the advice of the parish priest of Saint Peter's and insist that the students be punctual, even if you are reduced to having only four. Do the same for the other classes as for your own.

Please take care that the times of recreation are spent properly. You know that giddy laughter is out of place among us. Recreation is one of the things you must watch over most carefully. You do well to see that the Rule is strictly observed.

There is nothing I hope for more in offering you advice than to put your mind at rest regarding the things you write to me about.

I am told that the classes of Brother Étienne and Brother Isidore are falling completely into disorder. Please take steps to remedy this.

Brother Isidore's work is not to keep him from his religious studies, for it is more important for him to do these than to work. I think too that it is not right that he spend the time of the long recreation on Thursdays working.

Try to get your community to live a life of complete fidelity to the Rule.

I am, my very dear Brother,
Devotedly yours in our Lord,
De La Salle

Letter 18: To Brother Gabriel Drolin

EDITORS' INTRODUCTION: *Brother Gabriel Drolin, who took the "heroic vow" with De La Salle, had been sent to Rome in 1702 to establish the Institute there. Drolin entered a complex, highly clerical system of schooling, which neither he nor De La Salle understood before undertaking the mission. Many letters show De La Salle's impatience with Drolin's progress and incomprehension of his situation. Of course, their correspondence was made more tenuous due to the vagaries of the postal system of the day. Nevertheless, De La Salle urged Drolin to teach the poor and establish the Institute in Rome, thus leading to papal recognition. When the Brother sent with Drolin to Rome abandoned him, he carried on alone and stayed faithful to the Institute for twenty-six years. De La Salle continually promised to send another Brother; he never could. In 1728, nine years after De La Salle's death, Drolin was called back to end his days in France. Only in 1743 was a school directed by the Brothers firmly established in Rome.*

Paris
28 August 1705

I was indeed very surprised, my very dear Brother, at not receiving news from you for so long.

In the future please write more often, and it seems to me that it will be best if you do so every month.

Brother Michel and Brother Jacques died of typhus, one after the other, at Chartres, since I last received a letter from you. Please pray to God for them.

I am very pleased that you are no longer hampered by being at M. de La Bussière's house. But tell me, how do you live and on what?

You say that you do not like being in debt. It would be nice to know whether you are in debt and how much you owe, to whom, and why. That's just what you don't tell me.

I do not at all approve of your teaching Latin. You know quite well that it is contrary to our Institute practice. We must at all times remain firm in the practices of the Institute; otherwise, we lose everything, and God will not give our work his blessing.

I don't like these Saturday offerings of money received like this from the students. Although you get nothing out of it, it has a false ring about it in our schools.

If you need a class prayer book, know that we had books reprinted last year with all the necessary rubrics for use.

If there are any others you want, we can send them to you by way of Avignon. But I think we could have our books printed in Avignon, where they have been given official approval, and then have them sent on to you.

You must let me know how Christian doctrine is taught in Rome.

Like you, our Brothers in Avignon tell me that they suffer from the intense heat.

I am happy that you are now at peace and that you neither make nor receive visits.

Make sure that you take advantage of this time and of such a wonderful opportunity to try to give up worldly ways and to adopt a simple demeanor and the manners and way of acting in keeping with the Spirit of God.

With regard to the teaching of catechism, it seems to me that the right thing and the important thing is to teach it in your school.

Is it forbidden for a schoolteacher to teach catechism to his students in class?

I do not like our Brothers' teaching catechism in church. However, if it is forbidden to do so in the school, it is better to do it in the church than not at all.

As for myself, I do not like to make the first move in any endeavor, and I will not do it in Rome any more than elsewhere. I leave it to divine Providence to make the first move, and then I am satisfied.

When it is clear that I am acting only under the direction of Providence, I have nothing to reproach myself with. When I make the first move, it is only I who am active, so I don't expect to see much good result; neither does God usually give the action his special blessing.

I am told that the archbishop of Avignon, now of Genoa, is soon to be a cardinal.

The bishop of Vaison is asking for the Brothers. You know him.

I am, my very dear Brother,
Devotedly yours in our Lord,
De La Salle

Letter 27: To Brother Gabriel Drolin

Paris
14 February 1710

I was delighted, my very dear Brother, to receive your letter of 7 November, forwarded to me a few days ago by your brother.

I wrote you two letters, one in August and the other near the end of November, which Brother Ponce tells me he handed to the courier himself. I addressed them both to M. de La Bussière to be handed on to you.

If I am not to send them in care of him, let me know, and give a definite address, whether to you personally or in care of someone else, but please make sure it is safe.

I am delighted that you now have a papal school. That is what I have been hoping for.

I have asked Brother Ponce to call on the bishop of Cavaillon for me if he is in residence and to offer him my thanks for his kindnesses to you.

I must see to it that you have another Brother to keep you company.

I am pleased that you have left M. de La Bussière's house, and I am now writing to thank him for the kindness he has shown you and the hospitality he has extended to you. I will tell him also that I will not forget him but will pray for him and also have prayers offered to God for him and his family.

It is good to know that you have been on retreat to try to regain fully the spirit of your vocation and that of prayer. I pray that God will grant you this grace.

I know that it is a great misfortune to have to be in contact with the world, and it is much to your advantage that you have to a great extent broken that contact. Make every effort also to dissociate yourself from those candidates for ordination.

You may be assured that I will not fail to pray to God for you.

It is a great joy to me that you are now in excellent health.

I know that you have plenty to do and am happy that you have a great number of students.

I know too that there is a great deal of corruption where you are and that you have to be very careful and watchful over yourself not to get caught up in it. Blessed be God that he has given you the grace to keep free from it until now.

We have Brothers in Grenoble, Alès, Mende, and Mâcon, I think, since the last time I heard from you.

Pray for God's blessing on our Institute, and trust me, my very dear Brother.

Devotedly yours in our Lord,
De La Salle

Letter 32: To Brother Gabriel Drolin

Saint Yon, Suburb of Rouen
5 December 1716

It has been against my wishes that I haven't written to you for so long, my very dear Brother. I wrote to you several times without receiving a reply. I think that my letters were intercepted, as I know some of yours have been.

I have had many disappointments during this time. At present I am living in a house in a suburb of Rouen. It is called Saint Yon, and we have our novitiate here.

I assure you that I have a great tenderness and affection for you and often pray to God for you.

You can write to me as often as you wish. I have confidence that the Brother who is now in charge at Avignon will faithfully forward your letters to me. He is a very discreet man. I will answer them.

For nearly ten months now, I have been ill in this house where I have been living for a year.

The vacillations of the archbishop of Paris are causing concern among the bishops. I don't know what is thought of this in Rome.

I have been greatly encouraged by your last letter, and the assurance of your wholehearted affection gives me much joy.

Please let me know how you are getting along.

I was hoping to send you during the holidays a Brother who has been in Rome, knows a little of the Italian language, and is a prudent man and a good teacher. But we have employed him elsewhere in the belief that his usefulness in that position would be a matter of great importance.

The Brothers are preparing for an assembly from Ascension Day to Pentecost Sunday to settle many matters that concern the Rule and the government of the Institute.

I pray you to give your consent to the decisions that will be made at this assembly by the principal Brothers of our Society.

I believe that you are still teaching your classes. Please let me know how many students you have.

Your nephew came to see me, saying that he wished to be a Brother and that he had been to see you. He said that you were going to become a priest. As he is of changeable temperament, I sent him away to think it over. I haven't heard from him since.

I am, my very dear Brother,
Devotedly yours in our Lord,
De La Salle

Letter 41: To Brother Robert

EDITORS' INTRODUCTION: *Brother Robert directed the school in Darnetal. Note that De La Salle says that he should never take time from class, even for spiritual exercises, once again illustrating that ministry was as important to holiness as prayer.*

7 December [1708]

You do not tell me, my very dear Brother, why you have not been receiving holy communion. You should have given me your reasons.

Take care not to let yourself give way to impatience and to outbursts of anger.

There must be union between you both, genuine courtesy toward laypeople, and great patience with your students.

Be faithful to be present at the spiritual exercises and to go nowhere without permission.

It is better to omit some part of the spiritual exercises than to take time from class to carry out what is necessary, for you must not lose a minute from class.

Be very careful to speak softly in the house when you have to speak, and make sure that it is really necessary. You must never speak from a distance or from the window.

Don't dwell on thoughts about your class work during the time for prayer. Do everything at its proper time.

Make sure you don't reduce the number of students by your rebuffs, but teach them well so that they will not leave.

You must not take them on to a new lesson before they are ready. Be careful about this; otherwise, they will learn nothing.

You will have to see about buying books, provided they are good ones and that I know what sort they are.

You must have some shirts made up and other linen articles if need be, but let me have a list of what linen items you have and what you require.

You are not to accept the least thing from the parents of students or from the students themselves.

See that you both keep the rules and are closely united, and show great respect not only toward your Brother but toward people generally.

I am, my very dear Brother,
Devotedly yours in our Lord,
De La Salle

Letter 42: To Brother Robert

26 February [1709]

You can easily see, my very dear Brother, that you could have greatly scandalized the woman next door by speaking so angrily to her. You must always be prudent in what you say, especially when you are speaking to outsiders.

Show great charity also to the Brother in your community. Whenever you have anything to report, mention it to Brother Joseph so that he can set it right.

You will do well to send away people who come to speak to Brother during spiritual reading and during prayer.

Be sure not to eat other than at meal times; this is not to be tolerated. The hunger you think you have at such times is only a temptation.

Be exact in ringing the bell the prescribed number of strokes, for this is quite important in a community.

Take care never to tell untruths; that would certainly be a great fault. Don't give way to curiosity, for it is quite harmful.

Perhaps it is because you have done this that you find it difficult to apply yourself to prayer and to the other spiritual exercises.

Your whole concern during the student Masses must be to supervise the children.

Make sure that you don't strike the students, for it is a serious fault, and you cannot be too much on your guard against it.

You are quite right in trying to have your students make progress so as to increase their number and also carry out your responsibilities.

Be satisfied with starting class on time.

Take care that your school runs well and that your community is faithful to the Rule.

I am, my very dear Brother,
Devotedly yours in our Lord,
De La Salle

JOHN BAPTIST DE LA SALLE

Letter 60: To Brother Mathias

EDITORS' INTRODUCTION: *Mathias seems to have been changeable and discontent. In fact, he left the community a couple of years after these letters were written.*

23 March [1708]

I think you are as well off as you could be, my very dear Brother, and that you ought to be satisfied with the Brother who is charged with directing you now.

So try to carry out your duties well and apply yourself to your spiritual exercises, for they will sanctify you and lead you to God.

Resolve to become very recollected and to take all possible means to do so.

Act in such a way as to increase the number of your students as much as you can.

I am quite convinced that the Brother who is with you is not at all annoying and that you are satisfied with him.

Aren't you ashamed of saying, "Imagine such a handsome young man as I in such a vocation as this"?

You are very fortunate to be in your vocation, which is holy and leads to holiness and which does you honor both in this life and for your salvation.

What a wonderfully handsome young man you are! How can you talk about yourself like that! Is this the way a religious should speak?

If I am not satisfied with the letters you write, it is because you sometimes write offensively. Be careful to write more discreetly and more courteously.

Surely you see that it is very wrong to get angry and to harbor resentment.

You also see that it is very bad to lose your temper and follow your feelings; that is to act more like an animal than like a reasonable being.

Take care not to let yourself be carried away by impatience in class, for that is not the way to establish order or silence.

Answering back is detrimental to the obedience you should practice.

It is very wrong to let yourself be carried away by every idea that comes into your head, for many such thoughts are wrong.

Let yourself be guided by obedience, and you will see that God will bless you.

I beg him to pour out his graces on you, and I am, my very dear Brother,

> Devotedly yours in our Lord,
> De La Salle

Letter 64: To Brother Mathias

16 May [1708]

In reply to your two letters, my very dear Brother, I have to tell you that I have written to Brother Ponce asking him to go to Mende and put things in order. I think that he will be able to transfer you and put you in his community.

I am very happy to see that you are ready to go where I wish to place you. I am not prepared just now to bring you closer to Paris or to station you there.

I am very pleased that you are happy in the district you are now in and that in the future you wish to give me as much satisfaction as you have caused me displeasure.

I will see to it that you will have plenty of students, as you request, and that you will be eager to carry out your school duties, but please be as concerned about your spiritual exercises as you are about class.

I will not fail to pray to God that he may grant you perseverance to the end of your days, as you ask me.

Brother Ponce will provide for your needs. Show the breeches to Brother Antoine. You must do all he tells you.

Be assured that God will bless you insofar as you are obedient.

It is quite shameful to harbor those feelings of resistance against the Brother who guides you and to lose your temper with him.

Be on your guard that your distractions during vocal and interior prayer do not arise from thoughtless behavior and a preference for external things.

Try to practice recollection and submission, as you tell me you are doing, for they are very necessary for you, as you say. They are the main virtues you must endeavor to acquire.

You know quite well that you must make your spiritual exercises in the community and not go running about town. There is a walk on free days.

I am convinced that in the future you will be exact and faithful in doing nothing without permission and that you are anxious to keep the Rule because you want to carry out your duty, which consists in such fidelity.

> I am, my very dear Brother,
> Devotedly yours in our Lord,
> De La Salle

Your family has asked me to tell you to keep calm and not to write letters to them without necessity, as you have been doing.

Letter 127: To Brother Barthélemy, Superior General

EDITORS' INTRODUCTION: *Though still providing guidance to novices and others who sought it, De La Salle supported Brother Barthélemy completely. De La Salle wanted time and space for solitude, as these letters show. He wrote his last letter (134), "To a Brother," only a month or so before his death in April 1719.*

[1717–18]

I seriously think that since I have given but little time to prayer for so long, it is right that I should now spend more time in prayer to learn what God wishes of me.

To my mind, what I must ask of God in prayer is that he tell me what he wants me to do and that he inspire me with the disposition he wants me to have.

LETTERS AND PERSONAL DOCUMENTS

Letter 134: To a Brother

[February or March 1719]

Please, my very dear Brother, for the love of God, in the future you must no longer think of applying to me for anything at all.

You have your superiors, and it is with them you should discuss the spiritual and temporal matters that concern you.

From now on I wish to think only of preparing myself for death, which is soon to separate me from all in this life.

Last Testament and Final Words

EDITORS' INTRODUCTION: *The biographer Blain quotes De La Salle's final testament to the Brothers. He uses the term "associate" when he speaks of his relationship with the members of the Society, and attributes this association to God, who is the originator of the work. De La Salle recommended fidelity to the Roman church and to the pope. He believed in the church as the body of Christ, a foundational principle for his rejection of both Jansenism and Gallicanism, two errors that caused so much turmoil among French Catholics during his life. His final words summarize his entire life: He had faithfully followed God's lead in directions he would never have gone on his own. Now he could rest.*[4]

First, I recommend my soul to God and, next, all the Brothers of the Society of the Christian Schools with whom he has associated me. I urge them, above all else, always to show entire submission to the church, especially in these evil times, and to give proof of this by never separating themselves in anything from our holy father the pope and from the church of Rome, always remembering that I sent two Brothers to Rome to ask God for the grace that their Society might always be entirely submissive thereto. I also recommend to them to have a great devotion to our Lord, to love very much holy communion and the exercise of interior prayer, to cultivate a very special devotion toward the most blessed Virgin and toward Saint Joseph, the patron and protector of their Society, to fulfill the duties of their employment with zeal and disinterestedness, and to maintain close union among themselves and blind obedience to their superiors, which is the foundation and the support of all perfection in a community.

If you wish to preserve yourself in your state and to die in it, never have any familiar dealings with people of the world. Little by little you will acquire a liking for their way of acting and will be drawn into conversation with them, so that through politeness, you will not be able to avoid agreeing with their language, however pernicious it may be. This will cause you to fall into infidelity, and no longer faithful in observing your rules, you will grow disgusted with your state, and finally you will abandon it.

I adore in all things the guidance of God in my regard.

Notes

---⊹---

INTRODUCTION

1. Jean-Baptiste Blain, *The Life of John Baptist de La Salle*, Book 1, trans. Richard Arnandez, FSC, ed. Luke Salm, FSC (Landover, Md.: Lasallian Publications, 2000), 80.

2. Luke Salm, FSC, *The Work Is Yours: The Life of Saint John Baptist de La Salle* (Landover, Md.: Christian Brothers Publications, 1996), 15.

3. *Meditations by John Baptist de La Salle*, trans. Richard Arnanadez, FSC, and Augustine Loes, FSC (Landover, Md.: Christian Brothers Conference, 1994), 435.

4. Blain, *The Life*, Book 1, 150.

5. See the complete "Memorandum on the Habit" in Chapter 3 of this volume, especially numbers 60 and 62.

6. Blain, *The Life*, Book 2, 283–84.

7. See "The Heroic Vow," quoted in full in Chapter 8 of this volume.

8. Salm, *The Work*, 99.

9. Ibid., 101.

10. Blain, quoted in Salm, *The Work*, 120.

11. Salm, *The Work*, 163.

12. Blain, *The Life*, Book 3, 738.

13. See William Thompson, ed., *Bérulle and the French School* (New York: Paulist Press, 1989); André Rayez, "Lasallian Studies in the Mid-Twentieth Century," in Robert Berger, FSC, *Spirituality in the Time of John Baptist de La Salle* (Landover, Md.: Lasallian Publications, 1999), 81 ff.

14. For a more detailed survey of his major contribution, see Michel Sauvage and August Hermans, "Jean-Baptiste De La Salle," in *Dictionnaire de Spiritualité* (Paris: Beauchesne, 1974), 802–21. For a catalogue and analysis of specific spiritual themes see the series of volumes: Brothers of the Christian Schools, *Lasallian Themes* (Rome, 1992–95).

15. *The Letters of John Baptist de La Salle*, trans. Colman Molloy, FSC (Romeoville, Ill.: Lasallian Publications, 1988), 217.

16. *Meditations for Time of Retreat*, trans. Richard Arnandez, FSC, and Augustine Loes, FSC (Landover, Md.: Lasallian Publications, 1994), 436.

17. *The Letters*, 248.

18. The whole of the French School was noted for its practicality: "If we keep in mind the practical and theoretical sides of the French School, its refusal to separate ecclesial practice and personal development from theology and reflective spirituality, then we need to measure its fecundity on these two fronts. It is an irruption in the spheres of both practice and meaning" (Thompson, *Bérulle*, 80). As we have noted, this synthesis is embodied in his spirit of faith and zeal and the detailed attention he gave to both school discipline and the rule and practices of the teachers' lives.

19. Ibid., 84.

20. See World Council of Churches, *A Treasure in Earthen Vessel: An Instrument for an Ecumenical Reflection on Hermeneutics* (Geneva: World Council of Churches, 1998), no. 35; and David Tracy, *The Analogical Imagination: Christian Theology and the Culture of Pluralism* (New York: Crossroad, 1981), 107–15.

21. George Van Grieken, *Touching the Hearts of Students* (Landover, Md.: Christian Brothers Publications, 1999), 121.

22. In 1698, eighteen years after the founding of the Brothers of the Christian Schools, education was made compulsory up to the age of sixteen. However, this law was neither enforceable nor supported by teacher-training programs or financial criteria for teacher remuneration (see W. H. Lewis, *The Splendid Century: Life in the France of Louis XIV* [Garden City, N.Y.: Doubleday, 1957], 77). There were numerous initiatives for women in service of the poor through education, even though it was only in this period that experiments were taking place to provide for active communities in the world. Until this era women religious were bound to the cloister, so that only boarding schools for girls where the education would take place within the enclosure were possible. Pioneers like Charles Démia (1637–98), Nicholas Barré (1621–86), Adrien Nyel (1621–87), Peter Fournier (1565–1640), along with Alix Le Clerc (1576–1622), were among the influential figures of the period from whose contribution De La Salle was able to draw (see Edward Everett, "The Education of Teachers for Primary Schools in Seventeenth-Century France: The Influence on John Baptist de La Salle," in Lawrence Colhocker, FSC, *So Favored by Grace: Education in the Time of John Baptist de La Salle* [Romeoville, Ill.: Lasallian Publications, 1991], 1–34).

23. See Jean-Guy Rodrique, "Introduction," in *Meditations*, 9–28.

24. See Edward Davis, "'A Grace and Sweetness of French': The Vernacular in the Secondary Schools of France in the Seventeenth Century"; and Yves Poutet, "A Victory for Using French in the Teaching of

Reading: John Baptist de La Salle's French Spelling Book," in Colhocker, *So Favored by God*, 145–74.

25. See Edward Everett, FSC, "Introduction," in *The Conduct of the Schools* (Landover, Md.: Christian Brothers Publications, 1996), 37. This text was included in McGraw-Hill's 1951 series of educational classics. It has stimulated a plethora of practical models for engendering faith community rooted in the Lasallian approach to education.

26. See Jean Pungier, ed., *John Baptist de La Salle: The Message of His Catechism* (Landover, Md.: Lasallian Resources, 1999).

27. See Frances Ryan and John Rybolt, eds., *Vincent de Paul and Louise de Marillac* (New York: Paulist Press, 1995).

28. This conversion was not only an individual matter between the person, God, and the poor but also a corporate spiritual discipline. De La Salle's Brothers of the Christian Schools take a vow of "association for the service of the poor through education," which has evolved through various formulations over the years. However, even for this community, continual reassessment and reconversion to the poor has been a task (see Bruno Albago, *The Institute in the Educational Service of the Poor* [Rome: Brothers of the Christian Schools, 2000]).

29. Pedro Maria Gil, FSC, *Three Centuries of Lasallian Identity* (Rome: Brothers of the Christian Schools, 1998), 97.

30. See W. J. Battersby, *De La Salle: A Pioneer in Modern Education* (London: Longmans, 1949); and Gregory Wright, *St. John Baptist de La Salle: A Seventeenth Century Educational Innovator* (Manila: De La Salle University Press, 2000).

31. Gil, *Three Centuries*, 139.

32. It is clear that Voltaire had no use for popular education, social equality, or De La Salle's Brothers of the Christian Schools, who dedicated themselves to the service of the poor: "I am grateful to you [La Chalotais] for dissuading peasants from studying. I, who cultivate the ground, forward you a request for laborers, not for clerks. Send me especially some *frères ignorantins* to work my ploughs" (quoted in Battersby, *De La Salle*, 219). In the 1763 manuscript of La Chalotais, *Essai d'éducation nationale ou Plan d'études pour la jeunesse*, he had written: "The Brothers of the Christian Doctrine [sic] are ruining everything. They teach reading and writing to the people who ought never to learn anything but to draw and to handle the plane and the file....The good of society demands that the knowledge of the common people reach no further than their immediate occupation." The Brothers of the Christian Schools were known by

some as *frères ignorantins* because of their lack of a classical education and their rather strange habit.

33. In the context of the time, a conventional notion of the hierarchical nature of church and society was embedded in the consciousness of all spiritual traditions. While the Sulpicians were dedicated to clerical formation and service, one author notes: "Perhaps what we need to accent is Olier's notion of the priest as the experienced Christian in service to all, helping them to move toward perfection to which all are called. This preserves the place of the priest without denigrating the other members of the faithful. As we have seen, there is an attempted balance between clericalism without lapsing into anticlericalism" (see Thompson, *Bérulle*, 87). For De La Salle, the move into a nonclerical spirituality for his teachers was not the original insight, but resistance from the clergy, a Baroque liturgy that did not provide the most accessible spiritual resource for his students and their teachers, and the death of the first Brother sent to seminary, all convinced him of God's will that his movement be lay.

34. "De La Salle's determined insistence on the lay character of the society did not emerge from an a priori position about the relationships of clergy and laity (such as one could develop in contemporary theology and practice) but rather from pursuing particular commitments to which the events of his life had directed him"; see Michael McGinnis, "'Church,' in Brothers of the Christian Schools," *Lasallian Themes* 1 (Rome, 1992), 90.

35. Salm, *The Work*, 202.

36. McGinnis, "Church," 89.

37. For a review of developments in lay spirituality and theology in Western Christianity, see Kenan Osborne, *Ministry: Lay Ministry in the Roman Catholic Church* (New York: Paulist Press, 1993).

38. For a more comprehensive treatment of the work of our translators, see "Glossary of Words in the Meditations," Appendix B in *Meditations*, 479–82.

39. Michel Sauvage, "Lasallian Spirituality: Our Heritage," in Berger, *Spirituality*, 264.

40. Salm, *The Work*, 203.

41. See McGinnis, "Church," 89.

42. Van Grieken, *Touching the Hearts of Students*, 11.

43. McGinnis, "Church," 87.

44. Sauvage, "Lasallian Spirituality," 269.

45. McGinnis, "Church," 90.

46. Ibid., 89.

Chapter 1:
MEDITATIONS FOR THE TIME OF RETREAT

1. *Meditations for the Time of Retreat* are part 3 in *Meditations by John Baptist de La Salle,* trans. Richard Arnandez, FSC, and Augustine Loes, FSC (Landover, Md.: Christian Brothers Conference, 1994), 432–72. To gain a more complete understanding of De La Salle's use of biblical texts, see Luis Varela Martínez, *Sacred Scripture in the Spirituality of Saint John Baptist de La Salle,* trans. Francis Vesel, FSC, ed. Donald C. Mouton, FSC (Landover, Md.: Lasallian Publications, 2000).

Chapter 2:
MEDITATIONS FOR SUNDAYS AND FEASTS

1. *Meditations for All the Sundays of the Year* and *Meditations for the Principal Feasts of the Year* are parts 1 and 2 respectively in *Meditations by John Baptist de La Salle,* trans. Richard Arnandez, FSC, and Augustine Loes, FSC (Landover, Md.: Christian Brothers Conference, 1994). Attributing exact sources for the meditations has proven problematic because, as Jean-Guy Rodrique points out in the Introduction, De La Salle "took whatever was good for his purpose wherever he found it" (p. 9). Imminently practical and intensely busy, De La Salle offered only vague references to his sources. Rodrique does, however, identify three key sources for these meditations on principal feasts: the *Martyrologe* by Francois Paris (Paris: Hortemels, 1691); *Les Fleurs de la vie des Saints* by Pierre de Ribadeneira, SJ (Spanish edition, 1599; French edition, 1609); and *Breviare romain,* which De La Salle used in introducing patristic sources. For the meditations on Sundays, De La Salle relied on his own reflections on the gospel of the day (see Varela, *Sacred Scripture in the Spirituality of Saint John Baptist de La Salle,* for more on his use of scripture). For more on the sources of the meditations, see *Meditations,* 488–92.

Chapter 3:
RULE AND MEMORANDA

1. *Rule and Foundational Documents,* trans. and ed. Augustine Loes, FSC (Landover, Md.: Lasallian Publications, 2002), 199–202.

2. Ibid., 204.

3. All the elements of the "Memorandum on the Beginnings" are taken from Jean-Baptiste Blain, *The Life of John Baptist de La Salle*, 3 vols., (Landover, Md.: Lasallian Publications, 2000). The books and pages for each quotation are listed in the following notes.

4. Blain, *The Life*, Book 1, 68–69.

5. Ibid., 69–70.

6. Ibid., 71.

7. Ibid., 71–72.

8. Ibid., 73.

9. Ibid., 76–77.

10. Ibid., 79–80.

11. Ibid., 105–06.

12. Ibid., 107.

13. Ibid., 111–13.

14. Ibid., 114.

15. Ibid., 150.

16. Ibid., 151.

17. Ibid., 156.

18. Ibid., Book 2, 174.

19. Ibid., 307.

20. Ibid., 334–36.

21. Ibid., Book 3, 571.

22. *Rule and Foundational Documents*, 181–91.

23. The term De La Salle uses in the manuscript is *seminary*, but the reference is clearly to the teacher-training college, the first of its kind, that he established in Reims in 1687. As he makes clear in his Mémoire, the first Brothers are teaching only in cities or towns, where parishes or municipalities can afford to support a community of at least two members. Not wanting to refuse the requests of rural pastors for schoolmasters, De La Salle decides to establish a normal school to train religiously minded lay teachers for posts in the countryside, where they will have to rely on themselves.

24. The word in French is *rabat*, in Latin, *rabato*. This long, split collar is still worn on occasion by Anglican and Episcopalian priests and by some Protestant ministers, as well as by English barristers and judges.

25. The French word is *capote*. The overcoat worn by the Brothers is an adaptation of what peasants of the Champagne region wore at that time.

26. Saint Vincent de Paul (c. 1580–1660) founded the Daughters of Charity and the Congregation of the Mission (the Vincentian Fathers and

Brothers). The French used the term *Monsieur* (Mister) rather than *Père* (Father) when referring to diocesan priests.

27. This pastor of Saint Sulpice objected to the Brothers' distinctive habit.

28. Composed of passages from Blain, *The Life*, 379–81.

Chapter 4:
THE CONDUCT OF THE CHRISTIAN SCHOOLS

1. John Baptist de La Salle, *The Conduct of the Christian Schools*, trans. F. de La Fontainerie and Richard Arnandez, FSC, ed. William Mann, FSC (Landover, Md.: Lasallian Publications, 1996). For more on "a successful career" for teachers, see Edward Everett, "Introduction," in *Conduct*, 33.

2. *Conduct*, "Chapter 2: Breakfast and Afternoon Snack," 52–56.

3. *Conduct*, "Introductory Remarks on Corrections," 135–64.

4. De La Salle describes the ferule this way: "an instrument consisting of two pieces of leather sewn together. It should be from ten to twelve inches in length, including the handle, and should end in an oval of two inches in diameter. The inside of this oval should be stuffed" (138). It was to be administered rarely, only one slap on the palm of the hand not used for writing.

5. French has two forms of the pronoun *you* and its derived forms. Usually the singular, *tu, toi, ton, va, viens*, is used for family, friends, closeness, and familiarity; the plural, *vous, vôtre, vos, allez, venez*, shows respect, formality, and separation.

6. *Conduct*, "Causes of Absences," 159–63.

7. *Conduct*, "School Officers," 170–78.

8. *Conduct*, "Promoting Students from One Lesson to Another," 216–20.

Chapter 5:
THE RULES OF CHRISTIAN DECORUM AND CIVILITY

1. *The Rules of Christian Decorum and Civility*, trans. by Richard Arnandez, FSC, ed. by Gregory Wright, FSC (Romeoville, Ill.: Lasallian Publications, 1990). For printing information, see the "Introduction" to that volume, xx.

Chapter 6:
THE DUTIES OF A CHRISTIAN TO GOD

1. From *The Duties of a Christian to God*, trans. Richard Arnandez, FSC, ed. Alexis James Doval (Landover, Md.: Lasallian Publications, 2002). For a better understanding of *The Duties of a Christian to God*, see Jean Pungier, FSC, *John Baptist de La Salle: The Message of His Catechism*, trans. Oswald Murdoch, FSC, ed. Gerard Rummery, FSC (Landover, Md.: Lasallian Publications, 1999). Pungier remarks that De La Salle's catechism and those of his principal sources "had their roots in common soil: all were born of the multiplicity of catechisms that appeared at the time of the Reformation and the Counter-Reformation in the sixteenth century and into the seventeenth century" (p. 50). These catechisms were based in the *Catechism of the Council of Trent*. Manuel Fernandez Magaz, in his doctoral dissertation *Un Catecismo de gran siglo frances: Los Deberes del Christiano de San Juan Bautista de La Salle* (Madrid, 1968), does identify two sources for Part 1 of *The Duties of a Christian to God* from which the selection on prayer was taken: Jean Le Coreur's *Les Principaux Devoirs du Chretien* (Paris: Jean-Baptiste Coignard, 1689) and Claude Joly's *Le Devoirs du Chretien* (Paris: Pierre Le Petit, 1677).

Chapter 7:
EXPLANATION OF THE METHOD OF INTERIOR PRAYER

1. Selected and edited from *Explanation of the Method of Interior Prayer*, trans. Richard Arnandez, FSC, ed. and rev. Donald Mouton, FSC (Landover, Md.: Christian Brothers Conference, 1995).
2. Ibid., 21–24.
3. Ibid., 25ff.
4. Ibid., 83–85.
5. Ibid., 117–18.
6. Ibid., 134–37.

Chapter 8:
LETTERS AND PERSONAL DOCUMENTS

1. "Rules I Have Imposed on Myself," in *Rule and Foundational Documents*, trans. and ed. Ronald Isett (Landover, Md.: Lasallian Publications, 2002), 199–202.

2. Blain, *The Life*, Book 2, 289–90.

3. *The Letters.*

4. Blain, *The Life*, Book 3, 737, 738.

Selected Bibliography

———— ✠ ————

LASALLIAN PUBLICATIONS

The Lasallian Publications project is sponsored by the Christian Brothers Conference (the coordinating service for the Lasallian ministries and the De La Salle Brothers in the United States of America and Toronto, Canada). Lasallian Publications include English translations of all the writings of Saint John Baptist de La Salle (1651–1719), patron of teachers and founder of the Institute of the Brothers of the Christian Schools, as well as the three early biographers of De La Salle and a number of documents and commentaries on De La Salle and the first Brothers.

LASALLIAN SOURCES: THE COMPLETE WORKS OF JOHN BAPTIST DE LA SALLE

La Salle, John Baptist de. *Collection of Various Short Treatises.* Translated by William J. Battersby, FSC. Edited by Daniel Burke, FSC. Landover, Md.: Lasallian Publications, 1993.

———. *The Conduct of the Christian Schools.* Translated by F. de La Fontainerie and Richard Arnandez, FSC. Edited with notes by William Mann, FSC. Landover, Md.: Lasallian Publications, 1996.

———. *The Duties of a Christian to God.* Translated by Richard Arnandez, FSC. Edited by Alexis James Doval. Landover, Md.: Lasallian Publications, 2002.

———. *Explanation of the Method of Interior Prayer.* Translated by Richard Arnandez, FSC. Edited and revised translation by Donald C. Mouton, FSC. Landover, Md.: Lasallian Publications, 1995.

————. *The Letters of John Baptist de La Salle.* Translated and edited by Colman Molloy, FSC, and Augustine Loes, FSC. 2d ed. Romeoville, Ill.: Lasallian Publications, 2003.

————. *Meditations by John Baptist de La Salle.* Translated by Richard Arnandez, FSC, and Augustine Loes, FSC. Edited by Augustine Loes, FSC, and Francis Huether, FSC. Landover, Md.: Lasallian Publications, 1994.

————. *Religious Instructions and Exercises of Piety for the Christian Schools.* Translated by Richard Arnandez, FSC. Edited by Eugene Lappin, FSC. Landover, Md.: Lasallian Publications, 2002.

————. *Rule and Foundational Documents.* Translated and edited by Augustine Loes, FSC, and Ronald Isetti. Landover, Md.: Lasallian Publications, 2002.

————. *The Rules of Christian Decorum and Civility.* Translated by Richard Arnandez, FSC. Edited by Gregory Wright, FSC. Romeoville, Ill.: Lasallian Publications, 1990.

LASALLIAN RESOURCES: BIOGRAPHIES OF JOHN BAPTIST DE LA SALLE BY HIS CONTEMPORARIES

Bernard, Brother. *The Admirable Guidance Shown by Divine Providence in the Person of the Venerable Servant of God, John Baptist de La Salle.* In *John Baptist de La Salle: Two Early Biographies,* translated by William J. Quinn, FSC, revised translation with notes by Donald C. Mouton, FSC, edited by Paul Grass, FSC. Landover, Md.: Lasallian Publications, 1996.

Blain, Jean-Baptiste. *The Life of John Baptist de La Salle, Founder of the Institute of the Brothers of the Christian Schools; A Biography in Three Books.* Translated by Richard Arnandez, FSC. Edited by Luke Salm, FSC. Published in three separate bindings with continuous pagination. Landover, Md.: Lasallian Publications, 2000.

————. *The Mind and Heart of John Baptist de La Salle.* Translated by Edwin Bannon, FSC. Edited by Augustine Loes, FSC. Landover, Md.: Lasallian Publications, 2002.

Maillefer, François-Élie. *The Life of John Baptist de La Salle*. In *John Baptist de La Salle: Two Early Biographies*, translated by William J. Quinn, FSC, revised translation with notes by Donald C. Mouton, FSC, edited by Paul Grass, FSC. Landover, Md.: Lasallian Publications, 1996.

LASALLIAN RESOURCES: EARLY DOCUMENTS

Loes, Augustine, FSC. *The First De La Salle Brothers: 1681–1719*. Landover, Md.: Lasallian Publications, 1999.

Salm, Luke, FSC. *John Baptist de La Salle: The Formative Years*. Romeoville, Ill.: Lasallian Publications, 1989.

LASALLIAN RESOURCES: CURRENT LASALLIAN STUDIES

Berger, Robert C., FSC, ed. *Spirituality in the Time of John Baptist de La Salle*. Landover, Md.: Lasallian Publications, 1999.

Colhocker, Lawrence J., FSC, ed. *So Favored by Grace: Education in the Time of John Baptist de La Salle*. Romeoville, Ill.: Lasallian Publications, 1991.

Pungier, Jean, FSC. *John Baptist de La Salle: The Message of His Catechism*. Translated by Oswald Murdoch, FSC. Edited by Gerard Rummery, FSC. Landover, Md.: Lasallian Publications, 1999.

Varela Martínez, Luis, FSC. *Sacred Scripture in the Spirituality of Saint John Baptist de La Salle*. Translated by Francis Vesel, FSC. Edited by Donald C. Mouton, FSC. Landover, Md.: Lasallian Publications, 2000.

Würth, Othmar, FSC. *John Baptist de La Salle and Special Education: A Study of Saint Yon*. Translated by Augustine Loes, FSC. Adapted by Francis Huether, FSC. Edited by Bonaventure Miner, FSC. Romeoville, Ill.: Lasallian Publications, 1988.

OTHER TITLES

Aroz, Léon, FSC, Yves Poutet, FSC, and Jean Pungier, FSC. *Beginnings: De La Salle and His Brothers.* Edited and translated by Luke Salm, FSC. Romeoville, Ill.: Christian Brothers Conference, 1980.

Bannon, Edwin, FSC. *De La Salle: A Founder as Pilgrim.* London: De La Salle Provincialate, 1988.

Battersby, W. J. *De La Salle: Saint and Spiritual Writer.* London: Longmans Green, 1950.

Buckley, Michael. "Seventeenth-Century French Spirituality." In *Christian Spirituality III: Post Reformation and Modern,* edited by L. Dupré and E. Salieris, 28–68. New York: Crossroad, 1989.

Burkhard, Leo C., FSC. *Beyond the Boundaries; A Story of John Baptist de La Salle, Patron of All Teachers.* Lafayette, La.: De La Salle Christian Brothers, 1994.

Calcutt, Alfred, FSC. *De La Salle: A City Saint and the Liberation of the Poor Through Education.* Oxford: De La Salle Publications, 1993.

Campos, Miguel, FSC, and Michel Sauvage, FSC. *Encountering God in the Depths of the Mind and Heart: A Commentary on John Baptist de La Salle's Explanation of the Method of Mental Prayer.* Translated by Oswald Murdoch, FSC. Rome: Brothers of the Christian Schools, 1995.

Daniel-Rops, Henri. *The Church in the Seventeenth Century.* 2 vols. Translated by J. J. Buckingham. Garden City, N.Y.: Doubleday Image Books, 1965.

Deville, Raymond. *The French School of Spirituality; An Introduction and Reader.* Translated by Agnes Cunningham. Pittsburgh, Pa.: Duquesne University Press, 1994.

Koch, Carl. *Praying with John Baptist de La Salle.* Winona, Minn.: Saint Mary's Press, 1990.

Laube, Robert, FSC. *Pentecostal Spirituality: The Lasallian Theology of Apostolic Life*. New York: Desclee, 1970.

Mann, William, FSC. *John Baptist de La Salle Today*. Manila: De La Salle University Press, 1992.

———. *Lasallian Spirituality Workbook*. Landover, Md.: Christian Brothers Publications, 1994.

Mann, William, FSC, with Henry Dissanayke, FSC, and Isaias Tzegay, FSC. *Ambassadors for Jesus Christ: Prayer Meditations for Christian Educators*. Rome: Brothers of the Christian Schools, 1995.

Salm, Luke, FSC. *The Work Is Yours; The Life of Saint John Baptist de La Salle*. 2d ed. Landover, Md.: Christian Brothers Publications, 1996.

Salm, Luke, FSC, ed. *Beginnings: De La Salle and His Brothers*. Romeoville, Ill.: Christian Brothers Conference, 1980.

Salm, Luke, FSC, and Leo Burkhard, FSC. *Encounters: De La Salle at Parmenie*. Romeoville, Ill.: Christian Brothers Publications, 1983.

Sauvage, Michel, FSC, and Miguel Campos, FSC. *Announcing the Gospel to the Poor: The Spiritual Experience and Spiritual Teaching of Saint John Baptist de La Salle*. Translated by M. J. O'Connell, FSC. Romeoville, Ill.: Christian Brothers Conference, 1981.

Thompson, William M., ed. *Bérulle and the French School; Selected Writings*. Translated by Lowell M. Glendon. Mahwah, N.J.: Paulist Press, 1989.

Van Grieken, George, FSC. *Touching the Hearts of Students: Characteristics of Lasallian Schools*. Landover, Md.: Christian Brothers Publications, 1999.

WEB

www.lasalle.org (or its mirror www.lasalle2.org). The international web site of the Brothers of the Christian Schools.

www.cbconf.org. The web site of the Christian Brothers Conference, the central office and publisher that supports Lasallian ministries and members in the United States of America and Toronto, Canada. This site hosts the Lasallian Publications book list and order form.

Index

INDEX